Making knowledge work

Sustaining learning
communities and regions

Edited by
Chris Duke
Lesley Doyle
and Bruce Wilson

niace
promoting adult learning

© 2006 National Institute of Adult Continuing Education
(England and Wales)

21 De Montfort Street
Leicester
LE1 7GE

Company registration no. 2603322
Charity registration no. 1002775

NIACE has a broad remit to promote lifelong learning opportunities for adults.
NIACE works to develop increased participation in education and training,
particularly for those who do not have easy access because of class, gender,
age, race, language and culture, learning difficulties or disabilities,
or insufficient financial resources.

You can find NIACE online at www.niace.org.uk

Cataloguing in Publication Data
A CIP record of this title is available from the British Library

Designed and typeset by Avon DataSet Ltd, Bidford-on-Avon, Warwickshire
Printed and bound in the UK by Ashford Colour Press, Gosport

ISBN: 1 86201 246 6/978 186201 246 2

Making knowledge work

Contents

Contents

Preface

Pascal – Some challenges ahead

Jarl Bengtsson

Recently I had an interesting discussion with a man in his early sixties in a small village in France. The village is located in a poor rural region in the northern part of Burgundy. I have myself had a house in the village for more than thirty years, and I have known the man for the same period of time. When visiting me recently he noticed the word Pascal on some of my papers and he asked me if I was involved in doing some work about the French philosopher Blaise Pascal. I told him that was certainly not the case and I started to explain to him what our Pascal was about.

I explained to him that place management is how you can strengthen the empowerment of people at a local and regional level. His reaction was very positive and he said this is exactly what is needed throughout France. I then went on to explain to him what social capital was about. Here he got very enthusiastic and told me that in France social capital is being eroded everyday, and something urgent has to be done to restore it. So far, no problem in getting support for what Pascal is doing. But when I started to explain what a learning region is, he interrupted me and said this is nonsense. He said a region cannot learn, a region can only build an infrastructure for education, and if the regional politicians are clever they can work for and stimulate the creation of a learning culture that encourages people to engage in formal education and in formal learning.

I admitted to him that I found his definition of a learning region very convincing. He then went on to explain to me why he thought our region in Burgundy was so poor and lacking any developments for the future. The reason was, according to him, that the political community of the region was incapable of understanding the meaning of Pascal. But he wished Pascal all success for the future and wondered whether Pascal one day could come to visit the region and tell the political community what to do. I told him that would be rather unlikely in the near future, but that on the other hand Pascal has the ambition and capacity to share with all regions around the world information and advice about what works in developing regions in economic social and cultural terms through partnership in place management, social capital, and education and learning.

So you can say that Pascal navigates in a difficult and foggy landscape, trying to give new compass directions to regions so they can get a clearer overview of the landscape. One such compass direction that is particularly difficult to find is the balance between education and learning. This is a 2000 year old story. Most people would agree that learning is individual-based and education institution-based. Socrates was never thinking about learning in institutional terms. For him learning was above all self-development. His pupil Protagoras, and later Plato and Aristotle, started to lay the foundations for institutional education, which has been growing ever since. In medieval times, the church further strengthened the institutional aspect of education and learning, with a strong desire to control what went on in these institutions. The Humboldt scientific revolution in the eighteenth century was a major transformation for the universities in terms of content and purpose, but there was never any challenge to the institutional basis. The mass education of last century led to an explosion of education institutions. But at the end of the last century we saw also the birth of a new paradigm, namely lifelong learning. In the 1970s, OECD tried to make a synthesis between learning over the life cycle and the adaptation of educational institutions in this perspective. It was called *Recurrent Education, a Strategy for Life Long Learning*. It was on top of the policy agenda for about a decade and then more or less disappeared, to be was replaced during the 1980s by a returning concern for the front end model of education and back to basics. In the 1990s lifelong learning came back, this time based on economic and social concerns, but without any strategy as to what to do with the educational institutions. Today it is considered by all OECD governments as the future of learning and education, but still without a strategy.

In Thomas Kuhn's terms we are most likely in a paradigm shift between the twentieth century's enormous expansion of institution-based education and this century's search for a more flexible individual learning agenda over the life cycle. And still, according to Kuhn, in such periods of paradigm shift the two paradigms usually live in parallel for quite some time. For Pascal, this is a challenge – we must be able to respond to the concerns of the defenders of both paradigms.

Another compass direction that is equally difficult to establish for Pascal is that between the forces of a globalising economy and the role and value-added activities that a region can find and develop in this new economic reality. Often these forces, like international organisations such as the WTO, IMF and multinational enterprises, are detached from the specific concerns, realities and cultures of the people in regions.

We are all familiar with the powerful expression *think global and act local*. Most likely this will not be sufficient for the future for regional development. The challenge seems rather to be 'think global and act global with a local and regional touch'. But to find a distinct compass direction to overcome this challenge is still far ahead. Most likely there will be several to discover. The important thing is to be aware of the fact that regional development can no longer be seen only within the national economics and cultural contexts, but must also be seen increasingly in a global context. In this respect and given the fact that education and learning are becoming more and more inter-national, they will provide Pascal with a value-added tool in better linking regional and international developments.

It is in this new environment of fundamental changes in educational institu-tions and approaches to learning coupled with profound eruptions in the global economy, against the background of urgently needed sustainable development, that I prefer to see the mission of Pascal. It should over time be able to clarify and provide useful information and advice to regions about how they can find a value-added role for their activities in this new global environment. In parallel, Pascal also has an important and active role in stimulating and synthesising research, innovation and experimentation at local and regional levels and assuring that they can be shared with all.

I mentioned at the beginning that my friend in the little village in France thought I was involved in some activity related to the French philosopher and scientist, Blaise Pascal (1623–1662). I have never been particularly impressed by his work as I find him too influenced by religious concerns. But after the discussion with my friend I decided to read again some of his principal writings. And I discovered a man devoted to three passions:

- First, to be multidisciplinary in his thinking and scientific experimentation - for instance in mathematics and mechanics.
- Secondly, to try always to translate his theoretical work into practice and experimentation - for instance he invented the first ever machine to calculate.

- Thirdly, he was always totally committed to communicating his work, not only to his fellow colleagues but above all to the broader segments of society – for instance he produced a flyer for his machine to calculate and spread it widely.

So when it comes to further developing our methods of work, it would seem Blaise Pascal has something to contribute to our Pascal after all.

Contributors

David Adams
Executive Director, Strategic Policy and Research Division, Department for Victorian Communities and Adjunct Professor, School of Management, University of Tasmania.

Dr Alan Barr
Director, Scottish Community Development Centre, Glasgow, Scotland.

Paul Bélanger
Professor of Sociology of Education, Université du Québec à Montréal, Canada, Director of Centre Interdisciplinaire de Recherche et Développement sur l'Education Permanente (CIRDEP), and President of the International Council for Adult Education.

Dr Jarl Bengtsson
Former Director of CERI, OECD and Chair, Pascal Board.

Paul Carter
Leader of Kent County Council, England.

David Charles
David Goldman Chair of Business Innovation, Business School, and Director of the Institute for Policy and Practice, University of Newcastle upon Tyne, England.

Dr Lesley Doyle
Research Fellow, Pascal, Institute of Education, University of Stirling, Scotland.

Contributors

Sue Dunn
Head of Vocational Development, Kent County Council, England.

Chris Duke
Professor of Regional Partnerships and Learning, RMIT University, Australia, Chief Executive Officer, Pascal.

Donna Easterlow
Principal Research Officer, Environment and Rural Affairs Department, The Scottish Executive.

Dr Brian Findsen
Department of Adult and Community Education, University of Glasgow, Scotland.

Michael Hess
Professor, School of Management, University of Tasmania, Australia.

Norman Longworth
Vice-President of the World Initiative on Lifelong Learning, former President of the European Lifelong Learning Initiative.

Alasdair McKinlay
Community Regeneration Manager, Communities Scotland, Edinburgh.

Michael Osborne
Professor of Lifelong Learning and Head of DAICE, University of Stirling, Scotland.

Kate Sankey
Deputy Director DAICE, University of Stirling, Scotland.

Chris Shepherd
Former Chief Executive Dartford Borough Council, Director DICE Consultants, and Adviser to the Office of the Deputy Prime Minister.

Sue Warner
Head of Operational Coordination and Support, Communities Scotland, Edinburgh.

Dr Leone Wheeler
Manager, Leaning Community and Partnerships, RMIT University, Australia.

Bruce Wilson
Professor of Organisation and Work Design, Head of the School of Global Studies, Social Science and Planning, RMIT University, Australia.

Dr Shanti Wong
Executive Officer, Brimbank/Melton LLEN, Victoria, Australia.

Stuart Ogg
Chief Executive, Scottish Enterprise, Forth Valley, Stirling, Scotland.

Chapter 1

Making knowledge work

Lesley Doyle, Bruce Wilson and Chris Duke

Policy, politics and knowledge

Contemporary policy-making is now a highly complex business. As people have become better educated, as international relationships have become more intricate and unstable, as trans-national corporations and non-government institutions have become increasingly significant in their influence, so the pressures on governments and their agents to be more publicly accountable for their policies and decision-making have become more demanding. The emphasis on protocol and on adherence to tried and tested ways of doing things has been replaced by a focus on the quality of outcomes in a more unpredictable and competitive world.

These issues and processes are of deep interest and concern to the scholars, policy-makers and practitioners who have together formed Pascal. Their interest is in facilitating closer, more dynamic and productive collaboration among researchers interacting with regional governments in different parts of the world. The purpose is to enable the sharing of insights, and understanding of key issues that confront governments, in a timely way, and in language which bridges the divisions of culture and accountability which are too common.

Many people refer to the emergence of a 'knowledge' society or economy in which access to and utilisation of knowledge is a critical determinant of economic success. This, in turn, is understood to be the foundation of the social and cultural well-being of nations, regions and communities. The apparent attractiveness of this idea starts to fade, however, with grounded analysis of what it means in practice, or indeed even in policy. The examples of Silicon Valley and of various revitalised manufacturing areas do not present ready recipes for widespread and successful replication. Closer examination indicates that 'knowledge' is a multi-layered term. While it might indeed point the way towards the future, scholars, policy-makers and practitioners all need a more specific understanding of the relevance of different kinds of knowledge, and of how these can assist both economic growth and social development.

The emphasis on knowledge as an economic resource might be only part of the story. Yet governments and their public agencies have come to place increasing store by access to information as an essential resource for governmental decision-making. Data collection has become a major preoccupation, both as a means of better understanding a constituency and as a means of enhancing control. Here it is useful to make a distinction between information-gathering and the acquisition of knowledge. The raw data, the information gathered from the past and the present, does not constitute knowledge in its own right. The data have to be analysed, compared with other data and synthesised.

Such knowledge derived from various kinds of research projects has been used increasingly by governments at all levels to inform their decision-making. Typically, quantitative trend data have been most influential. Such data are seen as providing crisp insights. Reduced to small 'bites' of information such data help to sway a debate in one direction or another, irrespective of methodological issues. There has however also been a growing use of more qualitative research insights which can illustrate issues graphically and help in the exploration of complexity.

Yet the application of knowledge in support of policy-making is neither simple nor easy. Those who specialise in generating new knowledge, those who try out new ideas in practice, those responsible for advising on the allocation of public resources, are not necessarily aware of one another, or if they are, they are not necessarily able to communicate effectively. The nature of their work and the attendant pressures differ, and organisational arrangements can further hinder communication. Probity and other political and even legal concerns might also limit informal interactions amongst these stakeholders. It is these kinds of barriers that Pascal is concerned to address.

The focus of Pascal

Why does Pascal focus on learning communities and regions, and by implication, on the social well-being and relationships – the social capital –

of residents in these communities? There are other important policy areas where similar concerns about linking research and policy exist.

First and foremost, there is an interest in the nature and significance of learning because of the nature of the times in which we live. Irrespective of the differing ways in which knowledge resources are given priority, learning is seen unequivocally as an important and a central means of improvement in all parts of public life, social and economic. 'Learning' has long since taken on a character beyond the individual, not least in theories about organisational learning but also is in the ways in which regions and communities can seek better to position themselves in an increasingly global economic environment. Collective learning contributes to the development of social policies which strengthen communities and enhance the quality of life of their members. Writing about learning organisations Senge commented that:

> Learning organizations [are] organizations where people continually expand their capacity to create the results they truly desire, where new and expansive patterns of thinking are nurtured, where collective aspiration is set free, and where people are continually learning to see the whole together'. (Senge, 1990, p.3)

'Learning' is also a critical ingredient in communities themselves coming to understand the richness of their local resources, their relationships with each other, and in determining how best to deploy those resources in the interests of the whole community.

Pedler's work on learning companies is instructive:

> The Learning Company is a vision of what might be possible. It is not brought about simply by training individuals; it can only happen as a result of learning at the whole organization level. A Learning Company is an organization that facilitates the learning of all its members and continuously transforms itself. (Pedler et. al., 1991, p.1)

Place management, the third of the Pascal themes, is relevant because of the importance of place in focusing the transformation, whether at community, city or regional level. The concept provides the opportunity to relocate and contextualise policy-making and administration to respond to the needs and aspirations of communities rather than remaining locked in outdated divisions of labour. Like architects' 'lifelines' which try to anticipate the routes people

3

will take when designing pathways between new buildings, place management enables policy-makers to respond as well as to instigate.

Making knowledge work: a kaleidoscope of perspectives

The authors of this book bring many different insights to bear on these questions. They come from different experiences which reflect competing theoretical perspectives. They have contrasting ideas, and possibly different visions of how the Pascal venture might help regional and local governments in addressing current challenges. They write normally for different audiences, which accounts in part for the varying styles and orientations of the chapters that follow. All however share a common commitment to the importance of policy-making which encompasses social priorities as well as economic pressures. All share the view that we can learn from one another, and that a range of perspectives and experiences is of value. The most valuable insights may emerge where the most significant divergence appears to be.

Jarl Bengtsson, in the Preface to this book, illuminates the recent history of the priority on learning with speculation on the critical elements which will emerge in our understandings and debates about learning over the next decade. His concern is that although the rhetoric of lifelong learning is being considered again by OECD governments, there is as yet no strategy for its implementation. For all the benefits of the 'search for a more flexible individual learning agenda over the life cycle', as Bengtsson puts it, the institutions which have to deliver this are not yet clear on how best to do so. Nor is it clear whether as currently constituted they can deliver at all and – more crucially – whether they want to. A paradigm shift away from institution-based education, together with changes in the global economy and the need for sustainable development, highlight the role of Pascal as stimulant, synthesiser and depository of 'research, innovation and experimentation at local and regional levels'.

Bengtsson thus lays out the challenge for decision-makers – and in a lifelong learning society, this includes all of us – to think beyond the parochial and the short term, looking outwards to find the global context but retaining the local and regional as an integral part of that global perspective. In so doing, he sets the tone for the following chapters.

Such 'global learning' is finely illustrated in **Paul Bélanger**'s chapter 'Concepts and realities of learning cities and regions'. His concern is that cities are 'struggling at the international level for investment and for their future'. To survive they have to make lifelong learning their top priority. As important as financial investment is to develop a visionary and common purpose, ensuring that the city has the skills needed to make it sustainable, and to ensure that all, especially the young, have a stake in the city's future. Whilst this approach to learning would be immediately recognisable to Bengtsson's French villager, for Bélanger it has particular significance because it characterises the learning city.

Norman Longworth has more to say on this in the next chapter, 'Learning cities and learning regions: making the world a better place'. He describes how an early project as part of the European Commission Socrates programme made recommendations designed to enable cities and regions to achieve an 'outward-looking mission'. His is on the rationale for some of these subsequent initiatives linking learning cities and regions globally, and in particular on their value for developing countries and disadvantaged communities. The utility of internet and e-learning is emphasised, but Longworth also quotes Botkin (2002) on the need to '[respect] human diversity without asserting a cultural dominance over others'.

For Longworth, various lifelong learning projects from school through to the post-retirement years provide not only the individual perspective but also a gateway to learning in a collective, global sense. Universities have a particular role to play. They can use their long established worldwide academic and research networks to work with local authorities to build learning cities and regions. LILARA (Learning in Local and Regional Authorities) provides a good example of a university/local authority project. It is developing consultation tools to identify gaps in the learning of managers charged with the task of creating a learning city or region. The European Foundation for Management Development (EFMD) provides another example of this approach – this time being taken by businesses. The purpose of the global approach to learning, as opposed to the inward-looking approach of past times, is to create a 'global community'.

Longworth like Bélanger considers effective lifelong learning impossible if the resources available are not connected. Bélanger also makes clear that for this to occur, the city has to be prepared to learn about itself in order to develop new networks. This critical factor, he says, is 'in short, some kind of social capital'. A learning city has a full grasp of its internal actors, and of the population. It is able to mobilise them to act collectively. To reach this state definitions of social capital in common currency are not, Bélanger says, helpful because they do not embrace the vital need for a learning city to resolve conflicts of interest.

John Field and **Michael Osborne** in the chapter 'Researching social capital in Europe: towards a toolkit for measurement?' may provide a means to this missing social capital link. In a development from Field's (2005) work on social capital, they look at social cohesion, trust and participation in civil society, emphasising the close relationship of trust and networking to innovation processes and human capital investment. Their interest is in the significance of these three elements of social capital in the wider social and economic context, and they seek to answer the question 'what does the construct called "social capital" bring to the discussion that may be of value at the European level?' They list existing European datasets and identify six themes of analysis for which they offer relevant comparable data on social cohesion, trust and participation. These include examples such as levels of participation in formal and informal networks; information on social norms promoting collective action and social capital, and 'social governance' as a potential facilitator of policy implementation. This is a significant resource. However, they suggest that whilst 'there is little difficulty in creating a European toolkit for measuring and understanding social capital', the analysis of such datasets needs to be supplemented with qualitative data, collected within the 'lens' of national studies and aimed at interrogating the relationships identified through statistical analysis.

A central concern for Field and Osborne is to develop a collective approach for communities to learn about themselves, as a pre-condition for effective participation. How can communities tell whether what they are doing makes a difference, and how can those in power and with positions of responsibility best gather that knowledge and present it to communities?

David Adams and **Michael Hess** share the desire to balance social and economic performance. 'New research instruments for government: measuring community engagement' is written from an Australian, specifically Department for Victorian Communities (DVC), perspective. Here there has been 'a re-emergence of community as a useful category across a range of policy making and service delivery areas'. With the express purpose of establishing and consolidating the validity of this approach, they present the development and intended application of instruments designed to identify and measure the contribution of community engagement to policy-making and public management, thereby offering a balance to the existing market-oriented instruments.

Rather than the more easily measurable 'outputs of community engagement (such as increased levels of participation...)' Adams and Hess venture to explore the difficulties of developing indicators to measure the connection of these outputs to 'outcomes (improvements in implementation in crucial policy areas)'. Their research programme had 'a simple objective: to understand how to increase the confidence and capacity of Victorians to pay a greater role in socio-economic activity through exercising increased choice and control over their well being and prosperity'. The work has given them 'real' knowledge, new light on central problems of policy, and 'evidence on how "governance" factors intermediate both family and community level dynamics'. Over the past three years, Adams and Hess have been analysing existing datasets and new purpose-oriented data collected in partnership with local people, through organisations such as non-governmental organisations (NGOs) and local councils.

From a factor analysis of the characteristics of communities that Victorians think are important, they identify the differences between what Victorians feel is important from what they feel is present in their communities, so that they can locate the Department's community-strengthening capacity in the 'gap between what should be and what is'. They conclude that six areas require attention to achieve the levels and types of community engagement which have been shown to contribute to the creation of strong, resilient communities. Most important is the emphasis on recognising the crucial importance of knowledge invented locally, and not simply tapped through community consultation (Bauman, 2000). Community engagement activities are essential in the invention of that knowledge 'because they throw people together in endeavours which focus attention on local needs and capacities'.

This chapter exemplifies Pascal's work. This is a policy-maker/academic team: Adams is Executive Director of DVC's Strategic Policy and Research Division, but both he and Hess also have leading academic roles. They draw on theories of social capital such as we saw in the Bélanger and Field and Osborne chapters. They locate the DVC experience within the learning city framework as elaborated on by Bélanger and Longworth. Academic work is put to good use, at the same time as the Department's projects provide further experience for its development. Pascal's focus on place management as one main area of interest emanates in part from early recognition in Victoria that whereas market-based policy-making relies on knowledge and ways of working based on *interest, issues and beliefs*, community-based knowledge privileges *place*.

The next chapter addresses problems similar to those outlined by Adams and Hess: the need for policy-makers and communities to ensure some common understanding of the purpose and criteria for success of community involvement with government agencies. **Alan Barr** and **Lesley Doyle**, in 'Setting standards for community engagement', explain how on behalf of Communities Scotland, the Scottish Community Development Centre (SCDC) drew up standards and guidelines to engage agencies with communities. This was of value in itself, to combat the charges often laid at the door of the Scottish Executive that community participants frequently perceived a gap between intent and purpose. A community-led approach was adopted, with local agencies involved at all the stages. The standards – there are ten – address areas that frequently elicited negative feedback, such as the time-scales for consultation, the narrowness of the scope offered for influence on policy and practice, and the lack of openness. The detailed indicators associated with each standard have proved to be very popular, as measured by their 'mutual and voluntary adoption by community and agency partners in community engagement'.

Yet as we know, communities encompass a considerable diversity of interests, another theme reflected in different parts of this book. In 'Sustaining economic development through business engagement and mutual learning', **Stuart Ogg** approaches the issues from a business perspective. With the intention of identifying greater synergies between private business objectives and the interests and ambitions of the wider community he presents 'an attempt to help lay the foundation for developing a learning region'. More effective communication, knowledge exchange and learning between business and government agencies are now recognised as important in the armoury of local economic development. Without the necessary supporting mechanisms these processes cannot be enhanced or even sustained.

The Stirling Business Panel has been in existence for four years under the auspices of Scottish Enterprise Forth Valley. Its express purpose is to gather the views of the business community as a particular 'community of interest'. Its original design was to create a single channel to communicate with a large representative sample of businesses but it has actually provided 'a model for encouraging a wider exchange of ideas and knowledge as a bridge between public and private sectors'. Developing from an array of other community forums, assemblies and panels, it is a fine example of lifelong learning in community organisations, and of the new developments that Bélanger and Longworth see as necessary for an effective learning region.

Community rather than business consultation is also the subject of **Donna Easterlow** and **Kate Sankey**'s chapter 'Research, consultation and policy development for rural and remote communities in Scotland'. They consider accurate identification of the needs and aspirations of rural communities, and building the capacity for seeking solutions by engaging people in policy decisions. Two different initiatives are compared, and lessons drawn. The first relates to the Scottish Executive's *Closing the Opportunity Gap (CtOG)* strategy to tackle poverty and social exclusion. The second is *Community Futures*, a community participation approach to link community aspirations with strategic planning. Both initiatives used evidence-informed decision-making based on the premise that research and consultation evidence can contribute usefully. As Adams and Hess also found, these include 'identifying the problem to be addressed, deciding how to tackle the problem as well as evaluating the success of the chosen approach as a means of improving existing, and developing future policy'. Perhaps most important was the finding that policy-makers need to be aware of 'consultation fatigue', as well as cynicism within some communities about the value of research for practical purposes.

In the next case study, this time of learning community partnerships, **Leone Wheeler** and **Shanti Wong** begin with the traditional sense of learning. In so doing they speak in words that Bengtsson's villager would be likely to recognise. 'Learning communities in Victoria: where to now?' reminds us that learning brings the individual the benefits of personal growth, increased employability, broader interests and control over one's own future. It continues Longworth's theme (Longworth, 1999 and Chapter 3, this book) of the importance of inclusion to avoid marginalising disadvantaged groups. Here the concept of learning cities is about ensuring a networked approach to economic development and social inclusion.

According to Wheeler and Wong, a productive environment for such developments came with the election of a Labor Government in Victoria in 1999. This led to the establishment of the Victorian Learning Towns initiative, based on partnerships across sectors and the promotion of learning communities as a way of creating conditions for their sustainability. At this point the language becomes 'Pascalian', because such developments of themselves enter into the realm of learning organisations (see Senge, 1990). Wheeler and Wong draw our attention to a further, more focused and developed example of the learning city, which Longworth writes about in Chapter 3. They demonstrate that one of the key factors for the sustainability of learning communities is local government leadership when it is prepared to put pressure on central government for funds, selects good officers at local level with the ability to motivate volunteers, and ensure good coordination so that efforts are not dissipated through duplication.

Learning regions, cities and communities are presented by Longworth, Wheeler and Wong, and others in this book as an essential element in the fight against poverty and exclusion. In the next chapter, **Chris Shepherd** provides a timely reminder of the history behind such a philosophy, this time from a UK perspective. In 'Regenerating communities – or '*the poor are always with us*'. A UK experience', he treats us to his reflections on 20 years' experience as the Chief Executive of an English local authority. He begins with a brief historical overview of the route to local democracy and its impact on those who in the past were euphemistically referred to as 'the poor', and suffered from governance that 'was far from benign'. This led to growing demand for essential public services which now come from a variety of sources including central government agencies, local authorities, the private sector and the voluntary and community sectors. This can 'often lead to confusion by the public and a dislocated approach in service delivery'.

For Shepherd the advent of Local Strategic Partnerships, where the statutory agencies and other stakeholders work together and the Neighbourhood Renewal Fund provides the resources, is the latest and very positive step in essential service provision. Working to six common themes, for example education, housing, and their interrelationship with government-determined benchmarks, Shepherd sees the programme as an example of joined up government, echoing one of Wheeler and Wong's conditions for sustainability. Similarly, Shepherd emphasises that local self-determination is also important. He describes how the New Deal for Communities (NDC), intended to introduce the concept of community-led regeneration, puts this principle to front of stage. For these programmes to be sustained, Shepherd draws on his long experience and calls for 'robust data analysis, plausible interventions, good evaluation'. The need for Pascal to this work is again evidenced – in his further call for sharing and learning from the experience of others engaged in similar programmes.

The same concern with the complexities and confusion that can result from multiple sources of services delivery also prompts discussion by **Paul Carter** and **Sue Dunn**, In 'Vocational education and training: implementing innovation', she describes the way in which Kent County Council has addressed the English 14–19 education and training agenda at local level. As in previous chapters, and as in the April 2006 Pascal Hot Topic prepared by

Josef Konvitz of the OECD (Konvitz, 2006), the importance of the local authority is promoted as the main support for local communities. In Kent, these 'communities' consist of 23 clusters of schools and local authorities working together 'to deliver a flexible, demand-led, innovative vocational programme'. This highlights again the dual meaning of a learning community: the central purpose of the programme is to deliver an essential service, but the learning occurs not just among young people but also in, by and for those organisations – schools and colleges – that are charged with the provision of the service.

The essential ingredient, Carter and Dunn explain, is the collaborative nature of the vocational programme. Drawing on Michael Fullen's (2004) philosophy, they explain the need to sow the seeds of 'a moral purpose' for collaboration, to replace the potentially destructive competition with its accompanying mistrust, between the institutions. The success of the programme so far is put down in part to the adoption of this sense of moral purpose by individuals leading the institutions within the clusters, and by the clusters themselves, resulting in mutual trust, the development of a common understanding of the language used by the different providers, and the ability to produce and implement common curriculum frameworks.

Again a key question is the sustainability of the programme, which depends above all on support from local leaders. It is also essential to build on the body of knowledge available in the UK and internationally as to why some innovations succeed and others do not. Such an approach includes practitioners and policy-makers becoming fully cognisant of the research available, so that they can for example take advantage of the underpinnings provided by Senge (1990) and others on learning organisations.

As we have seen, learning cities, regions and communities depend on the active engagement of local people in governance. **Brian Findsen** looks at a section of the population which can provide essential support for a learning society. In 'Active citizenship and the third age of learning: economic and social dimensions', he traces 'the connection between third age learning, particularly in its non-formal and informal guises, and opportunities for older adults to be fully functioning members of society as active citizens'. Findsen starts from the base that older adults on low pensions are among the most marginalised, and that educational provision for them does little to alleviate the situation. Calling for a redress of this imbalance in formal learning, he reminds us of Field's (2002) observation that the lifelong learning agenda has been dominated by economic and vocational concerns, which leaves out older citizens. Further, the potential of senior citizens to effect social change goes largely untapped, counter-balanced as it is by 'the glorification of youth where to be old is to be "other"' (Biggs, 1993).

Findsen discusses the meaning of 'active citizenship', outlines current formal provision, and scans the types of informal learning provided, for example, by self-help agencies and mainstream providers. He concludes that the provision particularly impacts on those who have to put much of their effort into eking out a subsistence living, and who do not share an 'essentially middle class and primarily male' perspective. He identifies various arenas important for non-formal learning. These are where the value of older adults is most significant for a learning society, but most overlooked. Together these arenas offer a more inclusive package for older adults, as volunteers in non-governmental organisations and as political advocates for social change, also in the family as mentors to at least two generations. Findsen cryptically notes that 'the exigencies of economic survival and the reconfiguration of the workplace have influenced patterns of paid work for seniors, not all of whom can retire on superannuation or government/employer benefits'.

This volume concludes with two chapters that reflect on some of the tensions and challenges which policy-makers and researchers share in working together. Each raises serious issues that can complicate the application of knowledge in policy formation. Both are confident about the importance of 'making knowledge work', and point to conditions which will make this more of a reality.

Bruce Wilson's 'Policy-makers and researchers working together: dilemmas in making the connection' sets out a range of issues which affect the contribution of research to informing policy. He provides suggestions as to how the research and policy-making processes might work together more effectively, particularly in relation to social, economic and cultural policies. He questions the assumption that decisions by policy-makers are rational, because that in itself assumes that they have all the evidence at their fingertips and further, the means to understand the implications of that evidence. Indeed, the scope of the policy framework may itself be unclear. This, together with the complex interactions and relationships of the political environment, might suggest that the term 'decision' is altogether too generous. Other factors such as limited funding within difficult time constraints, the impact of pressure groups, and contradictory administrative divisions of labour also impinge.

In a development of Sandberg's (1985) concept of praxis research, Wilson suggests that relationships amongst policy-makers and researchers need to be understood in terms of intellectual dialogue. In this dialogue, researchers would communicate with clarity about the context from within which they work, while being open to the realities of policy-making; and policy-makers would engage in practice informed by theory, recognising how constraints might undermine the validity and reliability of the evidence available to them. Action research can provide a valuable approach connecting policy-making and research because it can engage stakeholders with competing interests. It also builds an environment in which policy changes can be accepted and implemented effectively. Through the story of a particular case study Wilson illustrates the relative effectiveness of the praxis approach.

Of course effective collaboration between researchers and policy-makers requires the use of shared and accessible language. This is a principal concern in **David Charles'** and **Chris Duke**'s final chapter. They draw on the experience of a European-funded project, 'City regions as intelligent territories: Inclusion, competitiveness and learning' (CRITICAL) to address explicitly the question how we go about the business of 'making knowledge work' – the title not only of this book but also of the Pascal Conference at the University of Stirling in October 2005. The formal aim of the CRITICAL project was 'to test the concept of a knowledge, or learning, society within the context of city regions, in order to assess how knowledge and learning can be utilised by cities within integrated strategies for their future development'. As such, the project had the explicit intention both of influencing European policy and of assisting city authorities in implementing policy. Charles was project manager for CRITICAL, Duke a participant observer, in a project involving four European cities and universities (Newcastle, Dublin, Tampere and Dortmund) together with a subsequent ancillary Australian partner (Melbourne).

The chapter documents intellectual and practical aspects of how the project took shape and was managed over a three-year period, paying particular attention to discussions *among* the four, then five, partners, of the challenge of identifying the essential features of a learning city-region. The authors reflect that it would have been an easier task if they had not been forever looking over their shoulders at what 'those who do' would make of the outcome, at how it could be used to examine and improve practice: 'uninhibited by such utilitarian considerations, it would have been so much easier to refine and elaborate the concepts, using the abstractions and special argot with which academics address themselves through their myriad of specialised journals'.

Language is a key theme of the final chapter, as is the use of metaphors as an important resource for communication. Like Wilson, the authors note tensions in the different priorities of policy-makers and researchers, including the challenge of sustaining a focus on learning, notwithstanding short-term pressures. There are practical difficulties to be addressed. Ultimately the increasing examples of 'co-production', the 'shared utilisation and exploitation of knowledge', which abound in universities, still leave government agencies with the challenge of disseminating the new knowledge. At the same time, the authors finish optimistically by noting that even just one or two 'listeners' in key agencies can lead to opportunities for dialogue and new modes of policy formation.

The emerging picture

What sense do we draw from this kaleidoscope of perspectives on learning regions, social capital and place management? In the first place, there is an emerging cohesiveness of theory and practice that was less evident when Pascal first embraced its apparently discrete concepts as the foundation of its ambitions. The concepts resonate with researchers, policy-makers and practitioners in all parts of the world, including less developed nations, even though meanings and possibilities can vary significantly. This reflects the significance of the increasingly transnational economic and political influences which shape people's livelihoods and their capacity for cultural expression, in quite unpredictable and volatile ways.

Yet, amidst this uncertainty and the challenges to the sovereignty of elected governments, these contributors demonstrate progress that has been made. Regional governments in different parts of the world are intervening in processes of change so as to give their citizens new opportunities to assert local values, and to enhance their economic and social well-being. This is reflected in their priorities, their resource allocation, and above all in the ways that government agencies understand their role and their relationships with each other and with communities.

There are few initiatives, however, which are readily generalisable across regions or nations. Part of the learning that is occurring is about how people and regional governments come to understand their potential for economic and social growth, and how to intervene. It is not easy to sustain the delicate balance which exists between people acting on their own behalf, 'self-managing', and acting as citizens led and supported by political leaders. The challenge is even greater now that transnational pressures for change are leading to greater social polarisation, and to a growing number of people who are excluded from employment, decent housing and the other attributes that are taken as the mark of civilised society.

Researchers can assist policy-makers in addressing this challenge through their capacity not only to document a diversity of interventions but also to examine closely both immediate and longer-term consequences. At the most basic, the authors represented in this book show the importance of providing policy-makers with evidence about the circumstances of their citizens, and of levels of need. More generally, research highlights points of intervention where regional governments can have particular influence, or can mobilise actions that will help to reorient the forces in play. Most provocatively, research and analysis can challenge aspects of government operations which contribute to polarisation and to diminishing the livelihoods of their citizens in the face of dramatic economic and cultural changes.

This book shows how the contemporary context of change requires respect for the quality of relationships among people in place, even though their world might be wrenched around in the most fundamental of ways – through, for example, the closure of a large local factory. It shows how willingness to challenge trends, and to build resources for critical thinking and for dialogue about possibilities, can produce learning leading to quite unanticipated outcomes. It shows also that respect for these qualities of local life can serve well as the foundation for good policy and programmes, notwithstanding tensions that can arise from the interests of local stakeholders. It shows, finally, that government agencies have much to learn about how they work, and work with each other, especially in intervening in local communities. *Making knowledge work* is about progress and possibilities. It points a way forward for researchers, for policy-makers and for practitioners.

Pascal, the network

Where does this leave Pascal in terms of how to 'make knowledge work?' This second book from the Pascal Observatory[1] was inspired by its third[2] international conference in October 2005. Taking the main themes of place management, social capital and learning regions, and assisted by the National Institute of Adult Continuing Education (NIACE), more than 120 public policy-makers, community development leaders and academic researchers from across the globe met at the University of Stirling to share knowledge and experiences of community-building, policy-making, regeneration and sustainability projects.

The conference generated papers from many different theoretical and geographical perspectives, all available on the Observatory website, at http://www.obs-pascal.com. This book builds on discussions at the conference but, more importantly, on work that has flowed from the conference. For example, Kent County Council is benefiting from new links established with the State of Victoria. New projects are underway which will engender support to improve local service delivery. The opportunity for a new Strategic Innovation Gateway at Québec, Canada was explored during the conference. Other similar opportunities have emerged.

Questions remaining important for further discussion include:
- What kinds of interventions work most effectively in achieving which goals?
- What are the implications of different kinds of partnerships for the effectiveness of various interventions?
- Are different kinds of interventions more appropriate for influencing some economic and social objectives rather than others?
- What lessons can be learned about the effectiveness of initiatives which have both economic and social objectives?
- What is joined-up government and is it important?
- How do initiatives allow or provide for joined-up government?
- What is the best model for joining up?
- How can policy-makers best utilise one another's skills and knowledge?
- How can social inclusion be made a reality in learning communities?

Pascal will continue to link researchers and policy-makers involved. This will enhance the development of learning cities and regions balancing social inclusion and economic development. The website provides an ongoing point of communication and connection. Pascal conferences, projects and other opportunities for discussion and debate extend and share understanding of how to build relationships amongst those generating new knowledge on these issues and those making decisions about policies and programmes – in other words, making knowledge work.

Notes

[1] The first was: *Rebalancing the Social and Economic: Learning, Partnership and Place* (2005) by Chris Duke, Mike Osborne and Bruce Wilson (eds).

[2] The first two were held at the University of Stirling in Scotland in March 2004, and in Melbourne in Australia in October 2004 (organised by a partnership of PASCAL, the Australian Institute of Public Administration, and the Department for Victorian Communities).

Chapter 2

Concepts and realities of learning cities and regions

Paul Bélanger

Late modernity cities are caught in a dynamic of inter-urban competition for their future growth and development. This is in response to crises produced by the rapid transformation of the world economy and a metamorphosis of their social fabric over the last three decades.

In this world of uncertainty, the development of cities relies on urban vitality and is less reliant on national agencies alone. Cities need to become the first agency of their future. It is in such a context that visions of *learning cities* or of *learning regions*, though often imprecise, have become in the last decades an emerging theme in urban debate and policy.

In order to grasp the moving notion of a *learning city* and its reality in different urban contexts, we have divided this chapter as follows: after exposing the socioeconomic context beyond this emerging vision of urban development and urban governance, we review various notions of a *learning city* and their different models of operations in order to offer, in the last part, a critical assessment of the moving and ambiguous reality of *learning cities.*[1]

The sociological context of this emergence

New meaning and position of cities in a globalised world

Cities of late modernity are compelled to compete for their urban develop-ment in response, primarily, to a multiple crisis of a socioeconomic nature. This crisis has been produced by the development of global communication networks and free trade, giving corporations more flexibility to relocate production and service facilities across national frontiers around the world, by the critical attrition of mass-production systems laying off less qualified active populations, and by the unpredictability of potential investments in national and urban spaces. In this context, cities have been compelled to re-image and re-imagine themselves in order to secure economic growth and development.

They are compelled to do so with a lessening of their ability to influence development (Chavagneux, 1997), since for well over a decade, several key factors have contributed to the enfeeblement of the nation-state. This weakened national autonomy can be explained by the trend toward the integration and interdependence of national economies. It goes hand-in-hand with the continued acceleration of communication, and with the transformation of the urban economic situation, now characterised by increased mobility and flexibility in the workplace, and by marked growth in the knowledge-intensive economic sectors (Reich, 1991; OECD, 2003). The changes occurring in the sites where economic decisions are made are twofold: a movement upwards, toward the boards of directors of multinational companies and their associated financial networks; and a movement downwards, to the level of large city states, which have become key actors.[2] While new supranational and invisible management of the economy has raised local awareness, and given rise to what may be called a 'global public opinion',[3] it also reawakens the need for cities to reassert themselves as semi-autonomous agencies.

There is a body of literature addressing this changing role of cities struggling at the international level for investment and for their future (Bélanger and Côté, 2005; Hannigan, 2003, Castells, 2003, 1996; Harvey, 1990; Judd and Swanstrom, 1994; Robins, 1997; Sassen, 1991). In this transformation, the uncertainty and the risks are huge. For each urban community – its municipal government, its economic actors and its civil local civil society – the search for strategies that can better position them in this global free trade world and inter-urban competition is imperative, though the process is not evident (Sassens, 2000). In this sense, one of the main issues for the cities is the capacity to project a bold image of urban vitality into the international marketplace,[4] yet the capacity of cities to develop from within and articulate this vitality goes much beyond.

It would be an overstatement to speak of a transition from nation-state to city-state. The late modern cities are not to be compared with the middle age city-fortresses, neither with the former autonomous Hanseatic cities of northern Europe. However, the tendency towards a greater capacity of initiatives on the part of urban communities, due to their centrality in contemporary economic, political and social life, is clear, as is their inclination to work alongside national governments, intervening directly to negotiate their terms of development (OECD, 2001a).

Confronted by the external context of the breaking-up of economic national borders, cities of late modernity are, also, challenged by the metamorphosis of their own socio-demographic fabric. At the same time as cities are becoming a focal point of identification for the city dwellers and a key cultural reference in the real life of people, their populations are becoming more and more multicultural, creating a stronger demand for a local democracy relying not only on equality of chances but also on recognition of differences (Taylor, 1994).

It is at the levels of urban communities and economic regions that individuals tend more to establish a sense of local identity and 'rootedness', and where they interact on a daily basis. It is here also that people go to work and, through daily contact, participate in society and in the economy. It is, again, at this level of proximity that the experiences of the multicultural and of potential inter-ethnic tensions are lived. It is here that they acquire, produce and transfer knowledge. And this growing sense of identity with the city creates a social demand for responsive regional or municipal governance. It is also here that the cultural plurality can either become an explosive context or a new asset.

Within this new urban context, the city appears as a risk society (Beck, 1992), having not only to redefine its attracting position on the global scene, but also to construct its very future.

The strategic urban resource of the city and the recourse to lifelong learning strategies

The more a city turns out to be aware of its necessity to become the main agency of its future, the more conscious it tends to be that the main strategic resource to take upon this challenge is the capacity of its citizens to act, to produce and to express themselves. This is true from both an economic and a socio-cultural perspective.

First, the trend towards specialisation of production and introduction of new technology as well as different work arrangements, contrary to the former Taylorist breakdown of tasks, is leading to multi-task job descriptions. And where these new information-intensive and relation-based work environments occur, precisely in the niche where the late modern cities are attempting to position themselves, work tends to become more abstract, more complex and more 'intellectual' (Bélanger and Federighi, 2000, chap. 4) It is precisely in such a perspective that the strategic resource of cities becomes their active population. A distributed and continuous development of the qualification and skills of the population, precisely in the context of a shifting economy towards more and more knowledge-intensive techniques of production, tends to be increasingly recognised as the main source of a renewed *urban vitality*.

Secondly, these work-related trends could not be isolated from a larger cultural urban trend, since it is the very same people who are the producers, the consumers, the fiscal contributors and the citizens of their urban community. To dissociate production from the subjects who produce – or to consider the changing mode of production separately from the increasingly competent people who are required to participate in it – would prevent any analyst from understanding the interaction between the new economic demand for a continuous development of local human resources and the emerging social demand of the 'local producers' and the local citizens, to give concrete meaning to their identification with the city. Moreover, one could even say that it is this shared sense of identity that creates the condition for a city to become a potentially organic, active agency capable collectively of intervention at this effective level.

If cities' futures rely on their urban vitality, which rests largely on the continuous development and pooling of the competence of the population in their positioning within the interurban competition, then one could grasp the reasons beyond the increasing recourse to the *lifelong leaning* discourse, in the cities' debate, on their necessary strategies. The continuing and generalised development of the urban population's capacity to act and express themselves is then becoming both a condition of urban vitality and a learning social demand of the population to join in the production of the future and in the distribution of its outcomes. Yet this seems often to be taken lightly, in the negotiation at play between the urban power elite and investors and developers.

One needs to reiterate that, in this context, the reference to the notion of lifelong learning, though *polysemic* (see next section), is critical, because no city will be able to rely on an increasingly competent active population, nor on a reflexive society and on vital interaction with and between its citizens without insuring an intensive multifaceted investment in education as a lifelong process that touches economic and other spheres of urban activity. In fact, it difficult to envisage a city reinforcing leading-edge economic sectors without also creating the conditions and environments that will support the population's ability to participate in these new economic sectors.

These are necessities for the implementation of projects of lifelong learning: a successful initial education for the young generation, together with significant increase of continuing education and training provision, and broader participation in adult learning. If any city ever hopes to compete efficiently and have a certain control over its future, that city requires a sustained mobilisation of its various educational agents.

New roles of cities to ensure the development and pooling of their collective intelligence

A big difficulty with this central reference to lifelong learning is that the redeployment of educational efforts, which is so needed for a city that strives to become an active actor of its future, both on the global scene and inside its boundaries, is not within its formal control.[5] In other words, the problem with this lifelong learning basic condition of their development is that cities have little or even no jurisdiction and governmental power over both initial and adult and continuing education. How, then, could a city ensure such development when it has no direct authority over it? Here, in this apparent contradiction, lies the challenge, the opportunity and the reason d'être of the notion of a *learning city*.

Not formally in charge, but deeply concerned, cities tend to develop new strategies to ensure the attainment of their lifelong learning ambition: the *learning city strategy*. A review of literature on this notion, and the observation of experiences, indicate different types of action.

The first and foremost action is the formation by the urban community of *a common and mobilising vision of its future*, a vision that attempts to integrate the economic, socio-political and cultural dimensions of a global strategy to deal with the uncertainty of its development. Prior and consecutive to the formation of such vision, a negotiation process takes place through which the different groups and institutions are invited to confer and explore common views and joint actions to deal with the uncertain future of their region and, more directly in education, to pool and join efforts. Often, an initial plural mechanism such as a committee or task-force plays a pivotal role in helping groups to identify what they have in common, and to work together on concrete projects.

Such a prospective imaginary linked to the creation of a large consensus on concrete urban projects that reflect and nourish it cannot, of course, emerge in one day or in one conference. It is the result of a mediation process that includes different actors with various interests; the amplitude of the process will determine to a large degree the legitimacy of the constructed imaginary. Then, such vision has its own force, creates momentum, and mobilises actors; it enlarges the economic and educational governance of the urban collectivity.

A second action, more directly focused on the educational scene, is for the urban community to intervene 'upstream' in the *expression of the social demand for initial and continuing education*. Without control over the various educational responses, the cities and the various actors involved could make a huge difference by supporting the identification and expression of learning needs, by helping to remove non-educational barriers to education and, beforehand, in the expression of educational aspirations. Dissemination of information on learning opportunities and celebration of atypical educational achievements are part of this line of action.

> A key concept of the learning community is the addressing of learning needs through partnership. It uses the strengths of social and institutional relationships to bring about cultural shifts in perceptions of the value of learning. (Cara, 2003, p. 3)

A third type of action, and certainly the one more frequently referred to in the literature, includes a series of *interventions with and as networks*. Within the notion of autonomous networking, the functioning network itself has its role and dynamic (Castells, 1996) and brings cumulative effects. Such connections are often best made at a municipal level, where the actors can better identify what is at stake and is required in developing and sharing the urban potential and collective intelligence (Brown and Lauder, 2001, p. 218). Yarnit (2000, p. 11) speaks of partnerships and the use of the *strengths of social and institutional relationships*. Within this framework, the municipal government is not viewed as a new instance of educational planning, but as an active partner bringing the various, strategic educational agencies and constituents into play.

Many authors refer here to the concept of *social capital*, which we will discuss later (see previous section). The interlinking networks strategy strives to implement each initiative in such a way as to lead to further actions (Cara, 2003), and to mutual reinforcement of investments (OECD, 2001a). The emergence of the learning city depends on being able to negotiate without formal mandate, and to link voluntarily different players and institutions. It implies the dissemination of initiatives and alternative responses which might otherwise take place in isolation, each mutually unaware of actions being taken elsewhere.

A fourth action, crucial though low profile, is one of *playing intersectorally*. Not the sole responsibility of education nor of the different other national ministerial areas, and yet, much interested in building a synergy between them, the cities and other actors try, with various success, to bridge and functionally integrate at their local level, the isolated intervention of departments of education, health, social affairs, justice, culture and public transport.

A fifth complementary and indirect but powerful way to act indirectly in education is through *the enrichment of the learning environments* in the city and its sub-regions. At local level, an entire structured and semi-structured learning ecosystem – with a thousand resources, formal and other – could be identified and connected which, then, could bring supportive learning resources and create a climate conducive to meaningful participation in structured educational activities. The notion of learning cities, indeed, refers not only to the diversification and promotion of learning opportunities but also to the diffuse impact of daily environments in which adult and young learners find themselves. The availability and animation of such stimulating environments at the work place and in the community is part of *learning community* strategies (Belanger, 2003).

One cannot refer to urban learning environment without recognising the ongoing *multiculturalisation* of cities. The coexistence of many cultures within the city may either feed racism and prejudice or pique interest and curiosity, or stimulate citizens' desire to learn. The literature on this topic offers various models of development (endogenous, synchronous and ana-synchronous) (Benfield, Terris, Vorsanger and Glendening, 2001; Walsh, 2001; Glaeser, 1991; Grossman and Helpman, 1992) which are of high interest in identifying strategies for the *learning city*. More generally, border-less access to informal and self-learning learning sites, centres, places and infrastructures has proved to be an indispensable support to correct inequalities arising from age, socioeconomic status, ethnic identity or employment status.

Definitions and models of *learning cities*

Definitions

The notion of *learning city*, as an emerging powerful urban imaginary, has been variously defined. Originally referred as a learning community[6] with a territorial base, the notion is

> ... used in a number of different ways within the education sector. In some instances, it refers to an overarching strategy developed by powerful partners to change learning behaviour in a large city. In others it relates to a tiny community-based learning initiative focused on a learning centre in a specific neighbourhood. (Cara, 2003)

European and Australian experiments have already produced many definitions of learning cities and regions:

1) [The learning city is] a city, town, village or region which harnesses and integrates its economic, political, educational, cultural and environmental structures toward developing the talents and human potential of all its citizens. It provides both the structural and a mental framework which allows its citizens to understand and react positively to change ... lifelong learning is primarily a response to the complexities of change, culture, and civilization in the modern world, liberating the creativity and spirit of individual. (Longworth, 1999, pp. 10–12, in *Udaipur as a Learning City*)

2) A learning city ... strives to learn how to renew itself in a time of extraordinary global change. Using lifelong learning as an organising principle and social goal, [it] ... promote[s] collaboration of the civic, the private, voluntary and education sectors in the process of achieving agreed upon objectives related to (... sustainable economic development and social inclusiveness). (Landry and Matarasso, 1998, in Candy, 2003, p. 1)

3) A learning city ... uses the strengths of social and institutional relationships to bring about cultural shifts in perceptions of the value of human learning. Learning cities explicitly use learning as a way of promoting social cohesion, regeneration and economic development, which involve all parts of the community through the range of resources they bring together. (Learning City Network, G-B, in Candy, 2003)

25

In this set of definitions,[7] one could observe common elements: a learning city or city region is one that identifies itself as a collective actor searching to reposition itself on the global scene. To that end, it holds on a logic of action based on three organising principles:

1. It retains lifelong learning as a key to ensure the development and pooling of the active population knowledge and competency in order to give the urban region a competitive advantage.

2. It relies, for inducing change, on the networking capacities and opportunities of the community and the feasibility, within its space, of developing cooperation between institutions (integrating space management).

3. In need of public support, it relates the economic goal of regeneration to the socio-cultural objective of social inclusion, attempting either to involve civil society in the decision or/and to ensure social cohesion.[8]

The learning city is then defined as an organic, active whole capable of intervention at an effective plane; addressing people where they live and work, where learning needs and potentials are concretely defined. With its tangible goals and the advantage of more direct relationships with the various actors, the city is seen as operating at a better, more suitable plane to mobilise the many agents and resources involved, and to cause a synergy between them.

Different operational models

At the core of the various projects for a learning city is the formation of a strategic network, in reference to the notion of autonomous networking (Castells, 1996). It is worth reviewing some of these models through their explicit description, better to grasp the social significance of the notion of *learning cities*.

Barnsley's model

Barnsley's model (see Figure 2.1) of urban regeneration (Yarnit, 2000) shows how, from the perspective of lifelong learning, a city can regenerate itself though the complementary and cumulative effects of formal and informal educational interventions, economic actions, social measures and cultural/intercultural practices. All the elements are shown as working in reciprocal movement. Thus one could imply that, according to this model, the cumulative effect could only take place if measures are taken not only for creating an attractive context and for investment but also for wealth

Figure 2.1 Barnsley's model

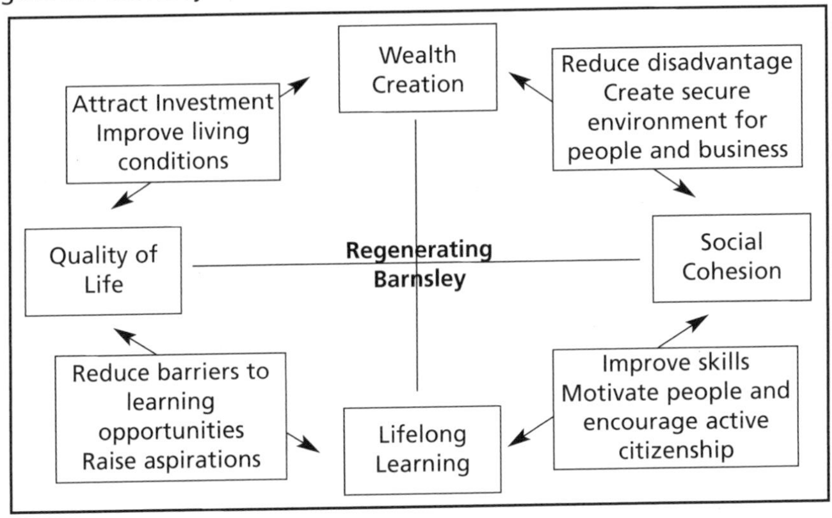

Source: *Local Economy, February 2000, p. 297*

distribution, social cohesion and the removal of barriers to learning opportunities and raising aspirations.

Steiner's model

Steiner's model (2002) (see Figure 2.2) illustrates the mutual influence of
various players in a learning city and the conjunction of factors and contexts
which can initiate a positive or unconstructive synergy. It then implies that
some interactions might work against the stated objectives, as in the case of a
city where players are isolated and 'weaker elements' are put aside. However,
the play of mutual influence can also, according to Steiner, be positive, but
only when preceded by a critical mass of 'bottom-up' action planning, along
with the establishment of common goals and an agreed general strategic
framework for action, including updating economic investment and
increasing opportunities for education, training and self learning.

Candy's model

Candy in Australia (Candy, 2003) proposes a similar but simpler model (see
Figure 2.3) of the synergistic growth potential that, assuming social
cohesiveness, could represent a sustained, endogenous economic
development of a city.

Figure 2.2 Steiner's model

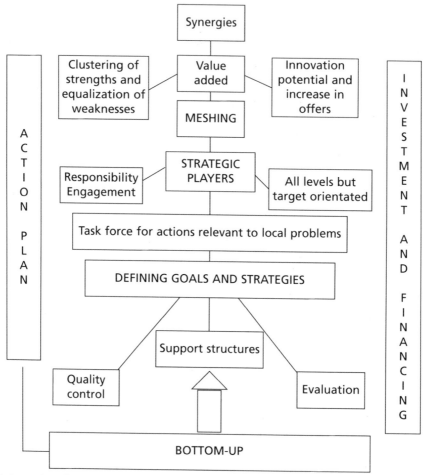

[Adapted and translated from the original German – Steiner, 2002]

Different orientations and levels of interventions

Through these definitions and working models, one can see two sets of orientations and four levels of interventions. In a minimal acceptance of the notion, *learning city* refers to the marketing strategy of an urban area in its effort to attract investment in knowledge intensive economic areas by exposing the innovation and creativity of its town (see Florida, 2002; Hall, 2000). What is notable in this narrow acceptation of the *learning city* as mainly a marketing device is that such urban development projects are largely *symbolic* and *ideological* in nature, conceived and constructed for their symbolic advantages.[9]

The reference to a *learning city* means, in other cases, the actual and projected intensity of educational investment both in initial schooling and in continuing education and training.

Within the Pascal Network,[10] the notion goes deeper (Duke, Osborne and Wilson, 2005): assuming the formation of mobilising vision, it involves the intensity of learning initiatives, an intersectoral space management approach and recognition of the potential contribution of active and interactive networks, that is to say the social capital of the city.

Looking back at the different types of actions involved (see above), one can see how, then, the same notion could refer to different strategies of various amplitudes.

Indeed, the prospective vision of a city could be the construct of few economic actors able to 'sell' it to a larger audience, or the result of a broader mediation process involving all segments of the urban society. One could speak of a continuum from the placing of a top down or hegemonic vision to a socially rooted process of creating a collective project.

Figure 2.3 Candy's model – Community capacity-building through learning

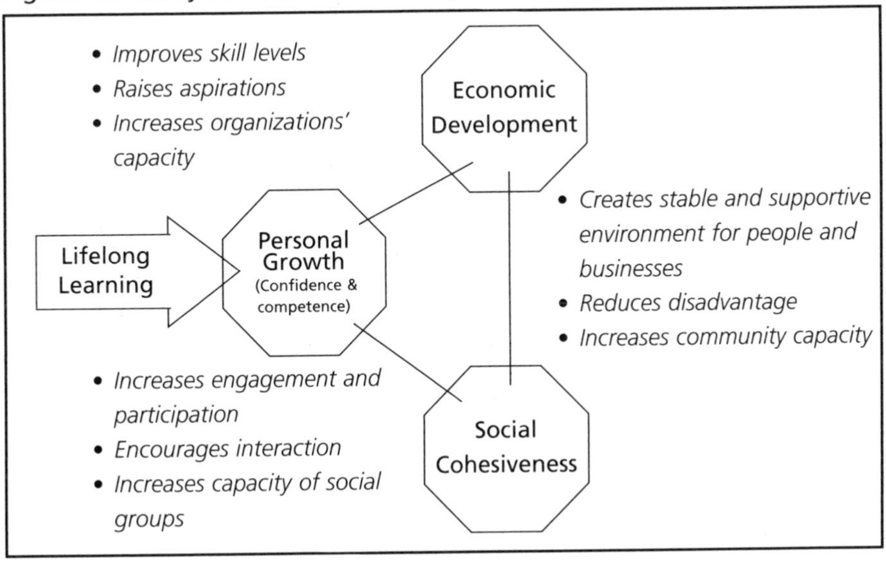

Of course, this continuum of *learning city* models is not neutral. Considering the diverse degrees of inclusiveness in the negotiation processes involved, and the consequent different legitimacy they produce, the continuum is not so continuous. The reality observed is moving; its ambiguity is indicative of both its social significance and its current ambivalence.

The moving and ambiguous reality of learning cities

From an anthropological perspective, a *learning city* is also a learning one in view of the complex integration process of the vision or discourse among the actors and the public opinion, and in view of its potential constitutive role in the adoption of new procedures of urban governance, also more profoundly, in the dynamics itself of social relations in this municipal society. It has to be seen as a social learning process even more so when one considers that both this shared and resonant imaginary of the future of the city and this built consensus on ways to develop synergy between initial schooling and continuing development and pooling of competency of the adult population are never ended.[11]

The 'city project', which can be described, in Touraine's terms (1988), as the definition of what the city is and wants to be and of how it agrees collectively to move toward this prospective identity, is necessarily a moving one. The project is crystallised and explicit enough to produce its expected mobilisation; yet, because of the mediation on which it is based, it will always be in evolution, continuously integrating new concerns and reflecting changing social relations.

The current general economy of lifelong learning

Lifelong learning is an ambiguous notion, not only because its meaning and value orientation are shifting from one agency to the other and from time to time,[12] but also because empirical evidence is showing that, in the current general economy of lifelong learning, initial educational systems and the organisation of adult learning provision tend to work as a cumulative process, positively for people with longer initial education and negatively for the others (Bélanger and Valdivielso, 1997).

Breaking with social reproduction of educational inequality in the city is a central issue. It has to do both with accessibility to prolonged initial education, and with the lifting of obstacles to participation in adult learning. Widespread sustainable and lifelong development of competency and curiosity, indeed, cannot happen without universal equality of opportunity in initial education. The recognition of successful educational experience in the initial part of people's lives as a critical factor for active lifelong learning biographies is well documented (Rubenson, 2003; Sargant, 1997; Bélanger and Tuijnman, 1997). For example, it implies the search for a suite of solutions against high drop-out rates among the young generation of its citizens. Entrance into the labour market of a significant number of young people without appropriate qualifications is, indeed, bound to create a serious threat for the future economy and the contribution of civil society in the municipal governance.

Cities see also their interest at stake in expanding beyond initial education and across the lifespan, through the upgrading and improvement of competence. On the rapidly changing industrial and social scene, cities cannot wait 30 years to renew the qualifications of their active population. Enlarged accessibility to initial education does not suffice to curb the trend toward reproduction of educational inequalities along the adult life course lifespan in the workplace and in daily life. A strategy for a society with the capacity for widespread initiative cannot work without freeing, for adult citizens, learning resources that are currently isolated and woefully under-utilised by the population.

To a significant degree, the emergence of such active learning cities hinges on the way the learning requirements of organisations and the local society, together with the individual aspirations of people, are expressed, and on how they generate wide and significant participation in formal and informal learning activities.

The learning demand is always a social demand, because it is composed of the new capacity for action of people required by organisations and systems in pursuit of their objectives, and the subjective aspirations and expectations of people in pursuit of their individual work and life project. Between these two dimensions in tension, a process of mediation and informal or formal negotiation is always at work.

The problem is not the social demand for learning, which is growing. In industry, the trend towards the introduction of new technologies, and specialisation and flexibilisation of production (Piore and Sabel, 1984; Lash and Urry, 1994), is demanding more competence and initiative. In the new information and relation-based environments in the service sector, work tends to become more abstract and more complex, requiring new abilities to manage information and an aptitude for interpersonal communication.[13] In society as a whole, it is not only the experts but also the 'secular' population that is being obliged to put its brains to work, to continually interpret new knowledge, technical information and expertise, to test these through a daily routine of trial-and-error, and to make the best possible decisions (Giddens, 1994). 'Safe' technical solutions are giving way to a reflexive citizenry; democratisation of formal democracy requires the recognition, reinforcement and renewal of citizenship, that is, citizens who are themselves reflexive.

The problem then is not the growing social demand for learning as such but first the imbalance in the operating definition of learning demand that most often, at the end of the day, will prevail and generate discriminatory responses and, secondly, the current conditions for participation in education that tend often to reproduce inequality.

An important issue is thus the creation of conditions, in all areas of the city and in all work places, for full expression of all learning demands. A multiple strategy is then needed: diffusion, also through media, of positive images of participation in learning activities, the creation of mechanisms for mediating learning demands through decision-making structures, dissemination of information on the various and often mutually unknown learning opportunities in the city, availability of local counselling and learning centres, services for recognition of prior learning, the involvement of museums, libraries and popular scientific diffusion centres such as the Planetarium, the organisation of Adult Learners' Week, and so on.

In cities, knowledge networks and opportunities for learning tend to form a series of comparatively isolated, though often overlapping, circles which vary in number. Part of the project of the *learning city*, as it is currently emerging, is to identify these formal and informal learning agencies and networks, to foster communication among them, and to make them known to the public, with a view to better responding to the growing and diversified social demand for learning.

The problem, hence, is not lack of social demand but its expression, and the creation of space and facilitating contexts whereby individuals can express their often implicit learning aspirations and negotiate their recognition together with external education and training requests, thus generating new mode of educational response among the various formal and non-formal agencies.

Take the case of Montréal. Its innate potential as a *learning city* is based on many indicators: the ongoing transition toward an intensive knowledge-based economy,[14] the quantity and quality of its learning and educational institutions at every level,[15] its multitude of informal learning resources, its social and communications infrastructures, and its diversity and cultural dynamism. Montréal is wealthy in educational resources of all kinds, and offers fertile soil for initiatives. However, its resources and its educational agents exist in near-isolation from each other and from the public. To create a continuum and generate a cumulative and diffused dynamic (Cooke, 1998, 1999) capable of reaching the population as a whole, these resources and practices have to act and interact differently. A critical factor is the creation of new networks and the activation and linking of existing ones across institutional traditional boundaries, in short some kind of social capital.

The ambiguity of social capital

In the literature on learning cities and regions, reference to the concept of social capital, though ambivalent, is pre-eminent. It is used to acknowledge the existence of ties and networks among and between individuals as effective channels of communication, as informal learning and inter-learning context, and as a factor of mobilisation for collective intervention.

The problem is that the meaning of social capital varies greatly and comes even in contradictory forms (Mowbray, 2005; Cavaye, 2005). For some, influenced by the consensual community approach of Putnam (2000), social capital means the measurable level of social cohesiveness and mutual trust that characterises a community. According then to the level, social cohesion constitutes a positive asset: the more social capital, the better-off a community becomes. Hence, through the construct of social cohesion as a key independent variable, recommendations follow on consensual community-building practice and policy.

For other researchers (Duke, Osborne and Wilson, 2005; Field, 2005), social capital refers to the extent of social connectedness and of various ties and networks as a strategic factor, unevenly present among individuals and among communities which derive advantage from these social connections. Social capital refers here to the structural dimension of social and economic life (Duke, Osborne and Wilson, 2005); it recognises social divisions and encompasses inevitable tensions between social integration and social exclusion. In that perspective, diversity and divergence of such networks could become 'essential elements in triggering the emergence of new processes' (Sotarauta, 2005). While social cohesion is the key word for the Putnam trend, the Pascal networks tends to use the terms of social inclusion and social integration: a significant shift.

The structure of relations between and among actors (Coleman, 1988) and the emerging networking character of societies (Castells, 2003) cannot be ignored. Social capital is a critical contextual variable and a potential strategic resource for individual and social actors. From an individual perspective, social capital refers to the ties and networks that a subject enjoys, and that influence participation in education as well as professional mobility. Social capital, wrote Bourdieu (1986), is 'the aggregate of the actual or potential resources which are linked to possession of a durable network of more or less institutionalized relationships of mutual acquaintance and recognition ... which provides each of its members with the backing of the collectively owned capital ...'

From a city or regional perspective, the existence of various tacit and organised networks constitutes a basis on which a city or region could rely and mobilise[16] in order to emerge as a collective actor with 'self-renewal capacity' (Sotarauta, 2005).

Social capital is thus a dialectical reality. It need not play only in the direction of accumulated resources used by agencies to reproduce inequality (Field, 2005). The investment strategies of a group or a city to draw on networks of relationships could aim at the reproduction of existing power relations as well as at changing them. Concretely it could function to preserve dominant social ties, but it could also, because of access to various connections and interactions between sub-communities, become 'highly effective ways for generating knowledge and enlarging access to skill development opportunities, for empowerment of communities' (Cavaye, 2005).

The relationship made between learning city or region and social capital is ambivalent. One should always assess, when such a relationship is made, the implicit definition given to social capital and the orientation that it carries, because it may ignore critical factors and lead to very different strategies.

Moreover, and beyond that debate, there is an important reality of social dynamics, involved in the *learning city* processes, which the concept of social capital does not capture. We mean the conflicts of interest inherently at play in the social relations of all social formations and, consequently, the inevitable mediation and negotiation processes that have to take place for the construction of a collective prospective vision that has legitimacy and leads to sustainable action.

Conditions for socioeconomic and educational efficiency of a learning city project

An active *learning city* project cannot emerge from one day to the next, nor can it result from any single decision taken by a municipal authority. Observations of on-going experiences and extrapolations of research evidences from similar actions at urban level indicate some basic conditions.

A first condition or favourable context is the rise of crises or quasi-crises coming out of the ongoing transition of the local economic structure, and the sense of urgency among the social groups in the city to explore and negotiate new production niches, substituting themselves to the weakening ones. Such crises will only become productive as long as the present economic infra-structure offers capacity for adaptation or transition, and thus constitutes incentives for bringing in new investments. The presence of emerging new economic niches in a city could create additional positive context, because of the propensity for geographical concentration of similar industries.

A second condition is the iterative construction of a vision of the city's future through informal talks, consultation, conciliation and arbitration. Such vision constitutes a possible operating mobilising discourse. The condition of social and political efficiency of such organising discourse is, then, the extent of its resonance (Jessop, 2004). The larger the range of local institutions and the types of public it reaches and involves, and the greater the scale (from meso to macro national and global) of intervention in which it finds echo, the greater its potential for effective consequences at economic, educational and institutional political levels. Observation of experience shows that the mobilisation is only sustainable when concentrated on a few major 'projects' that are amenable to monitoring and that could, complementarily, translate the vision into action and produce, both for the public and for economic actors, evidence that things are moving in the expected direction.

A third condition, related to the second one, is the possibility for a broad mediation process among all constituencies of the urban region. This process requires the existence of networks of connections, more or less institu-tionalised, that could support the informal horizontal communication and negotiation process. Without that kind of social capital, the process required for the formation of a mobilising vision could not take place. Only in such an environment could spatial integrating governance emerge, and broader local policy implementation frameworks appear.

The mobilisation itself of economic, social and education actors around such a collective imaginary of the city's future is based on its legitimacy and, consequently, on the give and take achieved between the economic, social, cultural and educational actors of the city. In the absence of this fourth condition, the *learning city* project remains minimal; either, as said earlier, as a marketing device, or as a top-down short-term political move by some local groups and decision-makers.

A fifth condition, more directly related to the explicit learning dimension of the project, is the recognition that, without agreement on high priority given to the achievement of equality of educational opportunity for all the young city dwellers, the project is bound to fail. It will fail not only because of the gaps in the qualification of the labour force of tomorrow, but also because of the lack of legitimacy that the project will suffer by negating the give and take condition precisely where the learning city takes its main significance, in education. It will fall short because of the impossibility for the less advantaged social groups of the city to *give* their consent without *taking* educational advantages.

A sixth condition, also directly related to the education dimension of the learning city project, is the agreement by local governance that, even without control over educational and qualification policies, the city can nevertheless influence significantly, indeed modify, the general economy and lifelong learning of the city by intervening upstream. This means creating spaces and allocating support for the expression of the learning demand, and making the various information channels available to inform the public of the various opportunities for learning. In that regard, the participation of libraries and museums in the project is critical because of their role as buttresses of self-directed and informal learning, the invisible portion of the iceberg that is the learning city (Livingston, 2001).

Conclusion

Urban contexts are contexts of ongoing complex change to which a city may adapt passively, or reassert itself as a community able to define its chosen project and organise its forces to implement it. Cities of late modernity, indeed, tend more and more to recognise the need to act, to be directly present on the international scene and, within their territory, to draw both on their citizens' readiness to develop qualifications in order to operate in advanced economic domains and on their capacity for various local initiatives. However the notion of *learning city* goes much further.

A *learning city* is one that has been able to define itself as a collective actor, a self-renewing entity capable of learning, and thereby of repositioning itself to intervene internally through mobilisation, and on the world stage where many of the forces that affect it are at work. The seeds of the *learning city* lie in this recognition of the city's ability to take the initiative.

Of course, one has to recognise the various meanings given to the *learning city*. For some it remains a marketing campaign of local government exposing internationally the competitive advantages of the *smart city*. In other cases the *learning city* has a much fuller meaning: it refers to the collective action of a city, involving mobilisation of the internal actors and of the population. The main operating force of the active and multidimensional *learning city* is, then, the shared and resonant imaginary of its future, and of agreed ways to construct it – a development that, to be sustainable, depends on the social legitimacy of this vision, and hence on the amplitude of the mediation process that produces it.

Such a project of the city as a collective actor includes not only the formation of a prospective identity but also a twofold plan of action to ensure, first, the creation or consolidation of new economic niches and, second, implementation of the agreed learning priorities and of the structured and informal educational approaches required. A manifold lifelong learning strategy is then put in place to thwart the social reproduction of educational inequalities, and to ensure the development and pooling of the collective intelligence of the city (Brown and Lauder, 2001[17]). In that perspective, inequality in learning opportunities is becoming, for cities, not only a matter of responsiveness to the growing sense of 'publicness' of its citizens, but also a question of sheer capacity to manage its economic future, and to ensure the manpower that it will require tomorrow.

However, in a society, 'everything is not equally possible or impossible' (Bourdieu, 1986). The learning city project, as studied here, is not a voluntarist enterprise or discourse; it is the rise of a new logic of action, involving a manifold strategy, that could only emerge under some conditions exposed earlier.

This chapter, based on available sources and direct observation made by the author in his own city, has attempted to grasp the different meanings and practices or strategies of *learning city* projects, and the conditions observed when such a project emerges. Further research is needed to document, in context, ongoing experiences,[18] to document the often informal mediation process producing the working vision, to better understand the diffuse influence of the urban different learning environments, to assess the efficiency and limits of such local strategy in the current neo-liberal global economic world, to look at cases where citizens resist to shape the collective urban future or have it shaped by others, to study evidence whether and how mobilisation pays off in any significant way for average urban residents, and, finally, to deepen our understanding of the intersectorality of this new logic of action, and of the conditions for its emergence.

Notes

[1] This chapter is partly based on earlier research done in cooperation with B. Paetsch (2004).

[2] See Lahrèche-Révil (2002).

[3] [Translated from the original French] 'Awareness of the damage caused by the world's economic, political and military management has marked the birth of a global public opinion' (Original in Massiah, 2003). See also the charter from the World Social Forum: <http://www.wsfindia.org/charter.php>

[4] David Harvey (1989, 1990) called this strategy 'the mobilization of spectacle' and noted that 'imaging a city [has become] a means to attract capital and people in a period of intensified interurban competition and urban entrepreneurialism' (p. 92).

[5] In most cities and, even when a city has educational responsibility, it remains limited to primary and secondary education.

[6] A learning community is one which 'mobilizes all its resources in every sector to develop and enrich all its human potential for the fostering of personal growth, the maintenance of social cohesion, and the creation of prosperity'. (TELS, 2003).

[7] The definition given in French-speaking literature is similar. See for example the definition of P. Destatte from the Jules Destree Institute in Brussels: 'Une région apprenante est une région caractérisée par une coopération permanente et efficace entre toutes les parties prenantes du développement régional, basée sur la conviction qu'offrir une formation de qualité, tout au long de la vie à tous les habitants, rendra ce développement régional plus prospère, plus humain, plus démocratique et plus durable'.

8 The definition of OECD (2001a) speaks to the two last dimensions: 'A learning city is one with plans and strategies to encourage wealth-creation, personal growth and social cohesion through the development of the human potential of all its citizens.'

[9] Like the organisation of sports mega events and spectacular premises (Gibson 2005).

[10] See http:www.obs-pascal.com

[11] One could read in that perspective the Landry and Matarasso (1998, p.3) definition: 'A true learning (community) is one which develops by learning from its experiences and those of others. It is a place which understands itself and reflects upon that understanding ... Thus the key characteristic ... is the ability to develop successfully in a rapidly changing socio-economic environment.'

[12] The discourse on lifelong learning was conceived by UNESCO (1972) and OECD (1972), and, after a silence of almost two decades, later developed by UNESCO in the Delors report (1996) and the Hamburg Declaration (1997), as well as by OECD (1999), and the European Commission (2002). Today it is a key component in national policy statements across the planet. For critical assessments of this notion see Bélanger, 1994; Alheit and Dausien, 2002; Field, 2001; Medel-Añonuevo, Ohsako and Mauch, 2001; Tuijnman and Bostrom, 2002.

[13] Of course one has to recognise the contradiction, in the needed flexibility of production, between internal and external flexibilisation, where external flexibilisation tends to break down activities into malleable sub-contractible units, using 'lay out – lay in' practices to produce flexibility, while internal flexibilisation puts emphasis on internal dynamic based, at the local level, on expanding learning programmes and accessibility and creating space for internal initiative in communities of practice, and, at the macro level, on active labour policies.

[14] In the domains of biotechnology, aeronautics, nanotechnology and of new media and cultural industries.

[15] Four universities (more than 200,000 university students) and 15 community colleges.

[16] 'The volume of the social capital possessed by an agent thus depends on the size of the network of connections he can effectively mobilize ...' (Bourdieu 1986).

[17] 'Collective intelligence can be defined as empowerment through the development and pooling of intelligence.' (Brown Lauder 2001, p. 218).

[18] See, for example, Sotarauta 2005, Simons 2005, Collins 2005.

Chapter 3

Learning cities and learning regions: making the world a better place

Norman Longworth

The TELS project – early soundings

TELS (Towards a European Learning Society) was one of the first European Commission Socrates programme's supported projects in the field of learning cities and regions. Between 1999 and 2001 it studied, not in a very scientific or systematic way, the understanding of leaders in 80 European municipalities and regions about the concept of the learning city and their preparedness for its implementation within their authority. Not surprisingly, it discovered that most of the authorities studied were unaware of the existence of the term, but could nevertheless demonstrate some movement towards developing activities that would today typify a learning city approach. More interestingly, many of them were eager to know more, simply as a result of their participation in a project that seemed to offer a glimpse of a vision they were seeking to articulate. The recorded results of TELS are gathering dust on a Brussels basement shelf, but these are some of the recommendations it made to the Commission:

1. Create a cross-sectoral strand in the Socrates programme to support the development of learning cities and regions. Name it after a famous civic leader or the Goddess of Communities.
2. Establish a programme for Cities of Learning similar to that for Cities of Culture. If necessary run a competition to decide which city it will be in each country.
4. Develop indicators which measure and monitor aspects of the growth of learning cities and the learning society, and initiate surveys and studies of these in and across member states.

5. Raise the awareness of learning community concepts in municipalities throughout Europe through high-visibility events such as the European Learning Cities week.

6. Develop a 'Charter for European Learning Cities' outlining the city's responsibilities vis-à-vis its citizens as learners, and its relationship to a wider European learning community, which cities sign up to.

7. Create a European network of one or more university departments in each country able to specialise in learning city research and development.

9. Promote Europe-wide interactions and partnerships between local government, industry and others for wealth/employment creation and international employability.

10.Establish links with global organisations and countries to share good practice and foster joint cultural, economic and educational development in the area of learning communities.

It is interesting to note how many of these comprise an outward-looking mission for cities and regions and how many have actually been implemented. Number 1 for example resulted in the R3L programme, which joined more than 100 European regions in 17 lifelong learning projects to promote collaboration between them. An example of number 4 is the INDICATORS project led by Stirling University, which developed and made available 'stakeholder audits', tools by which schools, universities, small businesses, adult education institutions and the local authorities themselves could measure their commitment to building a learning region. These are now also available through Pascal and the resultant network of expertise centres comprises the beginning of the implementation of number 7.

Towards wider horizons

But the focus of this chapter is on numbers 9 and 10. It explores the rationale for some of the initiatives that link learning cities and regions globally, whether or not the European Commission has become involved. It argues that thinking globally and acting locally can bring real benefits, notwithstanding the protestations of minimalist pressure groups to restrict responsibilities to local issues. Playing a much larger part on the national and global stage can often produce medium and long-term advantage. The unprecedented emotional and financial response to the Boxing Day 2004 tsunami crisis by people of all ages, incomes and political persuasions is but one demonstration of the extent to which people have advanced in their perception of this planet as a global, more holistic, village.

There is no shortage of exhortations to take this horizon-widening step. *Lifelong Learning* delivered the following warning back in 1996, identifying the so-called global demographic time bomb as an imperative for the development of lifelong learning attitudes:

> If birth rates in the developed world are too low for comfort, those in the developing world are uncomfortably high. In the poorer parts of the world a massive population growth, helping to raise the present number of human beings on this very finite planet from 5 billion to 11 billion by the mid-twenty-first century, presents almost insoluble problems. These are environmental, nutritional, educational, moral and, in terms of stability, they are dangerous not just for the countries themselves but, through the overspill of instability, for the rest of the world. Many of these new inhabitants of our planet are perhaps destined to live at subsistence level and below unless massive ameliorative projects are initiated. To even begin to touch the problem, emphasis will need to be put on fundamental Lifelong Learning principles and the use of the new development and delivery technologies. (Longworth and Davies, 1996)

Sir Christopher Ball takes up the theme in *An Action Agenda for Lifelong Learning for the 21st Century*:

> Equity requires management. So there is a duty, alike for national and local governments, organisations and individuals, to practise affirmative action to help developing countries, deprived communities and disadvantaged people, by ensuring that they receive a disproportionate share of available resources so that the gaps do not widen into gulfs. Those who most need it should receive most help. (Ball and Stewart, 1995)

Jim Botkin, in his search for a 'wisdom' society', sees a potential saviour in the effective use of modern information and communications technology:

> The human gap – the gap between global problems of our own making and our own ability or inability to find solutions to those

problems – has widened since the time *No Limits to Learning* was published. Nevertheless, the possibilities for corrective action are greater today than they ever have been. We have an internet and e-learning suddenly at our fingertips. In 1979, we didn't know what computers were, much less worldwide networks like the world-wide web. (Botkin, 2002)

But he offers also a caution:

We need to be cautious that technologically-mediated global learning doesn't become a new force for domination. If we can imagine a kind of global learning that respects human diversity without asserting a cultural dominance over others, then e-learning opens a flood of possibilities that we have only begun to explore. The philosophical question is: industrial technology helped create the human gap, can information technology help bridge it? (ibid)

Schools to the fore

And of course there is also plenty of activity to address these issues in local authority schools around the world. The *iEARN* network for example:

Imagine a world in which teachers and students all across the planet are able to work collaboratively on projects that make a difference in the world,' says its publicity, 'Among the tens of thousands of schools worldwide that participate in iEARN, there is no shortage of success stories to demonstrate the power of iEARN's vision, not only to make a difference in the world, but to deepen the learning that takes place in these connected class-rooms. (iEARN, 2005)

All projects in iEARN are initiated and designed by teachers and students. This provides powerful examples of how new and emerging technologies can make a difference in teaching and learning. Their projects involve a final 'product' or exhibition of the learning that has taken place as part of the collaboration. These have included magazines, creative writing anthologies, websites, letter-writing campaigns, reports to government officials, arts exhibits, workshops, performances, charity fundraising and many more examples of youth taking action as part of what they are learning in the class-room. More than 150 interactive projects, including 'the Atlas of Diversity',

'Global teenager' and the 'One world project' enable children to develop research and critical thinking skills, experience with new technologies, cultural awareness and the habit of getting involved in community issues.

The *Global SchoolNet*, a similar international schools network funded mainly by large American corporations, has a more overt, but no less interesting, rationale. In its own words it ' partners with schools, communities and businesses to provide collaborative educational, scientific and cultural learning activities that prepare students for the workforce and help them to become literate and responsible global citizens'. Like *iEARN* it provides learning tools and materials, and training courses for teachers. It concentrates on obtaining concrete outcomes, but the model is oriented towards giving schoolchildren the skills, confidence and insights that allow them to become future leaders in industry and public service. Both originated in the USA in the 1980s and both have extended their operations to more than forty other countries. With Schoolnet Canada, they are the largest of the many service-learning networks linking schools with each other around the world.

There can be little doubt in this digital age that the internet is compressing the planet and changing radically the way that people see the wider world. Many cities are already multiracial, multiethnic, multilingual and multifaceted. The tide of history is propelling them, sometimes reluctantly, towards greater understanding of, and cooperation with, other regions and other races, religions, creeds and customs. Austria's national goals for schools includes these words:

> Young people have to be able to develop independent judgement and understanding of and responsibility for social relations, sensitivity to the political and philosophical views of others, and the ability to contribute to the economic and cultural life of the country, Europe and the world. Humanity, tolerance, solidarity, peace, justice and ecological awareness are values that stimulate action in our society and interact with economic issues. (Euridyce, 2002)

These fine words are echoed in other charters throughout the world. The vision that makes them a reality has yet to manifest itself on a sufficient scale. But a start has been made. Almost every South Australian school has links with schools in other countries in South-East Asia, North America and Europe. It is a key part of the educational experience for their young people.

LILARA – widening awareness

The links among the city's stakeholders extend far beyond schools. *'Seniornets'*, linking pensioners in New Zealand, Canada, USA and the UK, have been operating for some time. Universities have been international organisations for many years, feeding into, and from, the worldwide academic and research networks that provide their sustenance. Those that work with their local authorities to help build learning cities and regions make the fruits of that research available to its leaders and professionals. The Pascal network of universities, cities and regions, described later, is an excellent example. Many of its members contribute directly to pushing back the frontiers of learning region knowledge and action.

The LILARA (Learning in Local and Regional Authorities) project for example is a European university–local authority project developing consultation tools to identify the learning needs of managers and professionals *vis a vis* the growth of learning cities and regions. It takes as its mantra the notion that learning regions, much like quality management, will not happen without the consent of their administrators and, eventually, the citizens themselves. It is vital therefore to research, design and deliver the learning that each one needs. Moreover, such activities encourage the delivery of the joined-up, holistic local government needed to cope with twenty-first century challenges. Six European nodes in Italy, Hungary, Norway, Ireland, France and the UK are collaborating in the project, and the State of Victoria in Australia has expressed strong interest in developing its own version of LILARA under the Pascal umbrella. The results of the project will open up the world of local and regional authority education to the new influences to which modern cities and regions must respond.

The PALLACE project – linking stakeholders

This is just one example of the advantages of bringing universities on board as stakeholder contributors to the development of local and regional authorities. There are of course many more. In many ways they are evidence of a shrinking world whose stakeholders must communicate in order to survive. The PALLACE project for example, a low-budget initiative from the European Commission, created an organisational infrastructure by which each of the seven partners would supervise a stakeholder sub-project to explore what it could do to help create a learning city. It called it a city-ring. The Finnish partner for example concentrated on cultural services and created a portable display giving information and inviting feedback about Espoo as a learning city that could be erected in libraries, museums and galleries. This raised a great deal of interest among those who saw it, not least because they were invited to offer their own opinion on the subject. The French partner created and trialled materials on learning cities for elected representatives and shared these with the city of Marion in South Australia. In the Auckland region, the Papakura Lifelong Learning Trust addressed the opportunity to link adult education institutions and, with France, tested materials to discover their role *vis a vis* the construction of the learning city. South Australia linked its schools with those in Finland to involve children, teachers and parents internationally in focused debate about the learning community and what schools can do to help create it.

There is an important add-on value to this concept in that it not only creates heightened awareness of what a learning city can be but also potentially mobilises hundreds of people to contribute to it, not least those future citizens who will eventually inherit its administration. Stan Salagaras, the Australian project leader, defined the following as positive outcomes:

a) It has reinforced that schools are in fact, as a result of the nature of their role, involved on an ongoing basis in the development of links with their surrounding communities to enhance learning outcomes for all – it is a fundamental component of their educative role and function.

b) It has emphasised the important role of schools in the development of learning communities and enabled individual schools to benchmark themselves with learning communities elsewhere. The very nature of a learning community means that it should be open to review and analysis.

c) It has involved children, teachers and parents as well as tertiary education providers, business and community organisations in a debate about what schools can do to help create a learning community. There is significant add-on value to this in that it not only creates heightened awareness of what a learning community can be, but also potentially mobilises hundreds of people to contribute to it.

d) It has stimulated the documentation in the form of case studies of a diversity of learning community initiatives. Two schools, Mawson Lakes School and St Columba College, have compiled comprehensive reports on their role in the development of a learning community through the PALLACE project.

e) When combined, these case studies identify innovative and practical outcomes which can help other schools to develop curriculum and methodological practices for collaborative work in schools, another intended outcome of the PALLACE project.

f) It has created international links between schools in South Australia and Finland, which will continue to grow and develop in the future.

Such outcomes could be realised on a local basis, but Salagaras is also convinced that the international dimension, and the fact of working with other countries, provided strong motivation and increased the quality of the final results. Certainly the Chinese city of Beijing, which is developing a lifelong learning facility for 800,000 people in its Xichen district, gained much from its participation in PALLACE, as well as contributing some key ideas.

Kent – increasing fruitful links

So why should a city or region, beset as it is by local problems and answerable to local residents and ratepayers organisations, become involved in international activities of this sort? Where is the benefit for its citizens? How far should it go to play its part on the larger global stage? How relevant is it to the city's mission? There are no easy answers to these questions, but where they do exist they lie in the scope of cities' visions, the extent to which they are planning for their future in a multilateral world, the depth of understanding of their leaders and the quality of their humanity. Many cities are already multiracial, multiethnic, multilingual and multifaceted. The tide of history is propelling them, sometimes reluctantly, towards greater understanding of, and cooperation with, other regions and other races, religions, creeds and customs. There are also, as we shall see, measurable advantages.

The county of Kent in the UK has long-standing links with the French region of Nord-Pas de Calais in France. 'Transmanche', as it is called, recognises that national boundaries no longer apply to commercial activity and that there are considerable economic benefits to be obtained from such cross-border cooperation. Other parts of Europe such as Oresund, linking South Sweden with the Copenhagen area of Denmark, and the Franco-German region around Strasbourg are other examples. But Kent goes further than this. In 2004 it began to discuss mutual advantages in links with the Hungarian region of Bacs-Kiskun. More recently it has been working with New Kent and the State of Virginia in the USA (Kent County Council, 2005a).

Not unreasonably in a country where euro-scepticism is high, Kent's European strategy takes a hard-headed approach to European cooperation. Its pivotal location within North-West Europe and its role within the UK as a gateway to the Continent offer obvious advantages, but the prime rationale is 'obtaining funding, influencing policy and co-operating on common interests with other regions' in order to 'help KCC (Kent County Council) achieve its core priorities and meet Kent's needs' (Kent Count Council, 2005b).

Economic benefit is therefore the main rationale, but Kent believes that much can be realised economically through an increasing number of links with both traditional and new overseas partners, and not just by attracting European regional funding. The sectors identified for joint working with the French Nord-Pas de Calais region for example reflect the responsibilities of the two regions: that is, transport infrastructure, economic development, training, scientific and technological research, tourism and the environment. The process starts at the political level by 'strengthening bilateral co-operation between the two Regional and General Councils, initiating regular contacts and meetings between the different political and administrative areas and establishing Joint Working Groups to maintain regular mutual exchange on key issues' (*ibid*).

The enlargement of the European Union in 2005 was seen by Kent as an opportunity: 'The County Council has recognised that the addition of more than 100 million people to the EU's market of 370 million people will result in increased business, project and other opportunities from which the people of Kent could benefit'. Among the objectives of the Bacs-Kiskun link are:

- developing projects which provide clear trade and business development opportunities for Kent firms, such as joint ventures and the provision of goods and services, including technical advice and know-how;
- participating in opportunities for institution-building and know-how transfer initiatives;
- identifying opportunities for projects on best practice exchange between KCC and the Central and East European Countries in a range of different fields related to core business priorities, for example, Social Services or Environmental Management.

The county intends to follow this up by exploring other opportunities in the Baltic Countries, the Czech Republic and Poland. Kent's links with the state of Virginia are similarly influenced by economic advantage, but here there is a much more wide-ranging interpretation of what that constitutes. The following activities demonstrate this:

- School-to-school links;
- Professional development of teachers on a study visit to Virginia;
- Virginia Indians hold a Virginia Indian Festival at Gravesend, Kent;
- Kent Tourism Alliance (KTA) launched its US Campaign, targeting the eastern seaboard of the US;
- Joint production of *Jesus Christ Superstar* between New Kent High School in Virginia and Astor College for the Arts, Dover;
- Kent features at the Smithsonian Folklife Festival in Washington in 2007;
- Centre for Innovation & Technology (CIT) in Virginia becomes a founding organisation in the Strategic Innovation Gateway Network (SIGN) covering Kent, Virginia and Hungary.

City-states and region-states

Clearly the longer-term advantages of inter-region cooperation are being addressed, much in the same way that PALLACE engaged the stakeholders of the future in debate about the city's, and their own, future. The link between the social, the environmental and the economic has always been there in local authorities. In cooperation projects such as this the solutions are becoming more internationalised. Of course, Kent is not the only region to establish fruitful links with other parts of the world. The city of Southampton's cooperation project with Xideng in China is yet another example of the proliferation of global interaction between cities and regions. For all parts of local government there are opportunities and benefits.

It is perhaps a reflection of the increasing autonomy and influence of regional government. John Eger, former adviser to two US Presidents, has gone so far as to suggest that there is a return to the concept of the powerful city and region-state that existed for example in the palatinates of Northern Germany before unification, and in Athens, Sparta and Venice in the more distant past. He bases this opinion on the increased power and influence now trickling down to local and regional government in many countries of the world allied to the enormous potential power of the new information and communications technologies for intercity, inter-institutional and interpersonal multilogue. And to a certain degree he is right. The opportunities do exist, and are being exploited by creative and innovative cities and regions. And yet the world of the early twenty-first century is hardly a safer or happier place in which to live. Perhaps a newer dimension is needed.

The PALLACE report anticipates this:

> There is whole new dimension to the debate when we discuss the global role of cities and regions for the future. Whatever model is adopted – city-ring, city mentoring, city-twinning, city network-ing – an even greater challenge occurs when we can include into these networks cities and regions from the less-favoured countries of this planet. (Longworth and Allwinkle, 2005)

And who can gainsay that this is a challenge?

EFMD – business and global responsibility

The European Foundation for Management Development (EFMD) adopts a similar focus in its Globally Responsible Leadership Initiative, a report produced by a group of senior representatives from companies, business schools and centres for leadership learning from five continents.

> The challenges facing humankind are large, undeniable and global. Economic, social, environmental inequalities abound and are increasing,' it says, 'Businesses are among the most influen-tial institutions worldwide and have a tremendous opportunity to shape a better world for existing and future generations. The obli-gation of the globally responsible business is to create economic and societal progress in a globally responsible and sustainable way. (EFMD, 2005)

It continues:

> The new global business context requires a definition of business that encompasses corporate aspirations, responsibilities and activities in realistic and contemporary terms that go beyond purely financially focused explanations. The purpose of the globally responsible business is to create economic and societal progress in a globally responsible and sustainable way. (*ibid*)

In its advocacy of 'the global exercise of ethical, values-based leadership in the pursuit of economic and societal progress and sustainable development', the report makes a powerful indictment of organisations that exist purely to satisfy their own narrow objectives. It suggests that, in a world beset by extremes of wealth and poverty, conflict and aggressive fundamentalism, all organisations have a new responsibility to expand their remit towards the alleviation of this situation. If they do not, then the undesirable outcomes of inaction will eventually overwhelm them.

Learning cities and regions – global opportunities

EFMD is of course echoing concerns that are well documented in papers, reports and recommendations from organisations of all types and all persuasions. So what is the responsibility of the city and region in this respect? And what can it contribute?

PALLACE suggests one approach:

> If we now imagine a city-ring comprising six or seven cities from the developed world, for argument's, and alliteration's, sake let us say Sydney, Seattle, Southampton, Sapporo, Stuttgart and Shanghai. And we now add one or two from South America or Africa or the poverty-stricken areas of Asia, each of them linking their schools, universities, adult colleges, companies, city administrations, museums, children, parents, seniors, teachers, researchers, under the guidance of an energetic, sympathetic, persuasive and knowledgeable set of leaders. (Longworthy and Allwinkle, 2005)

This is one way to start the process of alleviating global conflict, poverty and ignorance. If properly organised, it brings it much closer to the hearts, minds and capabilities of real people in real cities and regions, eventually bypassing the need for mass migrations of unfortunate refugees.

There are, perhaps surprisingly, real advantages. These are taken from *Learning Cities, Learning Regions, Learning Communities'*, a book that is also accompanied by learning materials adapted to each chapter (Longworth, 2006):

1. *It is a preventative measure:* the giant leap in mutual understanding and transformation of mind-set that takes place when people

and organisations in cities and regions worldwide communicate with each other and learn together. Through such understanding social behaviour improves, racism and ethnic hatred diminishes and cities and regions no longer bear the costs of picking up the pieces.

2. *It makes economic sense*: the profitable economic, trade and technical development that can result through increased contact between small and large companies in different countries, leading to increased employment and greater prosperity. Here is an attractive economic justification for greater learning city/region cooperation.

3. *It is incremental*: the transformation of mind-sets, attitudes and behaviours that occurs when thousands more people and organisations are contributing to the solution of social, cultural, environmental, political and economic problems throughout the world right across the age groups. Cities and regions, as learning organisms, can learn much from each other, and jointly help each other to cope with seemingly intractable problems.

4. *It is fulfilling for thousands of people.* This amounts to a huge increase in available resource through mobilising the goodwill, talents, skills, experience and creativity between cities and regions. It is a new resource, tapping into the knowledge of individuals, and turning human ingenuity and action into social and intellectual capital to the benefit of cities and regions

5. *It solves previously intractable problems.* All of this would potentially mean that there would be fewer refugees. Many of the developing problems can be anticipated and addressed through cooperation between cities at the moment of crisis.

6. *It is sustainable because it is so much more dispersed.* Governments and NGOs are no longer the only initiators of aid to the underdeveloped. Action is now shared with the cities and, through them, the people, who gain in understanding of the realities and problems of the modern world, and the extent to which they ameliorate the latter. Stakeholder organisations and institutions in the city/region have a real world-class focus and *raison d'être*, and a contribution to make to the construction of the learning city at home and abroad.

All of this suggests a new mission for cities and regions. No longer are they inward-looking entities with a responsibility only to provide services for their own citizens. They have a greater mission and a greater global responsibility, entirely consonant with the ideals behind the learning region concept: to open the eyes of their institutions and their citizens to the world outside, and to the contribution that they can make to improving it.

This is not hopeless, impractical, blue skies idealism. In so doing they are helping to re-create themselves into entities richer in every way, more prosperous, more resourceful, more knowledgeable, more sensitive, more participative and more creative, innovative and capable. With the application of such creativity, using the resources that are available in the community and from other organisms, this need not impinge heavily on local taxes. At the same time, it raises the city's and the region's profile in a world that needs, more than ever, the application of tolerance and respect for others.

Chapter 4

Researching social capital in Europe: towards a toolkit for measurement?

John Field and Michael Osborne

One of the objectives of the Pascal Observatory within the European domain has been to inform and respond to the social and economic priorities of the European Union. In this chapter, informed by recent debates over EU policy, we highlight some PASCAL thinking in the field of social capital.[1] In particular, this chapter considers social capital in the context of social cohesion, trust and participation in civil society.

Social capital: social cohesion, trust and participation

The European social model rests upon the belief that social cohesion, employment and economic growth are complementary rather than competing goals. This approach underpins the Social Agenda developed through the Lisbon strategy of 2000,[2] which seeks to develop an inclusive, tolerant and modernised pathway to a high performance economy. Much recent research into social capital is consistent with these values, with a number of studies having shown that levels of trust and civic engagement are related to economic performance. In particular, trust and networking are closely related to innovation processes and human capital investment (Field, 2003; Healy and Côté, 2001; Le Bas, Picard and Suchecki, 1998; Maskell et al., 1998; Tuijnman and Boudard, 2001; Whiteley, 2000).

There is also evidence of a relationship between trust and networking, and other aspects of individual and community well-being, such as health, education, job search or the likelihood of becoming a victim of crime (Campbell et al., 1999; Dika and Singh, 2002; Field, 2003; Halpern, 2001;

Korpi, 2001; Léveque and White, 2001). Conversely, studies of social isolation have demonstrated that the negative consequences are associated with a lack of social support networks and the absence of trust (Hyppa and Mäki, 2001; Phillipson, Allan and Morgan, 2003). It is also interesting to note that the recent Luxembourg Declaration on youth volunteering (albeit without specifically mentioning social capital) is replete with its social components, with discussion on issues around youth participation, trust, democracy, consultation, and active citizenship for young people (EC, 2005).

A growing body of empirical research points to the possible wider social and economic significance of participation, trust and cohesion. However, research also indicates that the construct of social capital is dynamic, complex and multi-dimensional. The term is used to encompass a broad spectrum of concepts about social networks (Christoforou, 2004). One level of complexity is the level at which social capital is defined, and this relates to the purpose of the application of the construct in policy research. Attempts to measure social capital at an international level have relied upon pre-existing national and multinational data collections, such as the European Household Survey and the World Values Survey. The use of such data sets is opportunistic and hence imposes limitations on the definition of the construct which lead to premature decisions on how social capital may best be measured. In particular, such batteries of indicators do not necessarily explain how individuals encounter and are affected by their access to social capital. Hence the question is what does the construct called 'social capital' bring to the discussion that may be of value at the European level?

To address this question it is necessary to recognise and work in conjunction with national and international initiatives to develop measures of social capital. For example, the OECD has identified the World Values Survey questions on trust as well established, and with cross-culturally and cross-nationally validity. This is certainly one important source of relevant evidence.

Even so, there are a number of issues that should be considered when applying such instruments in developing international comparative data sets. In this context the OECD has proposed a range of issues for consideration, which mirror issues raised in much of the well-known historic literature in comparative social science work, including that in education (e.g. Noah and Eckstein, 1969).These include:

- issues of cultural and linguistic translatability, and the context-dependence of measurement instruments, would need to be carefully considered when looking at both questions and guidelines;[3]

- countries are at different stages in the development, at national level, of social capital measurement instruments;
- guideline definitions of concepts like 'volunteering' might be applied to other forms of research as well as household surveys;
- guidelines are required which would be consistent with flexible application in national measurement; and
- data will need to take account of local needs and requirements.

These questions might be addressed by adopting an enquiry framework, rather than simply a descriptive reporting of indicators. Social capital can be described, measured and discussed on a number of geographical levels, such as the local village level, the national level and the European level, and these levels can be taken into account across a number themes within the field of social capital.

It is therefore possible to add value to what is occurring through international collaborations among national statistical offices by supplementing the analysis of such data sets with qualitative data collection aimed at interrogating the relationships identified through statistical analysis. This can occur through the analysis of qualitative data held at national level, where there exist deeper studies of trust, participation and norms promoting collection, for example the real world cases of social capital in their social, economic and cultural context in local village associations in Sweden.

Social capital has been defined in a number of ways. In an early essay on the subject, Bourdieu suggested that the concept encapsulated the *principle of the social assets* which was visible where:

> different individuals obtain a very unequal return on a more or less equivalent capital (economic or cultural) according to the extent to which they are able to mobilise by proxy the capital of a group (family, old pupils of elite schools, select club, nobility, etc.) (Bourdieu, 1980, p. 2).

Bourdieu's work is important in this context because he was seeking to examine the impact of social capital on inequality. From a different conceptual perspective, the neo-Tocquevillian, Putnam has described social capital rather more broadly as 'features of social organisation, such as trust, norms and networks, that can improve the efficiency of society by facilitating co-ordinated actions' (Putnam 1993, p. 167).

While there is general agreement on the importance of these factors, much debate has taken place over their measurement. One concern with broad measures of social capital is that they define social networks in class-related terms that may not identify social capital held in different forms by different groups in the community. The questions used in many surveys are class-based and hence the resulting relationships between claimed access to social capital and well-being may reflect primarily economic advantage. This is a further reason for the adoption of an enquiry framework.

In considering the related issue of deprivation in Scotland, Bailey et al. (2003, p. 39) recommend that a measure of individual deprivation be developed as a priority. They point out that individual measures need to be based on surveys of individuals, rather than area statistics. They conclude that relating individual and area measures may provide useful insights into deprivation (Bailey et al., 2003, p. ii). It follows that similar insights could be gained by relating area and individual measures of social capital.

Finally, systematic comparative analysis of survey data is highly problematic. First, despite recent discussions over international harmonisation in social capital measurement, actual progress to date has been limited. Second, even where standardised instruments have been adopted, the indicators themselves are concerned with values and behaviour that are norm-laden; people's responses will also be shaped by differing linguistic and other cultural factors. These cannot always be dealt with by careful translation alone, in part because even two words that denote precisely the same thing may carry quite different connotations or overtones. Because of these problems of linguistic complexity and cultural specificity, we believe that qualitative material should be utilised, particularly where significant ethnographic and interpretative research has been conducted, alongside survey data and other statistical evidence.

In a recent call from the European Commission,[4] six themes were presented as worthy of investigation as measures of social capital in the context of social cohesion, trust and participation across the 25 states of the European Union and its candidate countries:

1. Levels of trust in society and its institutions.
2. Levels of participation in formal and informal networks.
3. Information on social norms promoting collective action.

4. Information on social capital and 'social governance' as an element in economic performance.
5. Information on social capital and 'social governance' as an element in social performance.
6. Social capital and 'social governance' as a potential facilitator of policy implementation.

We now consider the feasibility of conducting an investigation focused on such themes. Our preliminary assessment of available datasets suggests that the following approaches would be appropriate for each of the six areas.

1. Levels of trust in society and its institutions

Research into generalised trust and institutional trust has advanced considerably in recent years. Sources at international level are now reasonably strong, and there are a number of relevant sources. Those which are of most interest include:

- the Citizenship module of the 2004 International Social Survey Programme (ISSP);[5]
- core modules of the European Social Survey (ESS);[6]
- the 2000–2001 World Values Survey (WVS);[7]
- certain of the standard EUROBAROMETER[8] surveys.

Furthermore it would be possible to propose further questions for inclusion in the 2006 ISSP, which focuses on the *role of government*.

Of the above datasets, the ESS and EUROBAROMETER would seem the most obvious core sources, since they allow for monitoring of change over time. ISSP and WVS would supplement the core sources. It would also be necessary to review relevant national level studies, quantitative and qualitative, for example Kumlin and Rothstein's (2005) work on how the causal mechanism between variation in the design of welfare-state institutions and social capital works. This empirical analysis, based on Swedish survey data, suggests that the specific design of welfare-state policies matters for the production of social capital.

2. Levels of participation in formal and informal networks

Recent debates over active citizenship and social capital have acknowledged the importance of both formal and informal networks. In general, quantitative sources tend to emphasise formal networks and organisation, and downplay informal ones. This distortion is to some extent inevitable, and this can be compensated in part by actively seeking qualitative evidence in respect of the influence of social capital on social and economic performance. Relevant information on both is available through the datasets gathered through:

- the Citizenship module of the 2004 ISSP;
- relevant core module of the European Social Survey;
- the 2000–2001 World Values Survey (WVS);
- EUROBAROMETER 62 (participation in sport);
- EUROBAROMETER 60 (citizenship and sense of belonging)

As with the previous theme, the ESS and EUROBAROMETER seem best placed to serve as the core sources. Furthermore, it would be vital to investigate the changing roles for networks, their densities, when they overlap, and those that are in decay. It would also be necessary to establish the extent of network strength and the relationship of that strength to kin, neighbourhood, work and religion.

3. Information on social norms promoting collective action

Trust is, of course, closely related to social norms. However, there are well-established proxy indicators for those norms which tend to promote collective action, particularly in social attitudes surveys. Thus Inglehart (1977) has identified those values that he believes to promote collectivist orientations, as well as those that he identifies as associated more with individualistic behaviour. As might be envisaged, there is considerable controversy over these interpretations. Data in this area would usefully be drawn from:

- the Citizenship module of the 2004 ISSP;
- supplementary module of the European Social Survey (2004);
- the 2000–2001 World Values Survey (WVS); and
- EUROBAROMETER 60 (citizenship and sense of belonging).

Again the ESS and EUROBAROMETER are the core sources. It would also be important to consider the norms or forces that undermine collective action, and their relationship to social cohesion and economic and social perform- ance, and provide links to the next two themes. There is also the difficulty of separating out those social norms that promote collective action that is directed against cohesion, for example campaigns against gypsy/traveller communities, sexual lifestyle groups or ethnic/national minorities.

4. Information on social capital and 'social governance' as an element in economic performance

A number of attempts have been made to demonstrate a statistical association between social capital and economic performance (Dasgupta, 2000; Glaeser, Laibson and Sacerdote, 2002; Healy and Côté, 2001; Whiteley, 2000). At a very general level, these studies tend to suggest that there is a moderate association between indicators of social capital (trust, participation) and indicators of economic growth.

Indicators of economic performance include both absolute measures of performance and indicators of growth. This is necessary because it is likely that for different member states of the European Union and beyond, coming from diverse economic backgrounds, any one measure of economic performance may be misleading. Moreover, economic growth can be very considerably affected by historical events; the collapse of communism in central Europe had very dramatic consequences for growth rates, just to take an obvious example, without necessarily also creating symmetrical growth in social cohesion. In the timeframe available for many research projects, it is not possible to demonstrate a relationship between social capital and economic performance, but this can be addressed in three ways. First retrospective analysis of data can be undertaken. Secondly, a set of international benchmarks can be established to enable continuity of research in the future. Thirdly, qualitative data can be explored to help inform the development of explanatory theories that can subsequently be tested quantitatively, both retrospectively and, especially, in future years.

One positive aspect of Putnam's work is his emphasis on studying long-term trends in data to identify the effects of social capital across different stages of economic cycles, and beyond the impact of isolated and atypical social events. This is an important corrective to some rather naïve studies relying primarily on survey-derived snapshots. For instance, the Social Cultural Planbureau (SCP) in the Netherlands – using just survey-studies – was heavily criticised recently. They reported that social cohesion in the Netherlands was rather positive. During the same time the social climate became very hectic because of the murder of a politician and much intolerance in society. Journalists and politicians remarked that the SCP was sleeping and used the wrong research methods. One alternative and rather more compelling explanation is that they were reporting on the underlying strengths of their society, whereas the politicians and the journalists were focused on the implications of the immediate events.

Apparently aberrant events are unlikely to be explained by sudden shifts in the underlying levels of social capital. Naturally, we should not rule out the possibility of dramatic growth – or decline – in the community's stock of network resources: Putnam's hypothesis of the 'long civic generation' draws attention to the importance of social capital accumulated during the bitter shared experiences and struggles of Depression and World War (Putnam, 2000). But these are exceptional cases, and tend to take place under circumstances that are relatively easily identified.

To address the broader issue of the effects of trends in the level of social capital it is desirable to explore the extent to which national trends can be established by seeking access to national data sets that have been collected for several decades. For instance, in the UK the 'General Household Survey' dates from 1971, and though the introduction of a dedicated social capital module is relatively recent in this as in other national-level surveys, a number of relevant questions have been posed over longer periods. Using this and other data sets that have a substantial time frame and that collectively address several indicators of social capital, trend lines can be established for UK society which can be used as a predictor of change in current levels of social capital.

Different data sets are available in other countries that can be used to generate an equivalent variable predicting change in current levels of social capital. The validity of this approach requires multivariate analysis at both the national and the international level. If successfully applied, trend analysis may help to differentiate between societies that may have similar absolute levels of social capital, but in which trends are different. It is postulated that those societies in which trends are positive are more likely to be experiencing improvements in economic and social progress.

In addition to research using econometric techniques, the relationship between social capital and economic performance can also be informed through qualitative sources. In particular, case studies of knowledge exchange/transfer and the spread of scientific and technical innovation are likely to draw on qualitative methods of research; the same is likely to be true of studies of social governance.

5. Information on social capital and 'social governance' as an element in social performance

Putnam has made a number of claims about the association between levels of social capital and levels of social well-being (Putnam, 2000). With relatively few exceptions, the overwhelming majority of research into this connection has tended to confirm Putnam's original assertion, albeit with varying degrees of strength (see Field, 2003).

Evidence of the association between indicators of social well being and social capital using data are best gathered from national studies, although the level of such data for each nation in Europe is undoubtedly variable. The proxy indicators of social well-being could include:

- Average levels of employment and income
- An aggregate index for health
- An aggregate index for human capital
- Average levels of personal crime and (where available) personal security.

In tandem with such measures, a Europe-wide analysis would monitor developments in public policy within each national jurisdiction, and summarise their significance for social policy. An example of this type of activity is the current work of the Schools and Social Capital Network[9] in Scotland. This is considering the impact of public policy in Scotland on social capital, and the implications for outcomes of schooling.

The relationship between social capital and social cohesion, whilst dominated by sociometric techniques, also draws on qualitative sources. In particular, case studies of anti-poverty strategies in practice are likely to draw on qualitative evidence; the same is likely to be true of studies of social governance.

If sufficient quantitative data is available at international level, a statistical meta-analysis could be conducted to seek to confirm the relationships that appear in data from national data sets. This would necessarily be a multivariate analysis in which international comparisons may make it possible to control for economic factors as a competing explanatory variable.

6. Social capital and 'social governance' as a potential facilitator of policy implementation

In his early study of the roots of Italian democracy, Putnam (1993) argued vividly that a vibrant civil society was central to the creation of good government. More recent research, summarised in Field (2003), tends to be inconclusive on this subject, at least in the sense of Putnam's argument. Rather, there is an emerging consensus that networks and partnerships can help to facilitate policy implementation, but often at the cost of a loss of central steering. Equally, attempts to retain control over partnerships and network are likely to hinder the process of implementation (NESF, 2003). Particular tensions arise in the case of partnerships created to promote social inclusion and foster user involvement in service delivery, especially if these arrangements are subjected to steering by performance targets and selective resourcing (Field, 2005, p. 138).

Using data gathered from national studies, it is possible to summarise recent research into the relationship between social capital and policy implementation. Many such studies are likely to draw on policy evaluations and case studies.

Some quantitative data are also available, including attitudes to government, in:

- the Citizenship module of the 2004 ISSP;
- the 2000–2001 World Values Survey (WVS).

Particularly in so far as these data sets allow us to disaggregate the findings for a variety of socio-economic, ethnic and national groups, they have some value. However, they suffer from severe limitations, not the least of which is that they neither enquire into the extent to which respondents might be service users, nor examine potential engagement in anti-poverty strategies of various kinds. Nor is it at all clear that survey data would help us understand these things, which seem far better suited to case study analysis and other approaches informed by qualitative data collection. This begs the question whether evidence-based policy can plausibly be developed on the basis of what will inevitably be a series of locally based and highly context-specific case studies.

Summary

We have provided a potential approach to gathering data about social capital across the European Union and within its candidate countries. In order for sense to be made of data spread across a wide and diverse geographical area, in the case of the first of the three themes, in the first instance, it would be necessary to construct a simple frequency analysis of the most recent data, for those countries for which data are available. It would then be feasible to add value to existing data sets by using advanced multivariate analyses, including multi-level modelling. As indicated above, differences in national data sets would require consideration of data in subsets from available sources. Statistical meta-analysis might enable aspects of construct validity to be explored and available qualitative studies may help to establish the concurrent validity of data. International comparisons might focus on the impact of elements of social capital on outcomes, and be based on multivariate methods in which proxy variables will be used to control any substantive differences that may be attributable to differences in types of data sets. This would of course be accompanied by an analytical commentary.

In the case of the fourth theme, we would recommend summarising recent existing research into the relationship between social capital and economic performance. While much of this research may use econometric techniques, much will draw on qualitative sources. In particular, case studies of knowledge exchange/transfer and the spread of scientific innovation would be likely to draw on qualitative methods of research; the same is likely to be true of studies of 'social governance'. It would be important to establish the robustness of all relevant research, be it qualitative or quantitative, into the relations between social capital and economic performance.

In the case of the fifth theme, we would suppose the analysis and synthesising of recent research into the relationship between social capital and the two variables of social well-being and social cohesion. In the case of social cohesion, whilst much of this research uses sociometric techniques, much also draws on qualitative sources. In particular, case studies of anti-poverty strategies in practice are likely to draw on qualitative evidence; the same is likely to be true of studies of 'social governance'. Again, the robustness of all relevant research concerned with the relations between social capital and social cohesion would be paramount in our considerations.

Similarly in the case of the sixth theme, we envisage assessing the robustness of all relevant research on the influence of social capital on policy implementation. Of particular importance here is the transnational research led by Kaase and Newton on trust in government and public institutions (see Newton and Kaase, 1995). For each of themes 4, 5 and 6, we would also recommend monitoring developments in public policy in each area, and summarising their significance for social policy

Concluding remarks

A key aspect of the approach that we suggest is the facilitation of on-going dialogue among policy-makers, researchers and key actors in civil society organisations. We believe that considerable potential exists for the development of a coordinated approach to monitoring and examining social capital and its consequences at the European level. A range of existing datasets could be mined systematically to create a rich and dependable set of social capital indicators that relate to at least six core areas of economic and social policy. We also believe that these indicators should be supplemented by evaluation of relevant policy initiatives, and enriched by the findings of qualitative studies. In principle, then, there is little difficulty in creating a European toolkit for measuring and understanding social capital. Indeed, much of the evidence already exists in readily capturable form, and simply requires systematic reworking and contextualising in order to produce a 'good enough' toolkit of indicators.

Such evidence, systematically analysed and clearly presented, could do much to improve the policy process. At the very least, as Vicki Nash sardonically observes, it would help policy-makers from inadvertently damaging the quality and character of people's relationships (Nash, 2004). But this would of course require changes by both policy makers and researchers to develop closer and more effective relationships. As researchers we will start by suggesting that the academic community should seek to communicate its ideas and evidence far more clearly than is often the case at present. While we have no difficulty with the use of complex concepts and precise terminology within our own specialist community, we also need to ensure that our findings are accessible to a variety of audiences, including policy makers and, ideally, interested citizens. We also need to be much more willing to argue the economic case for social analysis. Policy-makers are understandably concerned with the bottom line; social scientists should be able to demonstrate that all economic activities are embedded in social behaviour, social values, and social structures. The value of social capital as a concept lies at least partly in the way in which it allows us to engage with policy-makers by focusing on common policy problems through a shared terminology.

Notes

[1] We wish to thank the following for helpful comments on an earlier version of this paper: Fabio Sabbatini and Ralph Catts.

[2] Mogensen et al. (2004) provide a recent analysis of progress towards the Lisbon Strategy, and a useful analysis of baseline economic indicators.

[3] One simple example is the well-known difficulties of establishing the equivalence of 'trust', 'confiance' and 'Vertrauen' in the three major languages of Europe.

[4] Calls for tender VT/2005/025 for the 'Establishment of a network on Social capital (Social cohesion, trust and participation), as part of the new European Observatory aimed at informing the social policy debate and providing analytical input for the Report on the social situation in the European Union'. Online at http://europa.eu.int/comm/employment_social/calls/2005/vt_2005_025/tender_en.htm

[5] Available from the German Social Sciences Infrastructure Services (GESIS). Online at http://www.gesis.org/en/data%5Fservice/issp/data/

[6] The European Social Survey (the ESS) is a biennial multi-country tool first used in 2002/2003. Its central aim is 'to develop and conduct a systematic study of changing values, attitudes, attributes and behaviour patterns within European polities'. It seeks 'to measure and explain how people's social values, cultural norms and behaviour patterns are distributed, the way in which they differ within and between nations, and the direction and speed at which they are changing'. Available online at http://ess.nsd.uib.no/index.jsp

[7] The World Values Survey has carried out representative national surveys of basic values and beliefs in more than 65 societies. It builds on the European Values Surveys, first carried out in 1981. The most recent (and fourth) tranche of data gathering took place in 1999–2001. Available online at http://wvs.isr.umich.edu/

[8] The European Commission has been monitoring the evolution of public opinion in the Member States since 1973. Through the use of surveys and other instruments, the Eurobarometer has gathered data concerning European citizenship, including views about enlargement, social situation, health, culture, information technology, environment, the Euro and defence. Online at
http://europa.eu.int/comm/public_opinion/index_en.htm

[9] This is part of the Applied Educational Research Scheme in Scotland. Online at http://www.aers.ac.uk/aers/ssc_1.html

Chapter 5

New research instruments for government: measuring community engagement

David Adams and Michael Hess

Overview

Australian contemporary public administration is characterised by the re-emergence of community as a useful category across a range of policy-making and service delivery areas. The background to this introduction of social factors to balance the market oriented instruments of the New Public Management (NPM) has been the subject of considerable commentary (Smyth et al., 2005; Vinson, 2004; Considine, 2004). Less attention has been paid to the actual instruments needed to make community a practical part of policy making and public management. This chapter outlines progress to date in Victoria in establishing what could become a national measurement framework for engaging communities.

Initial findings may be summarised in terms of:
- The ability of the indicators to create new images of communities;
- The importance of local knowledge in shaping community engagement;
- The distinctively local nature of community strengthening patterns;
- The key role public administration plays in helping or hindering community strengthening;
- The centrality of local governments to shaping community strength; and
- The strong correlation between the relative strengths of communities and the relative risk and protective factors for family units.

Introduction

In recent years there has been a resurgence of interest in the nature and significance of 'community' in public policy deliberations (see for example Smyth et al., 2005). Engaging communities is seen to be a desirable end in itself linked to values of democratic participation as well as being of value, because of correlations between participation and improved levels of social capital. More recently correlations between engaged communities and economic growth have been promoted (Florida, 2005), igniting further interest in the dynamic of community engagement.

From a public policy perspective it has proved relatively easy to measure the *outputs* of community engagement (such as increased levels of participation in sporting, cultural, recreational and civic life) but much more difficult to measure the *outcomes* of community engagement (or indeed to agree on what they are or should be). This lack of clarity around outcomes and measurement has led to many governments winding back on their community engagement strategies or treating them as marginal enterprises within public policy. We have seen this as a mistake, and have attempted to enter the debate focusing on how community can be made part of the public policy and management mainstream (Hess and Adams, 2001). Our reasoning has been that since much of our life is lived locally in communities (be they communities of place, of interest, or of faith) understanding the drivers of community strength must be an important public policy activity. A principle factor in, and indicator of, community strength has emerged from our research under the general rubric of community engagement. Here we group all those interactions which allow individuals to participate in, and establish ownership of, their communities. Even where the logic of the significance of community strength and its correlation with community engagement is accepted, however, we lack instruments to give policy validity to this understanding.

Developing the capacity to measure this engagement is a vital activity if it is to be legitimised as part of the mainstream of policy-making and implementation. In this chapter we make the case for community engagement strategies to be in the mainstream of public policy precisely because the connections with important policy objectives and outcomes can be demonstrated and measured. Measurement becomes a central issue by connecting the process (community engagement) to the outcomes (improvements in implementation in crucial policy areas). The actual connecting point is through indicators that can demonstrate both process (e.g. rates of participation) and outcomes (e.g. improvements in safety and well-being). While we are concerned to consider the hard realities of measurement as a practical issue in policy, we also wish to take account of a particular subtlety the act of measurement can bring to the government community interface. It is our belief, based on the Victorian experience, that the act of measuring community engagement adds value to the policy process beyond the production of the numbers which provide decision-makers with such a sense of security and are, in any case, *de rigeur* for Australian policy advice. The subtle value in measurement in this case is that the indicators can also build a bridge between the theoretical abstractions (e.g. community engagement is democratic) and the practical reality (really knowing what a particular community wants/needs). The development of indicators creates metaphors and images which we have found helpful in illuminating the complexity of community engagement issues.

Our arguments are presented through the lens of the Victorian experience where over four years a consistent set of indicators has been established, and progress measured. The key policy agency has been the Department for Victorian Communities (DVC). The character and *modus operandi* of the DVC itself has become a central issue in the Victorian experience. This chapter provides a brief explanation of this, but is principally concerned with the DVC's research-based efforts to develop measures of engagement. These begin from a focus on providing a better understanding of the policy agency of community and the ways in which public administration might need to change to promote community oriented policies.

The research agenda required to achieve these outcomes is increasingly bringing together three themes. First, the focus on indicators of community engagement is providing real knowledge upon which to base continued learning for both public administrators and community players. These indicators have been used in the published and internal documents upon which this chapter is based (DVC, 2004; 2005).

Secondly, the indicators themselves are throwing new light on central problems of policy which have been overlooked in the recent past. These particularly include the risk and protective factors associated with social well-being and economic prosperity. The use of these indicators is providing us with an increased ability to compare the links between community and individual/family strength.

Thirdly, evidence is emerging on how 'governance' factors intermediate both family and community-level dynamics. This will be a focus for later research, but was partly why we have chosen to use local government area boundaries to organise our research. We believe that the robustness and outlook of local institutions – and how they choose to organise – are key determinants of community strength.

Ultimately our research programme has a simple objective: *to understand how to increase the confidence and capacity of Victorians to play a greater role in socio-economic activity through exercising increased choice and control over their wellbeing and prosperity.* At a policy level, the value of this research will be to inform governments and others on how better to allocate scarce resources, and how better to organise the planning and delivery of services. The research on which we report here is showing how public policy and management can (re-)capture the capacity to make and implement social policy.

Community agency and public policy

Internationally, efforts in market-oriented democracies to re-balance public policy after its long domination by the instruments of new public management (NPM) have seen the re-emergence of community as a significant public policy idea. Understanding the impact and potential of this involves both a consideration of the practicalities of making something as definitionally slippery as 'community' work in decision-making processes, and unpacking the concept to discover its intellectual legitimacy. Our argument is that community is important to contemporary government because it brings new sources of knowledge to bear, and that these are particularly relevant to contexts in which orthodox knowledge sources have failed to produce a satisfactory basis for decision-making and implementation.

Depending on the context, the type of knowledge which comes from community engagement may be more important than the knowledge frames upon which public policy has traditionally relied. It is also, however, based on very different assumptions. This makes it problematic within the organisational structures of public agencies. The symbiosis of appropriate knowledge and *modus operandi* in government under NPM reforms has reinforced a focus on expertise expressed as interest, issues and beliefs. This contrasts fundamentally with community-based knowledge which privileges *place*. While the claims of expertise are familiar and legitimate within our policy traditions and organisations, those of location are yet to be established – apart that is from their corruption into parochial pork barrelling. A brief discussion of some history and some epistemology will restate the argument that we have elaborated elsewhere for the significance and characteristics of community agency in public policy (Hess and Adams, 2002).

Australia, having spent two decades perfecting NPM, began following the trend (back) toward community engagement in the late 1990s. By 1998, Prime Minister Howard was using the language of the European liberal democrats in declaring to the World Economic Forum that 'we believe that social capital and the building of networks of trust and understanding in national and local communities are vital if those communities are to respond constructively to the challenges of change' (Howard, 1998). By the time of the Australia Unlimited Roundtable in April 1999 Mr. Howard was identifying 'a new social coalition of government, business, charitable and welfare organisations and other community groups – each contributing their own particular expertise and resources in order to tackle more effectively the social problems ...' (Howard, 1999).

This re-emergence of community as a policy factor at the conjunction of hard-headed financial management and soft-hearted social orientation clearly required explanation, not least because of the contradictions inherent in this logic. We have attempted an academic approach to these issues in earlier work (Hess and Adams, 2001). Back in the practical world of public policy and management the re-emergence of community was significant because of the new knowledge bases and processes it opened up, but these had not been spelled out in detail. Nor had they evolved into instruments for policy-making and implementation.

At the level of identifying the appropriate knowledge base for making public policy decisions, the problem facing governments was that for 20 years the NPM focus privileged expertise from market sources as the dominant knowledge source. As high policy, NPM attempted three things. First it attempted to diminish the role of the state and make the bureaucracy more responsive to political leaders. Second, it aimed for greater efficiency through the use of private sector management techniques. Third, it focused on the citizen as a customer and service recipient (Aucoin,1990, p. 16). As day-to-day public administration, this focus on market-based knowledge was reflected in almost all aspects of the public sector activity, from recruitment focus (towards managers and accountants and economists), through the types of strategies deemed relevant to address problems (user choice/user pays), to the instruments of implementation and service delivery (contracts and competitive tendering). Such ideas and instruments achieved normative status under NPM and, despite their relatively narrow knowledge base, were applied across the board to areas as varied as economic, social and environmental policy.

The ideas and practice of the NPM produced increased efficiency, and during the period of their dominance overall increases in productivity 'externalities' were significant. The narrow focus on economic knowledge, however, created difficulties of two kinds. The first were those that arose from the exclusion of consideration of other knowledge frames. The second had to do with the positivist basis of economic knowledge. Both have direct implications for the practicalities of policy and management, but are underpinned by some deeper intellectual problems. One has to do with epistemology – how the knowledge is created and valued. Our argument is that historically public administration applied ideas and used instruments arising from frameworks of knowledge and meaning which were relatively stable (Hess and Adams, 2002). They changed quite slowly over time and were closely linked to socially normative concepts underpinning and legitimising administrative action. In the 1990s NPM privileged functional knowledge drawn primarily from economics and management, pushing other knowledge frames into the background. This was consistent with earlier changes in so far as it continued the reliance on knowledge provided by experts even if they were drawn increasingly from outside the administration itself.

Community knowledge, by contrast, is interpretive, inductive and iterative. The implication of a community-based approach is that appropriate public knowledge is no longer seen as a given, to which administrations will have privileged access through expertise, authority and familiarity. It involves an understanding of the nature of relevant knowledge and of the issue of how to make it useful for solving a problem or taking an opportunity at the level of action. It starts from the assumption that knowledge needs to be constructed and mediated through a cooperative process of discovery with those affected by it. The level of certainty about the meaning and utility of knowledge is itself the central purpose of inquiry. Some aspects of how this might work out in practice can be seen from the way in which Victorian Governments have used the community focus to generate knowledge and processes which address problems beyond the scope of more orthodox approaches.

In the 1990s, Victorian governments went further than other Australian public administrations in implementing NPM (Alford and O'Neill, 1994). Since 2000 they have led the way in seeking to build on the financial benefits of those reforms, while balancing them with social considerations. In many ways these developments parallel those in other market-oriented democracies, as governments seek to balance economic and social orders of necessity in their management of public policy and service delivery. We have identified these changes in terms of the insertion of social knowledge and community-oriented instruments into the policy-making and implementation processes and have been concerned to illuminate both its theoretical underpinnings and practical implications.

In the aftermath of the 1999 Victorian election, the incoming Labor Government determined that one area in which it would differentiate itself from its predecessor was in its approach to public management. Under the rubric of 'innovative state, caring community' it developed a whole of government policy which bracketed NPM efficiency objectives with human and social capital areas, identifying place and community as the loci for these new elements (Victoria 2001).

The development of the policy was based on a broad appreciation of international practice. The actual implementation has, however, proven to require orientation to local circumstances in which the international models have proven less useful. The major structural innovation was the creation of a new Department, the Department for Victorian Communities, in 2002. The preposition, *for* rather than *of*, was intended to be significant. This new Department was not to be a vehicle for delivering policy in the particular location of communities – of doing something *to* communities. Rather it was to be an advocate for an approach to the development and delivery of policies focusing on communities of interest and places, through the medium of communities of location. It was to do something *in* and *with* communities (Hess, 2003). The ambition was to achieve an integrated, whole of government approach to areas of need for which the fragmented approaches of competing policy silos, working on narrowly focused expertise, had proven to have no answer.

The theoretical underpinnings of these policies range from economics' 'cluster theory' (Porter, 2000; Florida, 2003) to geography's new regionalism (Cooke and Morgan, 1998), social capital (Putnam, 2000) and complexity theory. What they have in common is an acknowledgement that place will be a vital and different category in decision-making. This has implications for the nature of agency. Traditionally public administrative action has been based on expertise, with agency resting with the experts in particular fields. Where place is privileged, however, agency shifts to networks. Political scientists have long identified policy networks as significant, and have mapped their influence (Rhodes, 1997; Considine, 2003). The networks that have emerged as significant in the Victorian experience of community engagement go beyond this, in that their claim upon the policy process is a claim based on place and the knowledge that arises from place-based engagement. While the Victorian experience is very much a work in progress we believe that it has taken significant steps to understanding the relationship between place, agency and the issue of how governments can best invest resources to strengthen community engagement. Among the lessons that we have been learning are some related to measuring community engagement.

The Victorian approach to measuring community engagement

DVC set out to measure factors related to community strength because of the increasing international evidence that, in market oriented democracies at least, social capital factors, captured in measures of community strength, played unacknowledged but crucial roles in determining the outcomes of policy interventions. Over the last three years, however, the focus has increasingly moved on to the extent and nature of community engagement. In part this is because strength measures generate league tables which may be unhelpful. It is also, however, because the fact of engagement of people in their communities has proved a better predictor of a community's capacity than the presence of other advantages. It now appears that it is in engagement activities that a community generates the knowledge it needs to be a successful partner in economic growth and social well-being.

This focus derives from the way in which we have come to view the characteristics that make communities strong. DVC defines strong communities as those endowed with social, economic and environmental assets *and* organisational structures that work towards their sustainable use and equitable distribution (DVC, 2004). Strong communities are built by community members who are engaged, participate, feel capable of working through problems and are supported by strong networks (Lin, 2001; Gilchrist, 2004; DVC, 2004). Strong communities can therefore be seen to arise from the interplay of four features:
- *the economic/natural/human/social capital assets* a community is endowed with – for example, schools and trained teachers;
- *the knowledge within the community* that allows for the sustainable use of assets – for example, how a community understands and values education;
- *the ability collectively to organise* in order to work through issues, determine priorities and make the best use of resources –

for example, actively engaged staff and parent bodies; and
- *local institutions* that provide governance structures through which collective action can be organised – for example, school boards and committees linked to government, other local institutions and businesses.

Because of the connection found between engagement and strength, the DVC indicators of community strength focus on aspects of connectedness and local networks that underpin governance arrangements. Some of the DVC indicators describe the outcomes of connectedness such as community safety, feeling that there are opportunities to have a say, tolerance of diversity and the ability to get help when needed. Others focus on the forms of participation that enhance social connectedness and lead to local network formation. Internationally there is evidence to suggest that the simplest forms of participation, such as attending events and helping neighbours, are the precursors of strong networks that ultimately lead to collective action and strong governance arrangements in local areas (Perkins, Brown and Taylor, 1996; Moen, 1992; Wollebaek and Selle, 2002).

The benefits of participation have also been shown to extend to personal and collective well-being reflected in: better physical and mental health; higher educational achievement; better employment outcomes; lower crime rates; decreases in maltreatment of children; and an increased capacity for a community to respond to threats and interventions (Granovetter, 1974; Coleman, 1988; Tomison, 1996; Vinson, Baldry and Hargreaves, 1996; Porter, 1998; Berkman and Glass, 2000; OECD, 2001; Lin, 2001; Szreter and Woolcock, 2004). Overall, this body of research claims that community engagement diminishes the impacts of social disadvantage (Gerard, 1985). Specifically in Victoria, the 2003 *Community Adversity and Resilience Report* (Vinson, 2004) showed that social cohesion, measured by participation in sport and ability to get help when needed, is associated with lower levels of negative social outcomes such as increased rates of imprisonment and early school leaving.

The association between participation and physical well-being noted internationally (Young and Glasgow, 1998; Berkman and Glass, 2000) is also reflected in the DVC findings (DVC, 2004). So participation also has an independent positive effect on health (Young and Glasgow, 1998). Given the weight of research opinion, it is hardly surprising to find that governments are trying many practical ways to enhance citizen participation as a means of addressing the specific problems and priorities of local areas (Coleman and

Gotze, 2001; Gilchrist, 2004). This logic culminates in the view that it is through the combined 'knowledge, experience and capability of different agencies, officials and community groups' that the solutions to the most complex and pressing problems are developed' (Considine, 2004). One dilemma this creates is that to enhance engagement with communities, governments will need to change the way they currently work. New institutional arrangements, instruments, toolkits, skills and cultures in public administration are needed to support and build the networks and local institutions that are critical to community strengthening outcomes (Hess and Adams, 2002).

Victorian measures of community engagement

Community engagement thinking and practice in Victoria have developed to the point at which they are generating data on which research findings can be based. DVC has gone about building this research from both existing data sets and new purpose-collected data. Where new data sets have been created, care has been taken to do this in partnership with NGOs, Local Councils etc. This acknowledges ownership and minimises transaction costs. Many of the data sets are generated as by-products of other pieces of research, piggy-backing on the work of others thereby putting our work into the mainstream of research related to particular policy areas rather than on the margins. This also enables important correlations to be explored, for example between community engagement data and heath status (VPHS, 2001–2, p. 40).

Often, long-established data sets relating to specific policy or service delivery activities contain unexplored relevance for measuring community engagement. For example, rates of default and disconnection from energy (i.e. the power being cut off) can tell us a lot about community dynamics. Digging into these data has provided evidence that levels of power disconnection have less to do with economic status than with social factors, such as how close users live to their electricity supplier. Where customers are able to access company staff readily they are less likely to suffer disconnection. By contrast, in communities that are distant from the supplier, trust between supplier and purchaser is lower, and disconnections more frequent. The point is that data on energy defaults has been available for the last hundred years – a rich source of information especially if it is cleverly correlated with other sources.

The most recent DVC research report, *Indicators of Community Strength at the Local Government Area Level in Victoria* (DVC, 2005) builds on the previous work of the *Indicators of Community Strength in Victoria* report (DVC, 2004). The latter took time series data relating to eleven indicators of community strength from the Victorian Population Health Survey, and applied it to four Local Government Areas (LGAs). The 2005 report adds to this by examining the indicators of community strength across all 79 LGAs in Victoria. It includes four new indicators not included in the first report: parental participation in schools; participation in organised sport; participation on decision-making boards and committees; and liking the community in which you live. The full set of indicators can be seen in Table 5.1.

Table 5.1 Community strength indicators from DVC Report.

Community attitudes
1. Feeling safe walking down your street alone after dark.
2. Feeling valued by society.
3. Feeling there are opportunities to have a say on the issues that are important to you.
4. Feeling that multiculturalism makes life in your area better.
5. Liking the community you live in.*

Participation
6. Attendance at a community event in the last six months.
7. Participation in organised sport.*+
8. Volunteering.
9. Being a member of an organised group such as a sport, church, community or professional group.
10. Being the member of a group that has taken local action in the last 12 months.
11. Parental participation in schools.*
12. Participation in decision-making boards and committees.*

Ability to get help when needed
13. Ability to get help from friends, family and neighbours when needed.
14. Ability to raise $2000 in two days in an emergency.

* New indicators not included in the first report (DVC, 2004)
+ Created from two years' data (mid-2001 to mid-2003) from the Exercise, Recreation and Sport Survey (ERASS)

These are not Local Government indicators. The phenomena they report on arise from the combined actions of local, state and federal governments, business and the community itself. LGAs have been used in this DVC research because they are the smallest area level that a sample can be drawn from in Victoria at reasonable cost. It is also a common area level used for the collection of other social outcomes data (education, police, etc.), which will allow for comparison with other data sets in subsequent reports.[1] One immediate problem in using LGAs for research on community engagement is that communities do not fall neatly into administrative boundaries. So for planning purposes these indicators need to be supported by other research that provides detailed information about communities.

The key finding that emerges from these local area based data is that community engagement has a different character across the LGAs of Victoria. Differences between rural and metropolitan LGAs are striking, with rural areas generally scoring higher than the metropolitan areas on all indicators. Every LGA has strengths, and no single area has low scores on all indicators. For example, Whittlesea in the north of Melbourne has lower levels of volunteering than other metropolitan areas, but has higher levels of parental participation in schools. Attitudes also vary greatly across areas. For example, the proportion of the population that feels 'safe on their street alone after dark' ranges from 40 to 90 per cent, while those that feel there are opportunities to have a real say on issues ranges from 41 to 75 per cent of the adult population across LGAs (DVC, 2005). In terms of participation, volunteering ranges from 35 to 68 per cent, and parental participation in school ranges from 50 to 75 per cent of all parents across LGAs. In terms of social isolation, as measured by the percentage of people who could not get help from friends, family or neighbours when needed, the level ranges from 8 to 22 per cent of LGA populations.

These differences emerging at the level of community engagement indicate a need for area-specific approaches. If community is to be a useful factor in public policy and management there can be no 'one size fits all' prescription. It is essential to consider the particular character of local areas when developing policies designed to improve community strength.

What Victorians think makes a good community

DVC research has been concerned to establish some benchmark data around the issue of public perceptions of community and engagement. Table 5.2 used factor analysis[2] to provide a broad-brush picture of what Victorians thought were the important characteristics of communities. The characteristics fell into four categories:
- activities which build a secure future;
- good local services and facilities;

Table 5.2 Factor analysis of the characteristics of communities that Victorians think are important.

	% of Victorians that consider important	% that think describes own community	% differ-ence
Category 1 Building a secure future			
People feel safe and secure	95	61	33
The government is responsive to local needs	78	23	55
People have opportunities to participate in the decisions made by government	72	26	46
There are good work opportunities available locally	70	28	42
Category 2 Local services and facilities			
Good local facilities and services (shops, childcare, schools, libraries, etc.)	92	73	19
There is easy access to parks, bike tracks and recreational areas	79	74	5
Category 3 Pleasant local people and environments			
People are friendly, good neighbours, help others	90	62	28
It's a pleasant environment, nice streets, well planned, open spaces, no pollution	89	68	22
People look after their properties	83	67	16
The community has a distinct character, it's a 'special place'	57	54	3
Category 4 Opportunities to participate			
There's a wide range of community and support groups (sports clubs, neighbourhood houses, etc)	79	62	17
It's an active community, people do things and get involved in local issues and activities	68	46	22
There are opportunities to volunteer in local groups	61	57	4
Local business's support local initiatives by donating time or money	68	42	26
There's a good mix of people of different age group, incomes, cultural backgrounds, etc.	68	70	−1

- pleasant local people and environments;
- opportunities to participate. (Table 2) (DVC unpublished data).

The outstanding finding to be drawn from these data emerges in the right hand column. This sets out the differences between what Victorians feel is important and what they feel is present in their communities. In order to have relevance, DVC's community strengthening strategy needs to be located in this gap between what 'should be' and what 'is'. Nowhere is the risk of not doing this more apparent than in the finding that while 'government that is responsive to local needs' was considered important by three quarters of Victorians, only one quarter felt this was the case in their local area.

Conclusion

How does this research contribute to our ability to understand what does and does not work in terms of community engagement?

DVC research indicates six areas that require attention to achieve the levels and types of community engagement that have been shown to contribute to the creation of strong, resilient communities. The first is creating images of community that have efficacy for public policy and management. Approaches that focus on programmes delivered by vertically-organised agencies produce distorted and fragmented views of community. DVC's use of indicators based on people and places creates a set of images of communities as they are experienced by the people in them. Moving the focus of data from the programme to the place contributes to a different policy perspective. More subtly and more importantly, however, this type of information creates a picture of how specific communities work. In doing this it provides essential baseline data for community focused policy-making and implementation.

The second area to which this research draws attention is that local knowledge is crucial. This is lost from sight in the modern programme-oriented world of public policy and management dominated by the cult of expertise, whether from within the bureaucracy or from 'independent' contractors. Local knowledge cannot simply be tapped into through 'community consultation'. It is not an objectified reality to be extracted and fed into the policy machine. As pre-eminent post modernist Zygmunt Bauman argues, local knowledge has to be *invented* rather than discovered (Bauman, 2000). We are only just rediscovering the parameters of local knowledge and its sensitivity to shocks, such as the loss of *agoras* – for example the rapid loss of public parks and other spaces in cities throughout the world. Engagement activities are essential to this invention of knowledge, because they throw people together in endeavours that focus attention on local needs and capacities. The knowledge this creates is about ourselves, each other and how we can work together.

The third area is that community strength is a distinctively local phenomenon driven by a mix of local and global factors. So far, our research shows just how much community strength can vary from neighbourhood to neighbourhood. This is, however, merely scratching the surface of the issue of how locality drives and changes needs and behaviours. Further research is planned to look more closely at the innovative potential of locality factors. Given that government policy tends to be programme- rather than place-sensitive, this is an important issue because current policy structures fail to comprehend locality, and therefore miss its innovative potential.

The fourth issue is that public administration matters. Many good community engagement ideas continue to come to grief here. For example, proposing indicators that are disconnected from the levers of government and resource allocation models is a guaranteed path to failure. The community engagement agenda challenges much of the orthodoxy of public administration, such as the dominance of the programme format. It takes time to work new ideas, new cultures, new structures and new instruments into the mainstream and away from the margins. Strong leadership, clear political authorisation, community backing and a good dose of resilience are critical to seeing this agenda through.

In the past, government policy has focused on providing assets and skills rather than on collective organisation and governance structures. However, it is collective organisation and governance structures that sit behind the effective claim over the use and distribution of assets and skills. Communities that have strong governance arrangements are better able to use and distribute their existing assets and make claims for resources that are appropriate for their needs. For governments this may mean directing investment in different 'connecting activities', such as recreation, learning and volunteering programmes, in order to build community strength in different areas. It may also mean changing the way services are delivered in order to be responsive to the differing local circumstances indicated in this report.

To researchers from earlier periods of public administration the next conclusion may seem obvious, but the extent to which local government matters surprised us. The extent of variations between local government areas was not merely an issue of geographical (dis)advantage. The research indicated that strong local governments that are well connected to their communities generate community strength. For example, in Swan Hill a local school had concerns about government funding for a stand-alone basketball court because they felt Swan Hill did not need another single-use facility. Instead they joined with their local government and other local groups to lobby State government for funding for a comprehensive sports and leisure centre that provides a range of services to all residents of Swan Hill, as well as to the school. This partnership led to the creation of a significant piece of infrastructure for the whole community that can be more easily managed than a large number of single-use, single-user facilities. In this example, a strong community has increased its assets in a sustainable way and has improved the quality of life for all its residents.

There are major implications here for the future of local government as the 'stewards' of community strengthening, an issue we are canvassing in Victoria (Considine, 2004; 2005). One of the more important implications is the need to invest in the capacity of all local institutions to create the conditions for the emergence of community strength. Those conditions involve, for example, distributed leadership; access to and valuing of local knowledge; local *agoras* or meeting spaces; and access to various forms of communication.

Not surprisingly, we are also finding considerable evidence that families, however they are constructed, will emerge as significant factors in community engagement and strengthening. The communities agenda is now at a point where we can forecast the next steps. We believe that one of those steps is to reconnect evidence about the drivers of strong communities with evidence about the drivers of strong families. In related research, strong correlations have been identified between community-level indicators and indicators of the risk and protective factors associated with individuals and families, and in particular with risk and protective factors for young people. Thus, for example, we are now able to specifically identify schools and neighbourhoods where low rates of participation and retention are correlated with low levels of community engagement. More importantly we are able to identify both 'causes' of low levels of engagement and those local strategies most likely to increase engagement. In short, local community level interventions can now drive improved educational participation retention and completion rates. This requires an understanding of both family dynamics and community dynamics.

It is the conjuncture of these that we believe will be the focus of research effort over the next few years.

The community engagement agenda internationally has a patchy record of changing the policy settings of governments. In part – as we have argued here – this is because of the failure adequately to ground new ideas and practices in ways that resonate with existing policy concerns of governments while simultaneously pointing to a different future. Indicators can form the bridge between rhetoric and reality, by highlighting in a common-sense way the workings of community dynamics. We may not fully understand the causal chain at work. Indeed there may be no causal chain, just a myriad of inter-connected influences at work. What we do know however is that features of strong communities are highly desired by the public, and that government levers can influence the emergence and sustainability of those features.

Note

We would like to acknowledge the contribution of DVC research staff to the production of this chapter, and in particular the contribution of Jeanette Pope to the development of the Indicator Reports quoted in this article.

Notes

[1] DVC is beginning to use the indicators of community strength at the LGA level in Victoria to track progress towards its goal of building strong communities. It is also examining the drivers of community strength and the relationship of the indicators to other outcomes that are important to government, such as education and crime.
[2] Factor analysis simplifies survey data by grouping responses that have a high correlation with each other and a low correlation with other variables.

Chapter 6

Setting standards for community engagement

Alan Barr and Lesley Doyle[1]

This chapter describes and explains a participatory action research and development approach employed in the preparation and application of standards and guidelines for the engagement of agencies with communities. A project for Communities Scotland conducted by the Scottish Community Development Centre (SCDC), the goal was to develop the basis for a compact between representative community sector organisations and those government and non-government agencies operating in communities. The focus was on supporting the effective implementation of community planning and community regeneration policies, although there is a very wide range of other contexts such as community care, health improvement, community learning and development, in which public agencies seek engagement with communities, for which the standards and guidance could also be relevant. They were developed with a view to their being agreed and endorsed on the one hand by the relevant key agencies, and on the other by representative organisations of the community.

Why were standards and guidance needed?

Community perspectives on participation

Practice experience and research evidence, together with feedback from community consultation[2] provided evidence to the Scottish Executive that community participants frequently perceived a substantial gap between the rhetoric of community participation and empowerment and the realities in their communities. In its 1999 guidance for research grant bids the Joseph Rowntree Foundation said: 'To date, the impact of community involvement on regeneration has been modest, and commitment to community involvement has been tokenistic'. Anastacio et al., (2000) found that 'community views tend to be heard only – or at least mainly – when these coincide with official or private sector views, or where they relate to relatively peripheral decisions'. In Scotland, the resulting contradictions from such perceptions and experience were breeding mistrust, which in turn was undermining new initiatives. This applied equally to neighbourhood and interest/theme-based communities.

The areas that frequently elicited negative comment included the time scales for community consultation, the narrowness of the scope offered for influence on policy and practice, and the lack of openness in providing access to relevant information. Also of concern was the lack of adequate investment in capacity-building for agency staff and elected members to develop the skills to practice in a community-responsive manner on the one hand, and a lack of consistent investment in capacity-building and mentoring support for community representatives and community-led initiatives, on the other.

Such negative experience is by no means universal; there are good examples of effective approaches to engaging with communities that are experienced as empowering. Taylor (2001) provides many examples in *Involving Communities – Handbook of Policy and Practice*. However, in Scotland the transfer of learning was ineffective and there was a need both to capture those principles and practices that enable effective community empowerment and to provide guidance that reflected the experience of communities.

The policy context of community planning and regeneration
There was a range of policy initiatives within which community participation and empowerment was seen as an essential precondition of effective implementation. The initiatives arise across all fields of public service provision, but are brought together in community planning.

From their inception in 1999, the Scottish Parliament and Executive have emphasised the importance of effective participation. Indeed a Policy Unit report (Scottish Executive, 2000) said that 'civic participation is an essential tool of modern government', and argued that 'inclusiveness in the policy-making process is a key principle at the core of the modernising government agenda' (p. 6).

The commitment to inclusiveness became enshrined in legislation in the Local Government in Scotland Act of 2003. It set out the basis for community planning as the means of establishing integrated public sector partnership working informed by community participation. Statutory Guidance from the Scottish Executive (2003) on Community Planning describes it as having two core aims:

- making sure people and communities are genuinely engaged in the decisions made on public services which affect them; allied to
- a commitment from organisations to work together, not apart, in providing better public services.

With a statutory duty to participate in community planning placed on local authorities (including all their professional services), health boards, joint police boards and chief constables, fire boards, Scottish Enterprise, Highlands and Islands Enterprise and the Strathclyde Passenger Transport Executive, the breadth of the obligation to develop effective community engagement became apparent. It is no surprise therefore that policy and guidance for the full range of public services has come to emphasise the adoption of community engagement not only by specific agencies but also as a collaborative requirement. The commitment can be identified in numerous Scottish policy documents, and in some instances in specific legislation both planned and enacted. Examples are the Housing Scotland Act (2001), which has created a statutory requirement for local authorities and registered social landlords to have tenant participation strategies in place, and the Planning (Scotland) Bill (2005) which the Minister for Communities has said: 'will make sure that local people's views will be properly listened to before developments can take place ...'

Nonetheless, evidence suggested that 'the tool of civic participation' needed significant improvement if it was to deliver the benefits that the Policy Unit report (Scottish Executive 2000) believed would flow from it: 'better policy, building ownership and consensus around some policy outcomes, accounting for actions taken' (ibid). Delivery of the benefits is central to community planning.

The strength of the shared visions and strategic plans that are to be developed though community planning should be measured by their relevance to achieving the well-being priorities of communities. Hence effective participation and partnership procedures are an essential element of the project. Given that community plans will draw on and integrate a range of thematic and local plans, participatory and partnership principles also need to be applied effectively at these levels. The standards framework was developed to be applicable at both levels.

Whilst the advent of community planning gives particular impetus to this proposal, there is a wide range of current partnership and participation initiatives in which the standards guidance will be beneficial. Since partnership and participation are at the core of the UK 'Modernising Government' agenda[3] they are set to become increasingly significant features of the practice of governance. They require a robust and authoritative set of principles for community engagement by public agencies.

It is in this context that the Scottish Executive Minister for Communities commissioned, through Communities Scotland, the development of standards for the conduct of community engagement.

Authoritative guidance

Whilst several helpful publications provide guidance on community participation (e.g. Chanan et al., 1999; Burns and Taylor, 2000; Scottish Executive, 2002) none carry the formal endorsement and authority of the main partners in community regeneration in Scotland, and none set out agreed standards between stakeholders.

The means by which the standards and guidelines were developed is critical to the authority that they will carry in practice, both with communities and with agencies. Hence the development of the standards guidance itself needed to be participatory. The final product could be expected to carry much more weight if it were arrived at through a transparent and accessible process in which community representatives played a leading role, and in which their experience of the strengths and weaknesses provided a template for assessing proposals. However, any standards guidance will only be authoritative if it also recognises the needs of, and issues for, agency partners. This dual engagement in development was central to the way in which the project was developed.

Ultimately, if successful, the critical difference between the guidelines that will be produced from this project and those that already exist will be their formal endorsement not only from the Scottish Executive but also from the Convention of Scottish Local Authorities, CoSLA, and the national community representative networks. Hence the intention was that the final product would not represent the particular perspective of one interest group, but a negotiated statement of principles and practice to which all signatories would be able to give assent.

Origins of the development process

The Scottish Social Inclusion Network (SSIN), an advisory group set up by the Minister for Communities, established at her request a sub-group to explore initiatives that would enhance community empowerment. The group included community and agency representatives who had been involved in the Scottish Social Inclusion Partnership programme, and in particular the training support programme 'Working Together Learning Together'. An issue identified particularly by community representatives in the programme had been the lack of clarity about ground rules for the conduct of community involvement. An initiative was proposed through the SSIN sub-group to improve the quality and experience of community engagement for all partners, by developing a set of national standards. The principal Scottish Executive agency with responsibility for community engagement, Communities Scotland, which is the national housing an regeneration agency, was asked by the Minister for Communities to take the idea forward. The Scottish Community Development Centre, together with a partnership formed between the Community Development Foundation (a Home Office funded non-departmental public body) and Glasgow University, was asked to work with key Scottish agencies, voluntary organisations and most importantly communities, to find out what issues the standards needed to address.

Communities Scotland wanted to generate awareness and interest in the standards from the beginning of the project to ensure maximum application. It contacted those organisations that would be most likely to use the standards, to get their input. This process of consultation was also seen as a pilot to see how the standards would be received and then applied.

It had become clear that there was a gap between the potential for community participation and the reality of how it currently worked. To release this potential, the standards were needed to enable agencies and local people to work together in areas such as public service provision and policy development. It was envisaged that a standard would be a measurable statement that could apply to either a community or agency partner, or both, stating how they should work together.

Process

Using a community-led approach, the standards were developed with local people in the lead, but with local agencies involved at all stages. The programme of work was conducted in two phases. Phase 1 was initiated with six geographic and four thematic focus groups designed to be as representative as possible of localities and interests. Both sets involved community and agency participants with a range of community engagement experience. The main themes they identified as in need of being addressed were equalities, purpose, structures, knowledge, skills and capacity- building. Once these themes were identified, working groups of community and agency representatives, made up of a mixture of participants who volunteered from the original focus group locations, developed draft standards.

The groups came across a number of practical problems. After a lot of discussion and trying different styles of writing they decided to view the standards as aspirational goals: a way of working that groups and organisations should seek to achieve. As some forms of community engagement involve large numbers of participants, for example, open forums and people's panels, guidance was written to accompany the standards, giving examples of where particular standards could be applied to wider forms of engagement.

Three national conferences were held for consultation on the draft standards and guidance; there was overwhelming enthusiasm for the project. The documents were then revised as necessary, and reviewed by a national advisory group, all involving a balance of community and agency representatives. A lot of useful feedback was offered on the standards – by this stage over 500 people had participated – and SCDC used this for improvement and refinement.

For Phase 2, six pilot sites were identified by SCDC and Communities Scotland, as far as possible building on contacts established in the original focus group areas. This ensured a range of partnership arrangements, and demographic and geographic characteristics. The contexts for the pilots ranged from the complexity of the whole of a local authority area community planning partnership, through to local interagency regeneration and community planning initiatives, to neighbourhood projects.

The objectives of the pilot stage were to:
- test the capacity of the draft standards to support effective community engagement in a range of different types of setting;
- enable revisions of the standards and associated guidance that respond to identified gaps and deficiencies; and
- achieve endorsement of an agreed set of standards by key national stakeholder agencies, organisations and networks.

Piloting also provided case study examples for the accompanying guidance.

The pilot programme identified five reasons for using the standards, to:
- plan what community engagement practices need to be in place;
- assess different community engagement approaches;
- monitor and review progress in community engagement;
- evaluate and review engagement processes;
- provide ground rules that everyone could sign up to.

SCDC worked closely with the pilots and identified some learning points and issues that helped to improve the final standards and supporting guidance. The learning points included:
- Facilitation – some facilitation had been required to use the draft standards, which raised issues about how easy it would be to introduce and integrate them into everyday practice without support.
- Ownership – how the standards were introduced was important because if they were viewed as being imposed, they may have faced resistance. It was necessary to help potential users to think about the standards as a tool of which they would have owner-ship, rather than as an additional burden.
- Operational cultures – in reality, external deadlines and policies frequently contradict the principles of the standards, which can be frustrating.

In addition to the six intensive pilots, other groups used the draft standards despite the lack of resources to support everyone interested. SCDC contacted those who had expressed an interest in piloting the draft standards and sharing experiences. They were interviewed to provide additional evidence that contributed to the final outcome of the piloting phase. All but one of the original geographic areas continued their involvement, with the application and testing of the standards which were revised according to the feedback received and further considered by the advisory group.

Throughout both phases of the process, a regular newsletter was sent to all those involved in the consultation process to keep them informed and to alert them in good time to the next stage. From the end of Phase 1, the standards were also available in draft form on Communities Scotland's website, and in addition the agency sought endorsement from key national stakeholder agencies, organisations and networks, for example, CoSLA, Audit Scotland, Communities Against Poverty and the Scottish Council for Voluntary Organisations (SCVO), which is the umbrella body for voluntary organisations in Scotland.

Launching and disseminating the standards

The National Standards for Community Engagement (2005a) were launched at three national conferences by key representatives of major stakeholders: the Minister for Communities, a Vice-President of CoSLA, and the Chief Constable of Strathclyde Police. To this point over 500 people had contributed to the development of the standards. A further 500 attended the launch conferences.

The standards provide ten straightforward measurable performance statements designed to be used by everyone involved in community engagement, to improve the quality and process of the engagement. They are accompanied by indicators that set out key principles, behaviours and practical measures that underpin effective engagement and will be of real benefit to Community Planning Partnerships in involving communities to achieve real and sustained results.

The standards are:
1. Involvement: *we will identify and involve the people and organisations with an interest in the focus of the engagement.*
2. Support: *we will identify and overcome any barriers to involvement.*
3. Planning: *we will gather evidence of the needs and available resources, and use this to agree the purpose, scope and timescale of the engagement and the actions to be taken.*
4. Methods: *we will agree and use methods of engagement that are fit for purpose.*
5. Working together: *we will agree and use clear procedures to enable the participants to work with one another efficiently and effectively.*
6. Sharing information: *we will ensure necessary information is communicated between the participants.*
7. Working with others: *we will work effectively with others with an interest in the engagement.*
8. Improvement: *we will develop actively the skills, knowledge and confidence of all the participants.*
9. Feedback: *we will feed back the results of the engagement to the wider community and agencies affected.*
10. Monitoring and evaluation: *we will monitor and evaluate whether the engagement meets its purposes and the national standards for community engagement.*

Reinforcing their commitment to community engagement, Ministers approved additional funding for 2005/06 to support the implementation of the standards.

All Community Planning Partnerships (CPPs), Community Learning and Development (CLD) partnerships and Community Groups associated with them, both geographic and thematic, were given the opportunity to access support to use and implement the standards. A total of 212 consultancy days were divided up between the local authority areas. The SCDC delivered the consultancy support on behalf of Communities Scotland. They were asked to make contact with Community Planning co-ordinators and Community Learning and Development lead officers in the first instance to discuss how consultancy should be used, with a strong focus on flexibility in using the consultancy to suit local needs.

Implementation of the standards

In addition to the standards booklet, introductory user's guide and illustrations for the pilots, there are National Standards for Community Engagement Support Materials (2005b). This is a detailed manual and reference document which draws on established knowledge and experience of community engagement to illuminate issues that may need to be addressed in practice. It is primarily designed for use by facilitators who are supporting use of the National Standards for Community Engagement. It is not intended to be read from start to finish, but to be used as a resource to focus on particular aspects of the standards, as circumstances require. Except for the section on using the standards, the sections of the manual correspond to sections of the standards booklet in the standards pack. The manual has therefore been prepared primarily as a web-based document that is 'hot linked' to the specific principles, standards and indicators that are described in the standards booklet. Much of the remainder of this chapter is drawn from it.

Defining community engagement

There are many styles and methods of engagement. The standards can be used in formal and informal, extensive and intensive community engagement with any groups of participants. The nature of the engagement will determine the standards that require most attention. The standards were written to ensure that they could cover the formal types of engagement that were emerging in the context of Community Planning. To make sure that this was the case, the working groups and advisory group for the project agreed the following definition:

> *Developing and sustaining a working relationship between one or more public body and one or more community group, to help them both to understand and act on the needs or issues that the community experiences*

This definition focuses on formal, representative, face-to-face structures for engagement between public bodies and organised communities that operate over time to address specified community needs and issues. In the context of Community Planning and regeneration initiatives, such formal engagement will be a common feature of local democracy, but formal structures are by no means peculiar to this context. To give just one example that is now common-place in Scotland, area committees enable representatives of a neighbourhood community forum to meet with representatives of local authority departments, health boards, police or other agencies. The agenda for such engagement will be clearly identified and there will be sustained effort over a long period to use the working relationship between community groups and agencies to make progress on the priority issues identified. Numerous other examples could be given of what has now become a common feature of local govern-ance in Scotland. All of the standards are seen as being relevant to them. However, the standards will also be relevant to less formal and sustained types of engagement, and to more populist and indirect forms of engagement. For example, an agency or partnership may use an event such as an exhibition about public services to create opportunity for dialogue with local people.

There are many other forms of engagement that illustrate differences in terms of levels of formality, time-scale, representation and other characteristics. As a result, some standards may be applicable to them all, for example, those relating to quality, accessibility and feedback of information. Other standards may only be relevant to some.

The principles on which the standards are based

The focus groups and the working groups involved in creating the standards repeatedly highlighted some key principles that should be present in the conduct of all community engagement. These have been incorporated into the standards booklet because they were seen as providing an explanation for the content of the standards themselves. In other words, the standards were seen as the means by which principles of good practice could be put into operation. Reading the standards it will be clear that while these principles are more prominent in some aspects than others, they are in fact threaded throughout. The principles are equality, purpose, learning from experience, skills, knowledge-building, capacity, and information. They are echoed in the capacity building literature, for example Skinner, 1997 and Skinner and Wilson, 2002. A brief elaboration on three of these provides an indication of the type of discussions held and the way they were concluded.

The principle relating to equality, fairness and inclusion was seen as overriding. Without it community engagement would fail to address the needs of, and issues affecting, those who have the greatest needs. A key point was to remind users of the standards that have been developed within a legal and/or policy framework that commits public agencies to equalities. To apply these standards it is necessary that participants have a clear understanding of the equalities principles, and of law and policies located in key pieces of legislation, and are referred also to the Scottish Executive (2004) *Good Practice Guidance* on consultation with equalities groups. The purpose of the principle is simple: there should be a commonly agreed purpose or purposes among all participants, but also the methods of engagement adopted should be suitable for the purposes that have been set. The principle of learning from experience was established because there is substantial recorded evidence of a tendency to rely on established methods; those who promote community engagement have a responsibility to investigate their suitability before they are put into operation.

Making use of the standards

The standards identify the main qualities that should be found in good community engagement. Each of the ten commitments is accompanied by a set of indicators that enable their users to see whether the standard is being met.

To make use of the standards, it is useful to think about three stages. Here, just a few examples are given of what has to be considered at each stage. The first stage is what needs to be considered before embarking on a community engagement process, for example to identify who has an interest in the proposed community engagement and to ensure that all those with an interest in the focus of the engagement have the opportunity to be involved; secondly, what the participants need to do as it starts, for example to ensure that support needs have been identified and are being addressed, and to create opportunity for participants to find out about one another – who they are, what interests they represent, how they see the engagement process.

Finally, what is needed to sustain its effectiveness. All the features of the engagement should be kept under review throughout the process. Continuing to work on them should be a normal part of the development of the engagement. Continually revisiting them is essential to enable any problems that are arising to be addressed and resolved. The only new areas that are likely to come into play will be agreeing how best to feed back the results of the engagement to the wider community and other agency staff, and monitoring and evaluating the engagement as it progresses, using the lessons to promote continuous improvement.

Unpacking the standards

Each of the standards is unpacked using a number of indicators. The 'involvement standard' is summarised here by way of example.

The involvement standard
We will identify and involve the people and organisations who have an interest in the focus of the engagement.

This standard deals with who should be involved and what characteristics should be evident in the way that they act. The standard places an obligation on all participants, but particular obligations are being placed on those who initiate community engagement. In most circumstance this will be a public agency.

> ### Indicator 1:
> *All groups of people whose interests are affected by the issues that the engagement is to address are represented.*

This emphasises equalities and inclusion. To ensure that everyone whose interests are affected by the engagement is effectively represented requires investigation of the issues and their impact from a community perspective. If key interest groups are not represented they may later express dissent about the engagement process and this can be undermined as a consequence. It is not uncommon for groups to complain that they have not been represented because they do not recognise those that claim to represent them (see also indicator 4 bullet point 5 and 6).

Indicator 2:

Agencies and community groups actively promote the involvement of people who experience barriers to participation.

This indicator relates to positive action for groups that may experience discrimination or exclusion. It recognises the reality that some people will find it more difficult to become involved than others, and sets an obligation within the standard to encourage and support them to become active. (Areas in which supports may be needed are identified in the support standard indicators 2 and 3.)

In discussing the underpinning principles of equalities and inclusion (see above) the range of participants for whom such positive action may be required has already been identified. But within the broad categories listed there will be widely different sub-groups. It will be important to consider the characteristics of potentially excluded groups, and to tailor promotional activity to their needs and circumstances.

Where the engagement is broad based it will be important to ensure that consideration is given to any potential conflicts that might arise between different groups, and address them before they become an issue. On the other hand, some community engagement will focus on specific groups that commonly experience exclusion. In this case all aspects of the engagement should be tailored to respond to their particular characteristics. If community engagement is about community empowerment it must serve the aspirations of the community that is being engaged.

Indicator 3:

Agencies and community groups actively promote the involvement of people from groups that are affected but not yet organised to participate.

This is again an indicator concerned with inclusion and equalities. It recognises that not all of those whose interests may be affected by the focus of community engagement may have established means by which they can explore concerns with one another and articulate these on a representative basis. If the engagement process is based around formal structures in which agency and community representatives meet, such interests are inevitably excluded. Action is therefore necessary to reach out to such sectors of the community. Through more informal means, their interests can be fed into more formal processes. The indicator highlights the need for deployment of community development support that enables communities to become organised, or at least for their concerns to be identified. This indicator requires that community development resources are available. They may come from a variety of organisations both statutory and voluntary.

Indicator 4:

The people who are involved, whether from agencies or community groups:

- *Want to be involved* (key determinant of positive motivation).
- *Show commitment to take part in discussion, decisions and actions* (exploring what is needed to enable people to participate fully is dealt with under standard 8: Improvement).
- *Attend consistently* (though more frequently a concern raised about agency representatives, it can apply equally to all other participants).
- *Have knowledge of the issues* (this is of key importance and is dealt with in more detail in standard 6: Sharing information).
- *Have skills, or a commitment to developing skills, to play their role* (both skill and knowledge development may be needed for agency as much as for community participants. (Standard 8: Improvement, deals with such development in more detail)
- *Have the authority of those they represent to take decisions and actions* (if the focus and purpose of an engagement process has been clearly defined, see Standard 3: Planning, it should be possible to agree the boundaries of its authority to act).
- *Have legitimacy in the eyes of those they represent* (senior officers or members can endorse the participation of their representatives. It may be less easy in more informal community groups. Nonetheless confirmation of the legitimacy of representatives is an important pre-condition for effective engagement).
- *Maintain a continuing dialogue with those that they represent.* Evidence that dialogue is maintained with their respective constituencies by all participants indicates the health of the engagement process. (Standard 9: Feedback, deals further with issues of feedback and dialogue with wider interests.)

This set of indicators focuses on the characteristics that should be evident among participants, irrespective of whether they come from agencies or communities. Participants and those that they represent need to ask themselves whether the characteristics are evidenced in practice. They have been identified as indicators for participation because they are seen as having substantial impact on the overall effectiveness of community engagement processes.

Further development

The support programme in the first year has focused on raising awareness of the standards. It has become evident that the range of people who regard them as relevant is huge. The statutory agency participants in standards events in just one community planning partnership have included managers and staff of the following: schools, colleges, community learning and development, housing, technical services, roads/transport and engineering, libraries and museums, corporate services, research, communications, archaeology, police, fire services, social work, business support and enterprise companies, community safety, health improvement, primary care, acute health services, sport and leisure, planning, architecture, building control, sustainable development/ renewable energy. What this illustrates is that community engagement is now regarded not only as part of the business of almost all services but also something in which most staff will have a role. The initial dissemination phase has also illustrated the need to address the awareness and skills of elected members, and highlighted the range of area and interest-based community and voluntary groups to whom they are relevant. As a consequence of all of this, Communities Scotland is commissioning further support work.

Many community planning partnerships and councils have formally adopted the standards and they frequently appear within their community engagement strategies. National bodies such as the Scottish Health Council are evaluating the patient focus and public involvement strategy of NHS Boards with explicit reference to the standards, Her Majesty's Inspectorate of Education has built them into its inspection framework for community learning and development, Communities Scotland itself is using them in assessment of Regeneration Outcome Agreements. But the most important indicator of the value of the standards is not in their use as an external tool by official bodies, but their mutual and voluntary adoption by community and agency partners in community engagement. Continued active use in the pilot areas illustrates the value of this approach. In many new locations work has commenced to apply the standards, and though the signs are positive, it is too early yet to be confident about their long-term impact. Communities Scotland is committed to commissioning evaluation of progress in their use, with a corporate target in the public domain to evaluate the impact of the standards by December 2007.

Notes

[1] With thanks to Alasdair McKinlay and Sue Warner of Communities Scotland.

[2] A consultation event on this proposal, involving 30 representatives of community agencies in East, South and North Ayrshire, was held on 22 July 2002.

[3] See http://www.archive.official-documents.co.uk/document/cm43/4310/4310-00.htm (accessed 20/03/06).

Chapter 7

Sustaining economic development through business engagement and mutual learning

Stuart Ogg

Overview

Business engagement processes can make a valuable contribution to the organisational infrastructure required for the successful application of the learning region concept. In Scotland, Community Planning and Local Economic Forums have created an important framework for promoting successful business engagement. On the ground, and in certain regions, efforts have been made to make the first tentative steps to create effective business engagement processes such as Business Panels and Assemblies. However, to sustain such processes requires considerable commitment from all parties concerned. There is a need to ensure clear purpose, based on the expectations of all parties. There need to be clear tangible benefits to all participants, leading to real and recognised changes, while constant communication is essential to reinforce and strengthen relationships, trust and openness.

Community Planning and Local Economic Forums and the Forth Valley

Scottish Enterprise Forth Valley is currently one of the 12 Local Enterprise Companies that comprise the Scottish Enterprise Network, the lead governmental agency in Scotland concerned with delivering the Scottish Executive's economic development strategy, Smart, Successful Scotland. In exercising its role as the main economic development agency within the Forth Valley, Scottish Enterprise Forth Valley has over time tried to employ a range of methods and approaches to use knowledge, ideas and insights to inform and influence the decisions and actions of individual businesses. The intention was to identify ways of developing greater synergies between private business objectives and the more strategic interests and ambitions of the wider community. This was in effect an attempt to help lay the foundation for developing a learning region.

Developing mechanisms that enhance and sustain more effective communication, knowledge exchange and learning between business and governmental agencies is now recognised as an important tool in the armoury of local economic development. This chapter examines some examples from the Forth Valley, Scotland, the context within which these mechanisms have been developed, their effectiveness and the lessons learnt from their application.

The processes reviewed can be seen to be integral to the successful development of a learning region. In this context 'a learning region is viewed as a geographical space in which local actors (individuals, firms, institutions and authorities) engage in mutual and/or interactive processes of regional learning. The continuous dynamic and complex process of regional learning is what characterises economically successful regions today' (Capello, 2002, p. 131).

As Florida (1995) has noted, learning regions provide a series of related infra-structures, which can facilitate the flow of knowledge, ideas and learning.

This chapter examines how in the Forth Valley, located in central Scotland between the two main cities of Edinburgh and Glasgow, efforts have been made to introduce mechanisms and processes that facilitate a more open and constructive dialogue between government and business. With the aim of creating the foundation of a learning region, the dialogue has taken many forms around basic principles relating to the exchange of knowledge and ideas. The general purpose has been to inform and influence the delivery of services, and the introduction of more effective networking between local businesses and public agencies, allowing them to harness the power of collective ambition and action.

Why is such an approach important in an increasingly globalised economy? Florida (1995, p. 532) has suggested that 'the new age of capitalism has shifted the nexus of competition to ideas. In this new economic environment, regions build economic advantage through their ability to mobilise and to harness knowledge and ideas'. Florida views successful regions as being based on high levels of personal, firm, institutional and organisational interactions. The focus in the Forth Valley has been on developing practical processes which have the potential to facilitate the foundations of a learning region based on higher levels of mutual awareness, knowledge exchange and trust between public bodies and local businesses. The intention is to locate and develop recognisable synergies between the individual ambitions and goals of firms and the broader social, economic and environmental goals of public bodies reflected in political priorities.

Conventionally, within the context of local economic development, business development has been based on the use of financial inducements for businesses to carry out actions faster, on a larger scale and/or to a better quality than would have been the case under 'normal' market conditions. Such inducements have been used to achieve individual business goals such as increased profitability, market share, new market entry and/or turnover, with the parallel aim of meeting broader 'public good' objectives in the form of employment and economic growth.

Essentially financial inducements have been used to address failures in the market mechanism at the level of the individual business, but with limited human and financial resources there is always a need to restrict the scope and coverage of such support. This has led to the allocation of support to businesses that are expected to show the greatest turnover growth and impact on the economy. At a national level, through Scottish Enterprise this has recently taken the form of a Consistent Customer Management process with businesses segmented into a number of categories according to their anticipated contribution to the economy. In parallel, a series of product intervention frameworks have been introduced to ensure the support provided is consistent across lowland Scotland. These processes are essential to ensure the maximum return on the investment of public funds, though there could always be latent potential within a local economy not being developed.

Within Scottish Enterprise Forth Valley, there was early recognition of this issue, leading to the question what other resources could be harnessed that were not as constrained, and that could be used to achieve a broader impact across a wider spectrum of businesses. Intelligence, knowledge and insights came onto the agenda. This happened at a time when the concept of the learning organisation was emerging as a possible avenue for exploration. Clearly, to be able to use knowledge and ideas as a way of influencing the actions of local businesses there needed to be a receptive audience. At this time Scottish Enterprise Forth Valley had been using a learning organisation methodology for internal organisational development purposes and there were close ties with the Investors in People framework being used to promote best practice in HR management with businesses.

Building on the idea of a learning organisation, it was clear that greater benefits could be achieved if it was possible to use knowledge and insights that could help local businesses respond more rapidly and possibly pre-empt changes in their local, regional and global operating environment, their market opportunities and their role and position within local, regional and national supply and value chains.

The early mechanisms used to share knowledge included:

- Sponsored business pages in the three main local newspapers as a way of promoting what the business community is achieving as well as the activities and support given by the public agencies. The aim was to raise the profile of business and enterprise, promoting positive aspects of economic development and an awareness of the support available from Scottish Enterprise Forth Valley.
- 'Insights' and briefing notes to promote respectively important ideas and thinking from relevant experts, and information/ knowledge about the current state of the local economy. Both were for a period of two years and distributed to every business within the Forth Valley. The aim of the former was to help local businesses raise their horizons from the tendency to think and act short term. The introduction and communication of ideas in a way that businesses could readily relate to and absorb was an attempt to inform future decision-making. In the case of the briefing notes, these were a series of facts about the local economy and local markets designed to help businesses understand their immediate operating environment.
- A monthly bulletin, *What the papers say*, circulated to a wide range of audiences and designed to raise the profile of economic development across the Forth Valley, again in a way that was easily digested and accessible to a wide range of audiences.
- Newspaper style annual reporting was introduced as a way of communicating to a broad audience what the local Enterprise Company was doing and how the company was working in partnership with local businesses to help them grow. At the time this was a significant departure from the normal glossy annual report, which because of cost inevitably had a much narrower and limited circulation.

- Extensive use of Plain English in all Scottish Enterprise Forth Valley communications, including strategy documents and other literature for general circulation. The aim was to promote understanding of the content of the communication; by having the Plain English recognition it was clearly a statement that the document was published by an organisation committed to encouraging engagement and understanding.
- Business Weeks involving a series of events highlighting key aspects of the global changes taking place and how these are being translated into real challenges and opportunities affecting businesses.
- Board lunches with stakeholder groups including business groups focusing on particular strategic and important operational issues. More recently these have been focused on specific customer groups as part of a broader Scottish Enterprise Network approach, which has concentrated on seeking the views of businesses that have received some form of assistance from the organisation or one of its constituent parts.

These methods, while valuable in their own right, tended to be one way communication processes focused on the transmission of information, knowledge and insights, with the aim of raising the horizons of businesses to the global challenges as well as possible ways in which such challenges could be addressed. The idea of using such mechanisms as tools for building commitment and confidence across a broad range of local businesses towards the achievement of an agreed economic development agenda was less well developed. Consequently, the potential to accelerate the creation of a learning region was limited at this stage.

Between 1999 and 2001 the emergence of Community Planning and Local Economic Forums in Scotland not only led to a much greater emphasis being placed on engaging all forms of communities of interest, including businesses in the design and development of public policies and services. They also created an infrastructure that had the potential to further accelerate and facilitate the development of learning regions. These created much more fertile environments for promoting processes and mechanisms that could nurture different types of relationships within a discrete geographical space. Both Community Planning partnerships and Local Economic Forums operate within specified geographical boundaries. In the case of the former they are based on local authority boundaries, while the latter reflect Local Enterprise Company boundaries.

The purpose of both Community Planning and Local Economic Forums is to create mechanisms for more effective communication, coordination and delivery of public services that more effectively meet the needs of local communities whether individuals, firms or organisations. Community planning 'is about agencies, communities and partnerships working together more effectively to improve services such as health, education, jobs, homes, transport and the environment. It is about joined-up government, recognising that complex and deep-rooted problems often require multi-agency solutions. The community planning process will secure greater engagement in conventional policy development and service delivery' (Scottish Enterprise, 2002a, p. 1).

'Community Planning is essentially a process to secure:
- Greater collective engagement by agencies with communities in assessing needs, policy development and delivering services which best meets these needs. Communities should be at the heart of community planning.
- Effective joint working between public, private, voluntary and community bodies.
- The improved connection of national priorities with those at the local and neighbourhood level.
- An overarching framework for Community Planning partnerships should be a means to coordinate other partnerships and where necessary rationalise other strategies and/or partnership mechanisms'.

Executive (2002, p. 9)

Local Economic Forums emerged from The Enterprise and Lifelong Learning Committee's *Inquiry into the Delivery of Local Economic Development Services in Scotland* report, published May 2000 (Scottish Parliament Committee, 2000). The proposal was to establish a Local Economic Forum within each Local Enterprise Company. These were established across Scotland in April 2001.

Essentially, Local Economic Forums are voluntary partnerships comprising representatives drawn from the public sector agencies providing support to local businesses (Local Enterprise Companies, local authorities, area tourist boards (now area offices of VisitScotland) further education colleges, Job Centre Plus, universities, etc.) and from the business community. The Forums operate under guidelines issued by the Scottish Executive Enterprise and Lifelong Learning Department, and their progress has been monitored by two

Ministerial Task Forces, one covering lowland Scotland (the Scottish Enterprise area) and the other covering the Scottish Highlands and Islands (the Highlands and Islands Enterprise area).

Forums do not have budgets or operational responsibilities, so their effectiveness depends on developing strong local relationships and partnerships between different public bodies and with the business community, underpinned by cooperative and collaborative values. The initial task set for the Forums was to eliminate overlap and duplication in the support services provided to businesses by public agencies, while the second major task was to develop local economic development strategies consistent with and contributing to the aims and ambitions of the national strategy set out in *A Smart, Successful Scotland* and reflecting local opportunities and challenges (Scottish Executive, 2001).

Community Planning and Local Economic Forums have very similar and complementary purposes. Forums are the main mechanism for providing the economic development input to Community Planning. Common to both are some key characteristics that include:
- Engagement of multiple stakeholders including the business community.
- Development of shared agendas through strategy development processes and ongoing dialogue regarding their implementation and impact.
- Sharing resources and avoiding overlap and duplication requiring an open and honest dialogue about services and their costs.
- Mechanisms for the regular exchange of knowledge and insights between public, private and voluntary sectors thus building internal and joint capacity and capabilities.
- Developing delivery mechanisms that are more integrated and therefore more reflective of the complex nature of the public policy issues being addressed.

Interestingly, while Community Planning and Economic Forums represent an extension of existing local partnership working within the economic development field, their formalisation through Scottish Executive direction and guidance created an infrastructure that if successfully developed and supported over time could become powerful drivers of emerging learning regions, albeit at the time this was not explicitly acknowledged.

Developing new models of business engagement

With the emergence and development of Community Planning and Local Economic Forums there has been a growth in the level of collaboration and cooperation between public agencies themselves, and with a broad spectrum of communities of interest. This has led to a parallel expansion in new processes for engaging these different communities of interest, including the business community, to inform and influence the way in which public services are delivered and strategic priorities set. Likewise, such processes have the added dimension of allowing a two-way exchange of knowledge and insights that has lead to mutual learning. This has been facilitated by harnessing the power of alternative perspectives, through encouraging their convergence towards the articulation and achievement of commonly held goals. In the case of the Local Economic Forums it has included mainstream economic development agencies, higher and further education, employability agencies, local authorities with their remit for delivering a broad range of public services, the police and different elements from the private sector in the form of representative bodies and individual business representatives.

Against this background, in November 2000 the Stirling Assembly, a civic forum for the whole of the Stirling Council area and one of the key strands of Stirling Council's innovative democracy strategy, debated with a group of local businesses the issues and opportunities they faced at that time. Much of the debate centred on concerns about the delivery of statutory services such as planning, environmental health, road maintenance, and so on. Very little time was spent on direct business development support. This happened at a time when Community Planning was in an embryonic state, with Stirling being one of four 'pathfinder' areas introduced by the Scottish Executive to 'pilot' the concept and practice (Stirling Council, 2000).

After that meeting it became apparent that while much had been achieved to engage and gather the views of many different communities of interest, very little had been formally orchestrated to collate the views and concerns from the business community as a particular community of interest. The experience of the Assembly meeting suggested there was an opportunity to create a new mechanism to gather knowledge and then use it to influence strategic policy and the design of public services aimed at supporting the growth of the local economy. From this realisation emerged the idea of the Stirling Business Panel. Following in the footsteps of the Stirling Citizens' Panel, which had been established earlier, this was seen as a way of collecting information about what was affecting the performance of businesses and getting some idea of the priorities, reflected by the views expressed by a representative sample of businesses.

The aims of the panel were originally set as:
- Enhancing the accountability of the organisations providing services affecting the performance of local businesses.
- Creating a sounding board to test policies and their implementation.
- Accessing underrepresented opinions.
- Establishing a baseline of information about the performance of local businesses that could be measured over time.

It is on record that at the time 'formal consultation with firms is less well coordinated and of a more ad hoc nature, (although we believe it is important to recognise that every contact which a Council officer and staff member of Scottish Enterprise Forth Valley has with a firm is an opportunity for consultation and feedback)' (Dempster, 2000, p. 3).

The original design of the Stirling Business Panel was to create a single channel to communicate with a large representative sample of businesses within the Stirling area, in support of both community planning and the emerging Local Economic Forum. It was designed in such a way that it would provide a basis for obtaining representative views and opinions from the full range of businesses across the Stirling area, as the basis for providing an objective view of the issues that businesses were facing. At this stage there was no attempt to see the panel as a model for encouraging a wider exchange of ideas and knowledge as a bridge between public and private sectors.

Initially, an invitation was sent out to over 2,000 businesses, with the object of gaining the interest of between 500 and 700 to become part of the panel itself. Eventually a panel of 600 businesses was established. To manage the panel, a management group was established comprising public sector officials from the Council and Scottish Enterprise Forth Valley together with the private sector representation. Funding for creating the panel and carrying out subsequent surveys has come from the two public sector bodies.

As the panel developed, and after each survey was carried out, a newsletter was produced and circulated to the panel to give them feedback on the survey findings and any information about how programmes and policies were being changed as a consequence. Recent findings from the panel have been presented to inform key Departments of the Council as to the issues facing local businesses. This was an initial attempt at embedding learning through two-way feedback into the delivery of services to the business community. At this stage the Stirling Panel has provided a useful starting point, particularly in having a mechanism to understand the 'demand pull' for services. However, it has had more limited value in achieving deeper business engagement.

The Stirling Business Panel has now been in existence for four years. A number of surveys have been undertaken and the results have been used to influence the delivery of business support processes where there has been the local flexibility to do so. With more consistent business support services being provided by Scottish Enterprise across Scotland, there has naturally been less latitude for local solutions, which has avoided duplication and overlap. Local authorities do still retain the capacity to remain responsive to local needs. Having acknowledged these constraints, the engagement and learning processes that have developed within Community Planning and the Local Economic Forums have allowed more effective local management of services and products to emerge.

Once the Stirling Panel had been established, the idea of Business Panels as a way of providing a permanent communication channel with the business community to help contribute to Community Planning and the work of the Local Economic Forum was promoted across other areas of Forth Valley, in Falkirk and Clackmannanshire. In both cases, the concept was eventually adopted, but further developed as more focused business engagement processes.

In the case of Falkirk, the initial Business Panel was established at an open meeting that a wide range of businesses was to attend. This was followed by a succession of individual sub-groups developing interests that had been identified by the businesses themselves, such as availability of skills, transportation and property. The initial flurry of activity and interest of the business community fell away. Recently efforts have been expended to reinvigorate the panel, highlighting the importance and necessity of resourcing these mechanisms and keeping them fresh for all parties concerned.

In Clackmannanshire a slightly different model has emerged, with European Social Fund support. Termed the Clackmannanshire Business Liaison Initiative, the basic principles are similar to those which have been developed for the Falkirk Business Panel. Notably, the direct engagement of businesses in workshop and meeting type settings has given a stronger sense of partnership between the public and the private sectors. It has also allowed businesses themselves to understand and help influence the overall direction and development of public economic development policies at the local level. A number of theme groups have been established to focus on specific issues, in particular improvement in public/private sector liaison in areas such as public sector procurement and regulatory services, support for tourism and retail sectors, environmental and waste management, management and workforce development, corporate social responsibility and networking and knowledge transfer between businesses. A senior member of one of the main businesses engaged in this initiative has publicly commented 'I have experience of working with other local authorities and enterprise companies but this is the first time I have seen such a comprehensive approach being taken to local business development support'.

Subsequent to the Forth Valley experience a Business Panel and an Assembly have been established in Fife and Edinburgh respectively. In Fife the model adopted is very similar to that in Stirling, while in Edinburgh the model is more participative and follows the Falkirk model though at a much more strategic level. The Assembly provides an avenue for the Council, Scottish Enterprise Edinburgh and Lothian and the business community to work together to ensure that public policies and initiatives fit in with the needs of business. 'It is proposed the Assembly will meet four times a year, twice with public organisations present and twice with them in attendance' (Edinburgh City Council, 2005, p. 1).

The Assembly's strategic approach is also emphasised:

> It is important that the Assembly focuses on the strategic issues facing the city. The concept behind the Assembly is that the key business and economic leaders are brought together to discuss the future and to give pointers to the Council and other bodies for action. The Assembly should not become involved in detail or localised issues. (Scottish Enterprise, 2005, p. 1)

In addition to business panels and assemblies, there has been a strong trend towards engaging particular groups of businesses in the development of strategic economic development plans. Most recently, Scottish Enterprise has reviewed its key industry and clusters plans with in-depth engagement of key players in each industry. It is now intending to create new Supervisory Boards for each nationally important sector. Again, while this is clearly a mechanism to promote constructive dialogue between economic development agencies and businesses so that a 'demand pull' approach can be adopted to the delivery of economic development support, the number of businesses actually directly engaged is by necessity limited.

In the context of creating a learning region through facilitating higher levels of business engagement in the economic development process, there will always be a need to balance the numbers engaged, with the depth of engagement required and the available resources. In addition, consideration needs to be given to which engagement processes are appropriate for satisfying which purposes. In some cases there will be a need for different mechanisms to be run in parallel. It is critical, however, that their effectiveness and ability to contribute to the wider learning process is constantly reviewed.

From this overview it is apparent that Business Panels, against a background of Community Planning and Local Economic Forums, are now making a positive contribution to the infrastructure of learning regions:

- As a source of knowledge and understanding about what drives and constrains business growth to inform and influence strategic development and service design and delivery.
- As a channel of communication with the business community to share and validate strategic analysis of issues affecting a local economy as part of the process of knowledge transfer and mutual learning.
- Consultation on specific policy issues, e.g. marketing proposition of an area so that there are closer ties between 'publicly' funded place marketing and that utilised by individual businesses.
- To pilot test new services and gather market intelligence as to whether innovations in service design and delivery would find a ready market and have the proposed impact. This can be contrasted with more conventional customer surveys targeted at existing customers to determine existing customer satisfaction ratings. While the panels in Forth Valley have not been used in this way, Scottish Enterprise nationally has regularly reviewed its customer satisfaction levels which are applied locally through the partnership processes.
- As a method for promoting business-to-business networking, mutual learning and support within a managed context.

Reviewing experience

The experience of Business Panels as a method of engaging businesses in the development of a learning region has highlighted some key conclusions about the different perspectives implicit in the approach adopted by public sector agencies. These are concerned with economic development and businesses operating in the market economy, as well as with the drivers and barriers to effective engagement.

Figure 7.1 offers a simple description of the different perspectives taken by the public and private sectors in the context of economic development partnerships and initiatives. In many senses these perspectives reflect the different underlying value systems of the public and private sectors. In designing engagement processes it is important to recognise these alternative viewpoints, in order to effectively manage expectations and design processes in order to create the right environment to develop and sustain meaningful and mutually valuable engagement between the two sectors.

Figure 7.1 Alternative perspectives

Private	Public
• individualistic and self-motivated	• collective and democratic
• immediacy with focus on short term	• driven by consensus
• results focused	• public, transparent and open
• private and independent	• accountable to broad range of stakeholders
• focused on managing costs, profit and return on capital	• multiple short and long-term objectives e.g. delivery of effective business support services and achieving long term economic growth
• narrower range of stakeholders mainly focused on investors, suppliers and customers	
• limited strategic objectives	
• emphasis on reducing uncertainty while dealing with increasingly competitive global markets	• multiple stakeholder environment e.g. political, communities, businesses, etc.
• customer driven	• managing and accommodating complex, uncertain social, environmental and economic systems
• corporate philanthropy, social responsibility	• provider/budget driven services
	• growing interest in more coordinated services

Similarly, the Business Panel process has helped define important drivers and barriers to effective engagement of the business community. These are set out in Figure 7.2.

Based on the experience of the Business Panels, a basic model combining the type, scale and depth of engagement, and the corresponding levels of mutual influence and learning that have emerged, is shown in Figure 7.3.

Flowing from the experience of business engagement so far, important critical success factors have emerged for achieving effective engagement within an economic development context. These can be summarised as:

- **A clear purpose to the engagement process** – this means there needs to be absolute clarity about what both parties expect to achieve from the engagement. This needs to be set out and agreed at a very early stage in the process. As noted in discussions regarding the Fife Business Panel, 'it was stressed by the representative organisations that businesses would only continually

Figure 7.2 Drivers and barriers to effective business engagement

Drivers
- Desire to contribute to the 'public good' and make a difference
- Recognition that there is mutual benefit through genuine engagement
- Clarity about respective/complementary roles (businesses as wealth generators and employers – public sector as provider of 'public' goods)
- Open minded (more inclusive approach to policy and service design/delivery)
- Commitment to open and honest dialogue
- Development of trust between parties
- Acknowledgement that engagement processes can be learning processes and that both sides can inform and influence each other

Barriers
- Technical/bureaucratic language reduces ability to communicate effectively
- Lack of trust and openness arising from the tension between public and private goals and accountabilities
- Different time horizons
- Entrenched views based on experience and underpinning values
- Potential conflicts of interest relating to different governance systems
- Engagement can be seen to be time consuming and of little or no relevance
- No clear end state defined
- Politics can be seen by some as an uncomfortable arena to participate in

Figure 7.3 Business engagement and level of mutual influence and learning

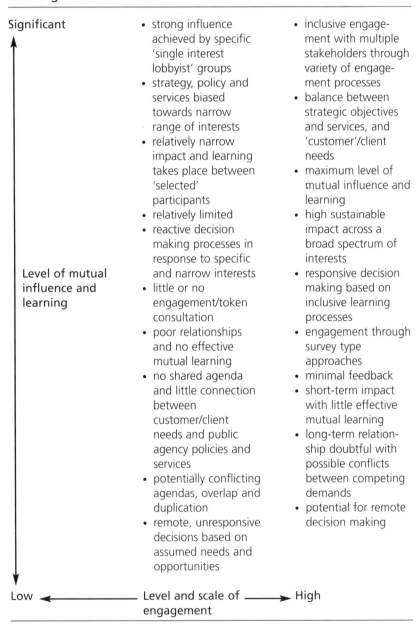

Significant

Level of mutual influence and learning

- strong influence achieved by specific 'single interest lobbyist' groups
- strategy, policy and services biased towards narrow range of interests
- relatively narrow impact and learning takes place between 'selected' participants
- relatively limited
- reactive decision making processes in response to specific and narrow interests
- little or no engagement/token consultation
- poor relationships and no effective mutual learning
- no shared agenda and little connection between customer/client needs and public agency policies and services
- potentially conflicting agendas, overlap and duplication
- remote, unresponsive decisions based on assumed needs and opportunities

- inclusive engagement with multiple stakeholders through variety of engagement processes
- balance between strategic objectives and services, and 'customer'/client needs
- maximum level of mutual influence and learning
- high sustainable impact across a broad spectrum of interests
- responsive decision making based on inclusive learning processes
- engagement through survey type approaches
- minimal feedback
- short-term impact with little effective mutual learning
- long-term relationship doubtful with possible conflicts between competing demands
- potential for remote decision making

Low ⟵———————— Level and scale of ———⟶ High
engagement

engage in a panel if they can see a clear and demonstrable benefit from their participation' (Fife Economic Forum, 2006, p. 1). In this respect the experience so far in Forth Valley and elsewhere in Scotland suggests that the idea can be applied very differently. Their purpose can range from data-gathering exercises using the panel as a standing panel to collect information from a broad range of participants which can be used to inform and influence policy and strategy and the delivery of public services, through to much more in-depth engagement with a more limited number of participants.

- **Relevant processes** – the appropriateness of the engagement processes and the infrastructure needed to support these is a critical factor affecting their success. For example, in the public sector there is a perceived 'meetings culture' based on the need to achieve consensus, unlike those running small/medium sized enterprises where 'time is money' so meetings are often not an attractive proposition.

- **Communication** – constant communication about the work and achievements from any form of engagement, to all participants, is a critical mechanism for cementing relationships, promoting understanding and influence and achieving an impact. In effect, feedback is a critical stage in the learning process, as it confirms what was agreed, reaffirms the shared knowledge and serves as reminder for action. As part of this process, it is critical that the language used is one that is accessible to all parties concerned and promotes unambiguous communication.

- **Action focused** – given that the private sector has a strong desire to be action-oriented and consequently short term, it is critical that there is a focus on developing positive and meaningful engagement which engenders learning and understanding between all parties concerned, and then to convert that into what is often termed early wins. An action-focused relationship is certainly one that is more likely to secure the commitment of private businesses rather that one which becomes a talking shop. Ultimately, there needs to be explicit evidence that the partnership and engagement processes have achieved a positive and recognisable impact within the areas of concern to the partnership.

- **Commitment and resources** – sustaining a managed engagement process needs resources and a long-term commitment. Relationships take time to evolve and become valuable to the parties concerned. Trust and openness take time to develop, yet are important drivers of an effective engagement process.

Looking ahead, much of the emphasis on learning regions has been on lifelong learning of individuals. In future there is a need to look more closely at how organisational development and learning can also contribute to the development of learning regions. Scottish Enterprise Forth Valley intends to be fully involved in these processes.

Chapter 8

Research, consultation and policy development for rural and remote communities in Scotland

Donna Easterlow and Kate Sankey

Overview – closing the opportunity gap, and community futures

This chapter reports on two research and community consultation approaches designed to inform and influence policy making. The underlying principle to be explored is that policy-making which is founded on community engagement and involvement will lead to better-targeted delivery of support services which are built on local evidence of the needs and aspirations of rural communities. The challenge for policy-makers, therefore, is to find consultation and participation processes which draw people from many parts of the community together to exchange information, express concerns and perspectives, and build capacity for seeking solutions and for engaging people in policy decisions. The success of such an approach will be demonstrated by activities undertaken by communities who are empowered and supported to improve the quality, well-being and sustainability of rural living.

We focus on two different initiatives that have sought community consultation and participation to inform policy development. The first relates to the Scottish Executive's work on improving access to, and quality of, services in rural areas,[1] as part of its 'Closing the Opportunity Gap' (CtOG) strategy to tackle poverty and social exclusion. The strategy is underpinned by ten targets, including one rural target,[2] which states as its aim:

> *By 2008, (to) improve service delivery in rural areas so that*

agreed improvements in accessibility and quality are achieved for key services in remote and disadvantaged areas.

This target reflects the Scottish Executive's recognition of the crucial role of accessible, high quality services – in the public, private and voluntary sectors – in combating rural deprivation and promoting strong rural communities (Scottish Executive, 2000a).

The second initiative discussed is a community participation approach called Community Futures, adopted by the Loch Lomond and the Trossachs National Park (LLTNP)[3] for engaging local communities early in a local action planning programme to link community aspirations with strategic planning for the Park. The National Parks (Scotland) Act (2000) provides the basis for National Parks in Scotland, and differs from other Parks in the UK and internationally by having a fourth statutory aim – to promote the sustainable social and economic development of the Park's communities. This was a significant driver, as the programme offered a unique opportunity for the views of the communities to inform policies and projects across all four of the objectives which are to:

- conserve and enhance the natural and cultural heritage of the area;
- promote sustainable use of the natural resources of the area;
- promote understanding and enjoyment (including recreational pursuits) of the special qualities of the area by the public;
- promote sustainable economic and social development of the area's communities.

Community Futures uses a strategic framework and a participative process to enable communities to develop local action plans. The process highlights the key issues and concerns that matter most from the community perspective, and so provides a more informed and locally sensitive insight behind conventional statistics. For example, we know the current demographic and structural changes which are taking place – increasing older population, outmigration of younger people, more second homes, a growing dependence on tourism, lack of public transport, and farming and forestry industry which is adapting to change, as support is altered through CAP reform. The Community Futures work enabled the consequences of these changes to be expressed by the communities in terms of the effect on provision of services and facilities, access to housing and employment, community vibrancy, local distinctiveness etc.

These two approaches reflect three key overarching commitments: to locally-sensitive policy making; to placing the views of the public at the heart of the policy-making process; and to the idea of evidence-informed policy-making. These commitments are echoed through many strategic and policy frameworks which deal with rural Scotland, in particular the Rural Strategic Development Plan (Scottish Executive, 2006). Local development agencies, National Park Authorities and LEADER+[4] local action groups have a critical role to play.

Furthermore, in Scotland Community Planning is a policy framework that is required to be enacted across all the local authority areas in the country. It was given a statutory basis in the Local Government in Scotland Act (2003). The Act places duties on:

- local authorities – to initiate, facilitate and maintain a Community Planning process;
- core partners (NHS Boards, Enterprise Networks, Police, Fire and Strathclyde Passenger Transport) – to participate in Community Planning;
- Scottish Ministers – to promote and encourage Community Planning, including local participation by Communities Scotland in Community Planning Partnerships (CPPs).

Closing the Opportunity Gap

It is significant that the rural Closing the Opportunity Gap (CtOG) target has deliberately not been specified in terms of the services and the levels of improvement by the Scottish Executive in a top-down way. Rather, it is one that will be based on a number of (different) local targets to be agreed as an ongoing process with Community Planning Partners who will hold overall responsibility for ensuring they are met. Twenty-two Rural Services Priority Areas (RSPAs) have been identified as experiencing particular problems of deprivation and service provision.[5] They are distributed across Scotland, include both island and mainland localities, and are the focus of the rural CtOG policy.

Working with Community Planning Partners is central to improving rural service provision and delivery. The very idea of community planning, as set out in the Local Government in Scotland Act (2003), is that local authorities identify and work with other important organisations, such as health boards, police boards and enterprise agencies, in a strategic way. Under the Act, CPPs must also involve the community itself as the main partner, by exploring community needs and views to inform community plans. In short, CPPs promote joined up government and service delivery, and community involvement at the local level.

It was in order to inform the dialogue between the Scottish Executive and CPPs in agreeing and setting these local targets, that the Executive commissioned a piece of research 'Service Priority, Accessibility and Quality'. Key objectives of this research were to:

- Identify and explore the service improvement priorities of people living in Scotland's Rural Service Priority Areas.
- Explore the issue of accessibility, and how access to key services might be improved, from the perspective of both service users and those who feel they do not have access to the services they wish to use.
- Explore the issue of service quality, and in particular the factors that determine satisfaction or otherwise, based on the qualitative experience of services.
- Explore any channels of communication open to rural community members to contribute towards shaping service provision and delivery, as well as interest in participating in such channels.
- Make recommendations on how to maintain ongoing dialogue between service users and providers in future.

The Scottish Executive has long been concerned with exploring issues to do with the accessibility and quality of rural services. It has drawn on the findings of a range of national surveys (such as the Scottish Household Survey and the Scottish Social Attitudes Survey), analyses and research studies to establish and measure the geographic availability, accessibility and quality of key services. By and large, these studies have been concerned with services that are 'known', assumed or taken to be important and/or for which data are available. They are also, moreover, usually based on particular, fairly limited, definitions of 'accessibility' and 'quality'. So, for instance, geographic availability has been equated with drive time (Scottish Executive, 2002). The Scottish Household Survey has asked about the 'convenience' of (a list of) services, and whether respondents agree or disagree that their local council provides 'high quality services' without a definition of what 'high quality' means. The Scottish Social Attitudes Survey has explored the issues of access to, and satisfaction with, services, particularly health services (Farmer et al., 2004) in more detail, but again using a pre-determined list of services.

In recognition of some of these issues, the Scottish Executive commissioned a piece of research that aimed to explore and go on to measure community perceptions of service quality in rural Scotland (Scottish Executive, 2000b). This was an interesting piece of work in that it employed a mixed method approach (including both focus group and survey research), and explored via qualitative research the issue of service quality. Participants' views were again sought, on a pre-determined list of 33 services. Furthermore – and crucially – qualitative views on what 'quality' means or how it is experienced were analysed in limited detail, and were condensed to 'degree of satisfaction' with services when 'measuring' perceptions and experiences of quality among a wider population, even though the researchers recognised the problems associated with this approach.

With all this in mind, the aim of the research discussed here was to be as open-ended as possible, and to explore rather than pre-empt service improvement priorities in access and quality terms for rural communities themselves.

Research methods and approach

The research comprised two key elements. A more detailed overview of the research methodology is available in the final report of the project (Accent, 2006). The first element was a review of the findings of local services research and consultation exercises across the 22 RSPAs, most of which, it was anticipated, would have been carried out or commissioned by community planning partners in order to meet the community consultation requirements of the 2003 Act. The aim of the review was to identify existing information and knowledge on local community needs and views with respect to service provision, for the Scottish Executive to be able to draw on its discussions with CPPs.

A further aim was to inform the direction of additional primary research – the second element of the overall research – in particular through identifying any gaps in the existing knowledge base. This work was intended to complement the research and consultation already conducted in each area, in order to meet the information needs outlined above. It included exploring *communities'* self-defined service improvement *priorities*, as well as the meaning and experience of the terms 'accessibility' and 'quality' in more depth.

Qualitative focus group discussions were selected as the most useful approach for exploring these issues. Qualitative research seeks to explore experiences, perceptions and meanings in detail. As such it was suited to the task in hand. Focus groups, in particular, would allow for both the expression of a range of individual views and discussion of, and where possible agreement on, the key issues and priorities for communities. The group discussions are described in more detail below.

Qualitative research, focus group interviews included, cannot and does not seek to elicit 'representative' community or population views. Focus groups typically include 8–10 participants. None the less the aim of this research was to include, as far as possible, a cross-section of the population of the RSPAs, including excluded and hard-to-reach groups. Thus the researchers sought to recruit participants across age, gender, socio economic, life-stage, length of local residency and ethnicity groupings, as well as Gaelic speakers, those without access to cars and disabled people.

Participants were invited to opt into the study. Recruitment was via a postal invitation to *all* households in the RSPAs. The letter of invitation explained the purpose of the research and the methodology, encouraging the recipient to pass on the information to other members of the household if they were not interested or able to participate. To compensate for the heavy investment in time and travel that would be encountered by many participants in coming together in central locations, a financial incentive and reimbursement for travel expenses was offered, and for those who had to travel particularly long distances, overnight accommodation. Those interested in participating were asked to complete and return a short questionnaire to provide the information in order to monitor social group profile.

This approach led to recruitment and attendance of between 7 and 12 participants – in most cases at least 10 – at each of the 13 focus groups, and representation of a range of social groups.[6] It did, however, lead to an under-representation of young adults aged 18 to 24. A key task of the workshop moderators was, as far as possible, to ensure that the experiences and needs of all sections of the community were considered. The group findings demonstrate the success of this approach, since many service priorities discussed were ones of importance to sectors of the populations who were either poorly represented or not represented at all within the actual group itself.

Focus group discussions

The workshops were facilitated by skilled moderators and supported with a topic guide. Gaelic speakers were available in all four of the groups that were held within Gaelic speaking communities to assist, if necessary, with any language issues.

The first task was to establish a list of services that the group agreed it was *most* important to improve for their community. This was achieved through the following process:

- Participants were encouraged to consider as many services – across the public, private and voluntary sectors – as possible. This involved drawing up a comprehensive list of services that they felt were important for both themselves as individuals and households, and their community, including both those that were and were not currently available.
- The group was then asked to prioritise the ten services that they thought it was most crucial to see improved in access and/or quality terms. The list could include the provision of new services or improvements to the provision of existing ones.

The value of this approach was demonstrated by the way that some of the services identified were not among those usually included in the services listed when views are sought in government surveys, for example local employment opportunities, pest control, fuel prices. Despite the range of services that people used or wished to use, generally the groups encountered little difficulty in reaching agreement, even where the service in question was only used by one attendee. There was one notable exception so that agreement was reached on nine priorities and not ten, as in the other workshops.

The second task was to explore the accessibility and quality experiences, needs and wants of the group in relation to the services identified. This was done with reference to a satisfaction pyramid as shown in Figure 8.1.

Participants were asked to use this model to assess current levels of access and quality of existing services, and to suggest what would be required to 'meet expectations' for new services. Then – for both existing and new services – they were asked to think about what improvements would be required to reach higher levels of satisfaction.

If necessary – this rarely proved to be the case – discussion was prompted by considering different delivery mechanisms, as identified in the literature review, which might enhance access and quality. This also involved an

Figure 8.1 Access and quality satisfaction pyramid

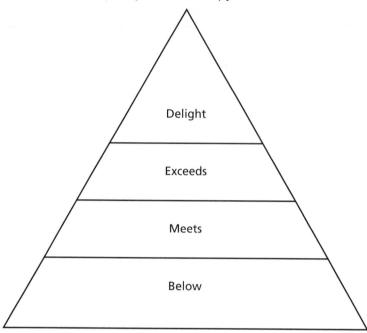

Source: Accent (2006)

exploration of participants' own ideas on innovative or alternative ways of improving access.

The final element of the workshop discussions was an exploration of participants' awareness of existing channels of communication available to contribute to the shaping of service provision and delivery in their community. Knowledge of CPPs, Local Authority representatives and individual service providers was explored, together with experiences of them, and how they could be improved. Alternative methods of communication were also explored.

The focus groups were taped with participant consent and fully transcribed. The results were analysed according to the particular service under discussion, as well as according to definitions of accessibility and quality emerging across all services. The findings were also discussed on a workshop-by-workshop basis, in order to provide detailed area information, and according to the social characteristics of the participants.

Findings

Service improvement priorities

Although there were some local variations, the focus group research identified a broad consensus in community service improvement priorities across the Rural Services Priority Areas. These priorities were not particularly surprising. They reflected the findings of other research, including that at the national level as well as at the local level. The priorities were:

- access to public transport, including buses, trains and planes and rising cost of private transport
- access to health centres, GPs and emergency health services
- access to other emergency services
- access to refuse collection and recycling
- access to post offices and retail shops
- quality of road maintenance
- access to and quality of communication services
- access and quality of utilities, water and energy.

Other services were identified as improvement priorities in some but not all areas. Access to and quality of housing and leisure, recreation and education was a concern for a sizeable minority of the groups, for instance. Other, perhaps unusual or unanticipated improvement priorities related to information services, a pier, pest control, trades services and farming advice services. These were confined to single focus groups and tended to reflect the local situations.

Most of the local variation came in terms of the different accessibility and quality problems currently being experienced with each of the services identified. So while a service might have been highlighted as a priority for improvement in a number, if not all, of the focus groups, the reasons for identifying it could be very different. It was these discussions in particular that resulted in rich information useful to the Scottish Executive and CPPs in thinking about the local targets.

Definitions of access and quality

Although focus group participants struggled to distinguish between experiences and expectations of accessibility and quality for some services, a range of definitions of the two were identified. These did, however, tend to relate to particular services or types of service, and are not therefore applicable to all services.

Access was variously defined in terms of:
- Travel time
- Opening hours, including phone lines
- Response time, including speed of answering calls and responding to requests, complaints and repair needs
- Regularity and/or frequency of service provision
- Services being brought into an area or to the home
- Service integration, particularly in relation to the coordination of public transport.
- Level of personal contact
- Physical access to buildings for those with mobility difficulties.

Quality was variously defined in terms of:
- Acceptable range of service, particularly in relation to range of goods available in shops and range of health services
- Cost
- Politeness, friendliness and willingness to help amongst staff
- Time allocated to service users, particularly with respect to GP appointments
- Services tailored to meet community needs
- Cleanliness of premises
- Access.

More detailed information on these definitions, to which services, and in which areas they relate, is available in the report of the research (Accent, 2006). The brief overview here highlights the usefulness of the research in identifying key aspects of service accessibility and quality that rural communities think need to be addressed, and which local targets could therefore seek to tackle.

Views on public consultation

The literature review found that CPPs and service providers are increasingly involving communities in the process of identifying the key services they require and where and how to locate and deliver them. A wide range of methods, involving face-to-face, postal, telephone or electronic contact, are used to consult the public on issues of importance to them. There are, however, local variations in the extent of research and consultation activity.

Focus group participants in some of the RSPAs still felt that more communication and consultation was necessary. There was a strong view in other areas, on the other hand, that there had never been so much consultation – yet so few results. These participants believed that councils, local government and the Scottish Executive should focus on 'getting the job done', rather than on discussing what needs to be done. This is of interest for any research project whose rationale is to seek community views on 'what needs to be done'.

Employing research evidence in the policy process

The detailed local research findings have been discussed with CPPS. Scottish Executive researchers accompanied policy officials on meetings with CPPs to present the findings, to answer any questions and concerns about the research, and to discuss the implications of it for each RSPA and the associated service improvement targets. At these meetings, it was emphasised that target proposals should be underpinned by the evidence base resulting from both elements of this research, and any other local information.

The Scottish Executive is now in the process of assessing the local target proposals. These will be assessed according to a number of different criteria. A key one will be to what extent they reflect community needs and wants, as expressed in research and consultation exercises.

The proposals cover which services will be the focus of the rural Closing the Opportunity Gap work and funds, and what improvements in terms of accessibility and quality are being aimed for. CPPs were encouraged to draw on the range of service priorities and definitions of accessibility and quality that the research identified. This will ensure that local targets will be set – and hopefully achieved – to reflect the needs of local communities and, crucially, be ones that they themselves believe will improve their experience of key services, and by implication the quality of life in their local area.

The Community Futures programmes

Small Town and Rural Development Group (STAR) promotes the principle that Community Futures is best undertaken through a programmed approach – where bottom-up planning meets top-down policy to create a new dynamic relationship between local communities and the agencies with responsibilities towards their area. Programmes are designed by STAR to enable communities to become active partners in translating their needs and aspirations into action. It is not a programme that would be described as having a research output; rather it is a participatory process which is applied across groups of communities in a structured framework, and is capable of being replicated and evaluated. The programmed approach enables communities to move beyond the planning phase and become partners in their own development. There are three key elements – community strategic planning, partnership and organisational development, and community project development.

Community Futures in the Loch Lomond and the Trossachs National Park was facilitated by STAR (2001–2005) through the three stages. Ongoing support is now provided through the Loch Lomond and the Trossachs Community Partnership, with directors drawn from the communities, the National Park and key public agencies. The work is supported by National Park staff in the Rural and Community Support team. Colin Roxburgh and Alan Tuffs have written a book telling the story of their work in the National Park (Roxburgh and Tuffs, in press).

Within the National Park there are 15,600 people living in 24 communities. Apart from the communities on the west and southern end of Loch Lomond with access to greater Glasgow, all communities are defined as remote or very remote. The Community Futures Action Planning stage (2001–2003), was supported by eight Community Agents, and was completed in three phases, each with eight communities. The communities carried out a series of activities including the following:

- 4,000 households completed a Community Views survey;
- 500 stakeholder interviews were carried out;
- 800 young people were involved through school and youth activities;
- 24 community profiles were compiled which documents the facts and figures about the community;
- 24 community workshops were held, attended by 1,800 people which identifies the main themes and issues that the community need to address;
- 24 Community Action Plans were published which describe the community's vision for its future and identifies priority projects and actions.

One of the major principles of Community Futures is that communities themselves should choose to take part in the programme – it should not be imposed on them. Building a partnership with communities requires a participatory approach from the outset. Voluntary buy-in to the programme was fostered through involving communities and partners in the design of the programme.

Local steering groups were established and a National Park–wide steering group was established with membership from the communities and partner public agencies. Communities were involved in the recruiting and training of local Community Agents to work alongside the communities, existing Community Councils and local organisations in the preparation of the Community Action Plan. Each community worked on the Community Action Plan over a five to six month period, with a launch event to celebrate. The whole Community Futures programme was funded until March 2005, enabling the process to move to the second and third stages of organisational capacity-building and project development.

Findings

Each Community Action Plan was different, but common priority themes emerged. These findings were reported in the State of The Park report (LLTNPA, 2005). Here is a flavour of the policy areas raised in the Action Plans:

- Infrastructure which impact on social and economic development:
  - Paths, trails and cycleways
  - Broadband, community websites and IT facilities
  - Environmental enhancements, litter, sewage treatment
  - Roads and traffic
  - Integrated public transport, community transport

- Social and Community Services and Facilities
  - Village hubs, multifunctional community facilities (post office, shop, café, youth venue, out-of-school care and learning centre)
  - Play and recreation areas
  - Affordable housing
  - Youth groups and activities
  - Access to learning and training opportunities

- Promotion, Tourism and Business support
  - Promotion and interpretative information
  - Branding and marketing of local goods and identity
  - Local Business support through networks, and available premises
  - Visitor management

- Environment and Heritage
  - Natural environment, waste management, paths and access
  - Built environment – improve shop frontages, car parks, toilets
  - Heritage centres, local history maps, trails, signage and publications

Promoting the sustainable development of the Park's communities will depend on understanding the social balance of communities. Imbalance in population structure is manifest in concerns for the viability of key services and facilities. The fragility of the economic base means that those most economically disadvantaged are reliant on public transport to access services, or require a private car, which is a further drain on limited resources, so community transport projects should feature in policy development.

The Community Futures process anticipated that as community awareness was raised, so too would be community expectations. It was therefore essential that mechanisms were in place to follow through from policy priorities being identified by the community in the Community Action Plan, to action actually being taken. Few of the issues raised are the responsibility of any one agency, nor can they be tackled by communities in isolation.

At policy level the outcomes of the 24 Community Action Plans have fed into the National Park Plan. They have also contributed to the wider Community Planning processes ongoing in the local authorities. At the local level the LLTNP Community Partnership has been formed from the original steering group, and a structure of four Area Networks provides the support for realising the aspirations through project development, funding and partnership working.

One example of this process was the priority identified to improve the quality of play and recreation areas in local communities. Some individual communities were working on improving existing play areas or creating new ones, supported by Community Agents as part of the Community Futures Programme. Thus there was an opportunity to share experiences and collectively achieve a Park-wide approach.

A vision for distinctive National Park play parks was agreed through a special Play in the Park meeting attended by 13 National Park communities. Here, excellent practice from Denmark and the UK (including Scotland) was presented. The Play in the Park initiative was supported by the National Park and LEADER+, and has resulted in a number of pilot projects coming forward, a series of design and training sessions, and a detailed audit of existing play provision across the Park.

The experience of this approach has been largely positive. There are now 18 communities that have set up Community Development Trusts. The community futures approach has moved into further stages, with a focus on support and training to communities. These issues link to key policy areas for the National Park. The draft National Park Plan (LLTNP, 2005) outlines the long-term aim for promoting balanced and sustainable communities, and proposes that it will be delivered under four areas of policy and action:

- Enabling strong and active communities
- Sustaining community facilities and promoting inclusion
- Improving transport for communities
- Improving access to housing.

Under each of these headings there are specific policies and actions which the National Park, along with partner agencies, will commit to. For example, under the second area there is a policy covering Local Provision of Services and Facilities. Here there are four policies to ensure that access by local communities to a range of key and essential services is sustained:

- Securing the retention and improvement of key local services and facilities within communities wherever possible.
- Exploring new and innovative ways of delivering local services and facilities.
- Facilitating social enterprise and community-led service provision.
- Ensuring that the needs of the Park's communities are recognised, such that access is sustained and improved.

The National Park plan itself was a consultation document, to be presented to the Minister later in 2006. The annual report for the programme indicates that targets are being met, and that the programme has had a sustainable impact on communities: 'Community Futures has drawn out the main priorities in the community'; 'confidence in the Trust is building – and other organisations are now working in partnership with us. Agencies listen to us now'. The communities have a voice, and are able to engage with policy makers and make a difference.

Reflections and lessons learned

Both of the examples of rural community engagement and involvement presented here have addressed the key aim of developing policy that reflects the needs and wishes of rural communities themselves. The vehicle to achieving this has been evidence-informed policy-making. There are a number of points in the policy making process where research and other evidence can have an input. These include identifying the problem to be addressed, deciding how to tackle the problem, as well as evaluating the success of the chosen approach as a means of improving existing, and developing future policy.

The approaches described here were based on the idea that research and consultation evidence can usefully contribute in all these ways to the same policy. The local Closing the Opportunity Gap targets will reflect community views on what the service provision problems in their local areas are and what is needed to address these. The Closing the Opportunity Gap strategy as a whole, including this particular element of it will, in time, be evaluated to assess what has 'worked' and what has not.

The Community Futures programme was designed so that the evidence provided through the Community Action Plan could feed into National Park-wide policy and also bring the policy into an action phase. Evidence that this has worked will be judged against the National Park Plan, and will be an iterative process. The strength will lie in the ability of the National Park to maintain the dialogue with the communities through the Community Partnership and the Area Network framework. The communities now have the capacity and support to engage with strategy and policy in the Park.

One key finding of the Closing the Opportunity Gap research has been the experience of 'consultation fatigue', and cynicism about the value of research in terms of what it achieves in practical terms amongst some sections and communities of the public. This has a number of implications. First, it is important that not just the findings of research and consultation exercises are communicated to participants, but also the actions that will result. Participants of the focus group research are being informed then of the key findings and of the local Closing the Opportunity Gap targets being set for their local area *and* how the two relate.

A second key finding is that wherever possible, use should be made of the existing knowledge and evidence base in informing policy.

These findings are echoed by the experience of the Community Futures pro-gramme. The voice of the communities was actively sought by the National Park, and engagement with the process was positive. There was value for the communities themselves, as a consequence of this engagement. They had access to a Community Agent for support, and consequently better access to the key public agencies that are the gatekeepers for the services.

There is a growing role for policy makers to engage in community consultation of the kind which both influences policy development *and* provides a dialogue framework for communities to develop confidence, skills and knowledge to take forward projects and initiatives themselves, in collaboration with service providers.

Notes

[1] The Scottish Executive classifies rural communities as 'accessible rural', 'remote rural' and 'very remote rural' (Scottish Executive 2004). Accessible rural communities are defined as those with a population of less than 3,000 but within 30 minutes drive of a settlement of more than 10,000 people, remote communities are defined as those with a population of less than 3,000 and within a 30–60 minutes drive of a settlement 10,000 people and very remote communities are those with a population of less than 3,000 with a drive time of over 60 minutes to a settlement of over 10,000.

[2] More information on the 'Closing the Opportunity Gap' strategy and the ten targets, including the rural target, is available at:
http://www.scotland.gov.uk/Topics/People/Social-Inclusion/17415/opportunity

[3] Details of the Loch Lomond and the Trossachs National Park and the Community Futures Partnership can be found on the following web sites:
http://www.lochlomond-trossachs.org and
http://communityfuturespartnership.org.uk

[4] LEADER+ is a European Community Initiative for assisting rural communities in improving the quality of life and economic prosperity in their local area. See http://www.defra.gov.uk/rural/leader/default.htm

[5] More information on the method of selection of the Rural Services Priority Areas is available at: http://www.scotland.gov.uk/Topics/People/Social-Inclusion/17415/CtOG-targets/ctog-target-h

[6] For information on the locations and population profiles of the focus groups, see Accent (2006).

Chapter 9

Learning communities in Victoria: where to now?

Leone Wheeler and Shanti Wong

Over the past 10 years, the State of Victoria has seen a number of initiatives, some Government funded, others not, that come under the banner of learning community partnerships. They usually involve a coalition of key stakeholders and a networked approach to economic development and social inclusion. This chapter summarises what happened, describing the current state of learning communities, and teases out some of the issues in taking the learning community movement forward. What can community workers and policy-makers learn about building sustainability into pump-priming projects, in order to ensure that gains made are not lost in the long term?

The Victorian context

In the twenty-first century, the new disadvantaged will be those who do not know how to learn. They will be unable to adapt as they are faced with ever more information and change. But learning is about more than getting by. Our ability to learn is what enables us to shape our own future. We are born curious and our ability to continue to learn is what defines us as individuals, as communities and as societies.

Learning brings benefits that include:
- personal growth and expanded horizons;
- increased employability and career potential;
- broader interests and social participation;
- control over your own future.
  (Campaign for Learning, 1998–2006; Clark, 2001)

Learning cities are a twenty-first century response to age-old dilemmas. As the pace of life quickens ever more rapidly and information technology becomes a primary means of communication in our societies, those people who were always at risk of being marginalised – the poorly educated, the unemployed and underemployed, people from a non-English-speaking background, people with disabilities and other minority groups – will have even greater difficulty in developing the skills to participate effectively in their community (Longworth, 1999).

The global effects of economic downturns impacted on Australia, as it did elsewhere, during the 1990s and community development approaches surfaced in different ways in attempts to provide a direction for the future in the prevailing political culture of economic rationalism that existed in the State and Federal Government during that time. In this climate, the economic imperatives of efficiency, productivity and unrestrained competition were regarded as the basis for progress (Goldsworthy, 2001; Kenny, 1999). Governments withdrew from interference in society, and public health, education and welfare were starved of funds (Kenny, 1994, p. xi).

It is no coincidence that the election of a Labor Government in Victoria in 2000 saw the implementation of many initiatives designed to improve social inclusion and the empowerment of local communities. The government seemed genuinely interested in testing strategies for developing stronger communities where local people determined and developed the options for their future. Models that creatively engaged individuals and communities and allowed more complete community participation were encouraged. Even learning partnership projects that were commenced by the former government changed to a more participatory model, such as the Victorian Flexible Learning Network project. The emphasis moved to connecting Victorians and the creation of a learning society (DPC, 2001; S&RD, 1999). All this was set in the international background of the 5th Unesco World Adult Education Conference (known as CONFINTEA) held in Hamburg in 1997. This among other things called for lifelong learning for all adults and the creation of a 'learning society' (Unesco, 1997).

Local, national and international interest in community capacity-building has become a feature of the early years of the twenty-first century as the 'link between strong communities and good economic outcomes has … caught the attention of governments internationally' (Department for Victorian Communities, 2002b). In Australia, as in the UK, Canada and the USA especially, learning was beginning to be more widely recognised as adding value to organisations, communities and individuals, and as a new means of economic and community renewal (Blackmore, 2002, p. 3).

Learning Towns and Cities was one of the strategies piloted by the Victorian Government as a component of *Growing Victoria Together* (DPC, 2001). The development of learning communities was also supported by *Knowledge and Skills for the Innovation Economy* (Kosky, 2002), *Respect: The Government's Vision for Young People* (Office for Youth, 2002), the *Blueprint for Government Schools* (Kosky, 2003) and *Taking Young People Seriously* (Youth Affairs Council of Victoria, 2003).

The input of individuals and communities into ways to change and strengthen communities was also specifically requested by the Department for Victorian Communities through its demonstration projects in Community Building (Department for Victorian Communities, 2002a) and the Department of Human Services Neighbourhood Renewal projects. 'In the longer term the intent is to drive more fundamental service delivery reform across the public sector' (Department for Victorian Communities, 2002b; Department for Victorian Communities, 2004). This was echoed by the introduction of Local Learning and Employment Networks (LLENs) – community networks focused on improving the outcomes for 15–19 year olds.

This, then, was a more supportive environment to be experimenting with modern ways of engaging those who do not have the skills to participate effectively in our twenty-first century communities, by learning 'about the dynamics of where they live and how it is changing' (Landry, 2000, p. 267).

The evolving nature of learning communities

Apart from the broad range of learning partnership projects that have been mentioned under the banner of learning communities, there is a distinct brand of learning communities in Victoria known as Victorian Learning Towns. In 2000, ten towns/areas were designated as Learning Towns. The objective of the initiative was the formation of a coalition in each Learning Town, which supported, promoted and valued lifelong learning. The idea was to create strategic links between Adult and Community Education (ACE) organisations, education and training providers (TAFE, schools, universities and registered training organisations), public sector organisations (local, state and federal), community organisations, business and industry (Sheed and Bottrell, 2001). The Learning Towns were funded by Adult and Community Education within the Victorian State Government. Sheed and Bottrell (2001) note while each location developed in quite distinctive ways, they were also influenced by the conceptualisation of learning towns and cities in both the UK and Europe.

At the time of the establishment of the Victorian Learning Towns project the learning community concept was very broad, but most definitions emphasised the importance of partnerships across sectors and the promotion of lifelong learning as a way of addressing economic growth and social disadvantage (Cara and Ranson,1998; Kearns, 2001; Kearns et al., 1999; Longworth,1999). Faris and Peterson (2000) also identified the development of learning communities as a way of creating sustainable futures for communities. They believed that this involved capacity-building with individuals and groups in communities to enable sustainable economic development, promote social inclusion and cohesion, and encourage civic and social participation.

The term 'learning community' was also used to encompass terms such as learning cities, learning towns and learning regions (Faris, 2001; Henderson et al., 2000; Yarnit, 2000).

The interest demonstrated by interstate and international communities endorsed the focused development of the Victorian Learning Towns through the government project, and indicated that communities were willing to learn from the experience of others. Within Victoria there were expressions of interest in supporting and encouraging the development of new learning communities. The pilot project communities were in an ideal position to mentor the development of emerging communities and maximised their capacity to do this through their informal network known as the Victorian Learning Towns Network (VLTN).

The opportunity was ripe for the Victorian Learning Towns to assume a leadership role that was based on relationship development and trust. 'Learning Towns now have the opportunity to proactively engage (with others) as a 'teacher' rather than a 'student'' (Cavaye, 2002, p. 39).

The Victorian Learning Towns developed a distinct learning community model of social change through their foundation in the ACE sector. This has been significant in determining the characteristics that have developed. The model is characterised by an action-based approach rather than a theoretical one (Australian Learning Communities Network, 2002). The Learning Towns emphasised engaging with people and problems, and getting into action as quickly as possible.

One of the tensions the Learning Towns had to negotiate was the tendency to 'short-termism' identified by Faris – in *A model for developing learning communities* at the annual meeting of the Australian Learning Communities Network (Faris, 2002) – when governments support short-term radical intervention at the expense of longer-term systemic change. This results in the perpetuation of existing problems once the short-term effect has worn off. Governments (understandably) require quick results. The tendency to focus on the immediate rather than on long-term systemic change mitigates against profound changes in culture.

Using their skills in partnership and collaboration, the Victorian Learning Towns successfully negotiated compromises in their agreements with the project funding bodies, and continued to develop leadership and mentoring for other areas within Victoria to implement the learning community concept in order to facilitate long-term change. For example, Hume City, the Yarra Ranges and Melbourne's West, driven by local government, are taking a systematic approach to addressing issues of economic and social disadvantage. The work is underpinned by policies of lifelong learning and joined up strategies to address participation in learning, skills and employment (HGLV, 2004; Shire of Melton, 2005; Yarra Ranges, 2003).

The concept is evolving. Yarnit (2006) notes, in an evaluation of testbed learning communities in the UK, that these communities are new models for planning and delivering learning, skills and employment based on partnership, collaboration and community engagement, linked to local strategic planning. Yarnit now seems to be defining the term learning community more narrowly, and this is in line with emerging models in Australia. For example, the vision, strategies and projects that underpin the development of the Hume Global Learning Village are directly linked to Hume City Plan 2030, and a regional approach is taken to local initiatives in an attempt to avoid costly duplication and encourage collaboration.

Sustainability

Sustainability is a challenge that must be considered in one-off or short-term funding, particularly in relation to programs such as Learning Towns. How can such programmes benefit a community and ensure lasting change?

'Funding from agencies and government programmes is generally time-limited and designed to build resources that support enduring change. Sustainability derives directly from the nature of community and so needs will vary over time' (DCITA, 2005). It is important to explore how sustainability applies to a variety of community settings.

Ife transfers the ecological principle of sustainability to evaluation of the long-term viability of changes to existing systems and their impact on other systems. He challenges the idea that many 'new' ways of doing things are sustainable. He points out the incongruity of the terms 'sustainable development' and 'sustainable growth' – 'blatantly self-contradictory term(s)' (Ife, 2002, p. 42). He says that this confusion allows the desirability of growth to go unchallenged, believing that 'unbridled growth and unnecessary consumption' are unacceptable. In advocating for development (including technological development) to occur for socially and economically determined reasons that transform the 'existing, blatantly unsustainable order' (Ife, 2002, p. 42), he supports the local evolution of systems that meet the needs of particular circumstances.

So in order to evaluate the sustainability of a learning community it will be necessary to consider whether it will require increasing levels of resources or whether it seeks more 'steady-state' solutions. Ife draws attention to the importance of recognising that continual change and restructuring are incompatible with sustainability, but rather require a change in existing practice to ways that have not even been considered (Ife, 2002, p. 75).

Long-term sustainability of a learning community can also be linked to a community-strengthening approach, such as that provided by the Strengthening Communities Unit, New South Wales Premier's Department (cited in Kenyon, 2006, p. 17):

> Sustainable communities maintain and improve their social, economic and environmental characteristics so that residents can continue to lead healthy, productive and enjoyable lives. Sustainable development in these communities is based on the understanding that a healthy environment and a healthy economy are both necessary for a healthy society.

This view is supported by Faris, who believes that a commitment to the triple bottom line increases the likelihood of success in the long-term development of a learning community (Martin and Faris, 2005). The inclusion of an environmental approach is founded on respect for the land and recognition that human communities are interdependent with their surrounding living systems. Fostering broad coalitions based on partnerships is likely to support the sustainability of a learning community initiative. This asset-based approach builds on the stock of human capital (mainly formal learning) and social capital (including non-formal and informal learning). Lifelong learning is regarded as an organising principle and social goal.

Learning communities show that the ecological principles of sustainability and diversity underpin progress and successful community change. Local solutions developed by local people may be modest, but with a greater likelihood of being locally relevant and absorbed. The partnerships developed by learning communities maintain and conserve existing resources, while adding value through collaborative effort, problem-solving and innovation.

Critical Success Factors

The erratic application of the government policy that recognises the value of lifelong learning and supports it with resources has been a feature of Australian education at a national level. It remains a problem today (Sodoti, 2003). The leadership of the Victorian Government in supporting the Learning Towns has provided the research and the practice platform for proactive local governments to investigate the potential of learning to address social and economic disadvantage. Local bodies need to be cautious about going off and 'doing their own thing' (Ife 2002, p. 44) as this may affect others negatively and dissipate the effort. Locally devolved community work requires coordination; local government is the best placed enterprise in our communities to do this. Leadership by local government has proved to be crucial to the sustainability of learning communities, a position argued by Kearns (ALCN, 2004) and by Considine who describes the 'impressive record of achievement in the field of community strengthening (by governments in Australia), perhaps because the unique patterns of urban concentration and rural distance often require active intervention by government to support local resilience' (Considine, 2004, p. 3).

John Cain, Chair of the Advisory Board, Hume Global Learning Village, also advocates that local government should lead a learning community initiative, and that this should be backed up by policies from State government. Like Cavaye, Cain noted that while governments need to invest in initiatives such as learning communities, in his experience, things will happen effectively when you have a few committed people, with good officers chosen and a champion who drives it (Cain, launch of VLCN, November 2005; Cavaye, 2002). Learning community volunteers and workers who cultivate organisational relationships and ensure the necessary resources are acquired are crucial to the successful development and sustainability of local community strengthening strategies.

Learning communities have demonstrated the strategic value of developing resources and networks that already existed into a coalition with the potential to influence and change the circumstances of marginalised and vulnerable sectors by opening up the circuits of power. Good partnerships take effort and commitment from both sides. The networks that have developed through learning communities have been used to validate ideas, support initiatives and raise commitment.

Networks strengthen communities and build positive social capital. 'Strengthened communities are positive and resilient ... (they can) bounce back from challenges ... and respond to future challenges' (Department for Victorian Communities, 2002b).

Networks, relationships, knowledge and integration will be key features of economic and social success in a less structured society in the twenty-first century (Australian National Training Authority, 2004, p. 2; Blackmore, 2002). The networks that have been established and strengthened by learning communities are an example of 'new models of planning and service delivery' that have demonstrated the 'modern approach to prevention' that the Department of Victorian Communities has sought (Department for Victorian Communities, 2002b).

The Shire of Melton Community Learning Plan 2005–2007 outlines a sophisticated model of networks and the linking of infrastructure. The Melton Community Learning Board has representation from key organisations across the Shire involved in learning, including the local university, schools, employment services and adult community education. It also links to a range of state, national and international networks. Key organisations now align their strategic plans to goals in the Community Learning Plan. They are actively contributing to the funding of joint projects to address common issues – for example, mapping the aspirations of young people across the region (Peter Blunden, Chair, Melton Township Learning Precinct at VLCN, Nov 2005).

The strategic focus and planning of current learning communities seems to align with a set of principles that derive from Landry's model of the Creative City (2000) – communities that:

- reflect and respond;
- display creativity and leadership;
- value learning in individuals and organisations;
- are equipped to cope with change;
- see opportunities in the unexpected and insignificant;
- turn weaknesses into strengths;
- learn to manage change through democratic processes.

Challenges and Dilemmas

The prolific use of technology, combined with new understandings of ourselves and the way we interact with social systems, means that we are leaving behind a way of looking at the world that is built on a belief in stability and controlled change as ideal. In a world that operates dynamically at every level, challenges are posed for community leaders, for governments and for businesses. The more docile workforce of the mid-twentieth century is being replaced with individuals who have an appetite for learning. Yet education and training, let alone lifelong learning, are still treated with suspicion in many enterprises (Campaign for Learning, 1998–2006; Kearns, 1999).

Other issues that require debate include the insistence on aspiration and assumptions that all growth is desirable. A lack of motivation, a lack of role models and a lack of aspiration can be reinforced by the formal education system and its uneven connection with training, qualifications and career progression. A learning community can address these issues through action and reflection on its learning. The challenge remains to sustain and develop the commitment of partners to result in significant change through the extension of lifelong learning opportunities to individuals in the community.

The sustainability of learning communities is likely to be determined above all by local circumstances. For example, the establishment of a regional coalition of local governments in Geelong, known as 'G21', has supported the development of a community culture that learns from its experiences, reflects on them and plans for improvement by practising these principles in its own implementation. It devised strategies that include people who are marginalised and economically disadvantaged. It fostered a collaborative approach to community development that recognises that 'investment in learning underpins the development of functional communities' (Cavaye, 2002, p. 39).

These emerging learning communities in Australia provide examples of the new models of planning and service delivery referred to by Yarnit (2006). The key messages for policy-makers, service providers and local government are that joined-up strategic planning across a city, shire or town, which links to state and local government policies, can cut out costly duplication and encourage the linking of key policy areas such as education, health and community services. Learning community initiatives can link service providers to make better use of community infrastructure, problem-solve in creative ways and, most importantly, link grass roots initiatives to a broader context.

Conclusions

Learning communities seem to have a resilience and appeal that has ensured their continued development through the early years of the twenty-first century, despite erratic funding and inconsistent policy application. This may well be because they have become a 'movement' rather than an 'initiative', characterised by an emphasis on group identity, values and lifestyles rather than, or in addition to, developed ideologies. The movement demonstrates a tendency to emerge more from middle than working-class constituencies (American Studies, 2002). The development of an international movement may ensure the survival of learning communities, because they are being driven by the community and by people with vision who have capitalised on this.

The Victorian experience has been used to strengthen the concept and to develop partnerships nationally and internationally. The VLTN has become well established and has supported the establishment of the Victorian Learning Communities Network (VLCN), an informal network that includes learning communities that are not in receipt of 'Learning Towns' project funds.

In March 2004, Australia's unemployment rate of 5.6 per cent crept up into 'the good half of the OECD range', although 11 of the other 29 countries have unemployment rates below 5 per cent (Colebatch, 2004). At the same time, Victoria was the State that was the furthest advanced in its key indicators for young people – that is, engagement in education, training or employment. The longevity of this improvement requires the sustained backing of integrated, community-based responses (Sodoti, 2003). A national policy on lifelong learning would contribute to the effectiveness of social inclusion strategies in supporting economic improvement.

The interest and models being developed by communities such as those in Melbourne's West, the Yarra Ranges, Hobsons Bay and Hume, that have identified lifelong learning as a valuable strategy in strengthening those communities, is a powerful indicator of the impact of learning communities. They have contributed to demonstrating that community partnerships that value lifelong learning can effect social change and build communities that are viable, socially inclusive, democratically aware, adaptive and successful in a rapidly changing environment.

Next Steps

McNulty (2004) suggests that as learning communities gain some traction, there are higher order questions for them to pose:

- What can we do *now* in order to be able to do tomorrow what we are unable to do today?
- How does our leadership *each day* contribute to developing the culture of our learning community?
- Where in the culture web can we intervene most effectively to trigger positive change?

The work of learning communities in Australia has only just begun. They have been successful in extending participation – in learning in particular – but it would be untrue to claim there has yet been widespread improvement in other forms of social participation, leading to genuine transformation. Recent racial and other social tensions in this country are providing a real test of the cohesiveness of our communities, as they have in the UK. The opportunity to 'mix and match' discourses such as social capital, lifelong learning and community-building that the learning communities movement presents however offers fertile ground for the development of innovative strategies to ensure that these became legitimate concerns for public policy development.

Chapter 10

Regenerating communities – or *'the poor are always with us'.* A UK experience[1]

Chris Shepherd

Introduction – the evolution of modern local government

Local democracy in the UK is a relatively new phenomenon. Most urban communities only received their Royal Charters a little more than one hundred years ago. Prior to the wider establishment of local democracy, the dominant governance came from the government in Westminster and from the established Church and landowners locally.

This governance was far from benign, with much of the population poorly housed and badly nourished, with poor health and little or no education. This situation changed slowly over time, often in response to pressure from below; labour strikes, revolts and the threat of revolution spreading from France concentrated the minds of the ruling classes.

Much of the local democracy we see today has its roots in the development of the Church in society in the nineteenth century. Often the church was the largest building in the town and was the focus for community life. Churches doubled as markets, courts of justice and meeting places. There are even examples where the Church authorities set up the first enterprises to supply public utilities.

There was little evidence of any concerted effort to address the issues affecting the poorest sections of society, and any support was often harsh and frequently hastened an early death. Nevertheless, for the more fortunate in society the Church set up schools, medical support, a sense of purpose and a moral code. The established Church was closely aligned with the monarchy and the national government. It had considerable influence over society in general and communities locally.

The move from the country to the towns during the industrial revolution in the eighteenth century, and the growth in population in the nineteenth century, put considerable pressure on the physical infrastructure supporting the new urban settlements. Serious health issues developed due to the lack of clean water and the proliferation of poor sewage disposal. Boards of Works were established to provide the necessary infrastructure. They were normally governed by local people of influence and took on local tax-raising powers.

In many of the larger cities and towns these Boards of Works formed the basis of the new elected municipal authorities and Royal Charters were first presented at the end of the nineteenth century. For the first time this gave local people a say in what should happen in their areas. However the legislation controlling their activity was almost non-existent, such that some municipalities ran factories and restaurants, whilst others ran public utilities and parks.

Progressively legal constraints were introduced by the central government, which circumscribed what a municipality could do either by placing a duty on a municipality, or through enabling legislation that permitted certain activities. Over time these powers and duties have changed, with some added and others taken away. The end of the Second World War saw the greatest change in service provision at both state and local level, with the nationalisation of industries including health and transport, changes in education and housing, land use planning, policing and welfare.

These changes were a consequence of the time and the urgency to address the many issues that arose as a result of the War. Money and resources were scarce but there was an expectation by the general population that things would improve radically and rapidly. They did not. Damage to the physical and social fabric together with economic decline as a result of the War left many people homeless and unemployed. It took three decades before significant improvement was visible across the UK. Even then there were large geographical disparities between regions and their communities

Whether the changes in society and the way it is governed today came as a result of opportunism or benign paternalism is hard to say, but one thing is certain: it has always been top down, with many people feeling it was done *to* them, rather than *for* them or *with* them.

Changing times?

Since the Second World War, governments have been concerned about the poorest sectors in society, whether that concern is motivated by the cost to the tax-payer or by the government's desire to improve their well-being.

Communities that experience multiple deprivation vary over time and place. At one time the inner cities were often the place where the poorest people lived, with the more affluent moving out to the leafy suburbs. Furthermore, the construction of these communities constantly changes over time, being affected by inward migration, demographic change and local economic factors.

The costs of transport and congestion have recently led to a reversal of the trend for the more affluent to locate out to the suburbs. Their return to the inner cities has displaced many poorer people to marginal estates, where work is hard to find and the cost of travel into the city is prohibitive.

For the last two decades the British government, supported by the European Union, has established programmes that try deal with the causes of multiple deprivation. They have concentrated considerable resources, both regionally and locally, to tackle the problems. Despite the large sums of money involved, only some of the initiatives have been effective. Others seem to have brought about only a marginal improvement in certain areas, which may often be temporary in nature.

Some of the least effective initiatives to deal with deprivation have occurred where governments have intervened in the local economy, propping up failing industries. More effective has been the approach to some of the housing renewal areas and the development of new skills for the jobs of tomorrow.

Unfortunately, one of the main problems in trying to tackle deprivation in defined localities has arisen from successive governments centralising power and decision-making to Whitehall, leading to a 'one size fits all' solution to service issues. The tightening of controls centrally is usually followed by loosening in due course. However, this cycle of change from central to local and back to central control gives little encouragement to local democratic institutions to try to address the problems. It leads to even less confidence in the most deprived communities in society.

Demographic change is influencing the whole of society, particularly the most deprived. An aging population and much publicised issues around the funding shortfall in pensions will change the structure of the workforce, with extended working lives, increased health care needs, changed housing requirements and new learning requirements. An aging population in the most deprived communities often already lives in unsuitable homes, suffers poorer health and inadequate health services, experiences higher rates of crime and is poorly equipped in terms of skills and the basic educational standards. As the numbers increase this is likely to worsen.

A more recent change in the country's economic performance, and the enlargement of the European Community, have also had a significant impact on the most deprived communities where the skill gap is largest. Employers require higher levels of skill in the new economy and these skills are increasingly difficult to obtain for people in some communities. Traditionally, some of the people unable to up-skill successfully take the more basic jobs in the local economy. However, much of this basic work is now undertaken by foreign workers on temporary contracts and low wages.

Partnerships

The essential public services provided to communities come from a variety of sources including central government agencies, local authorities, the private sector and the voluntary and community sectors. This can often lead to confusion by the public and a dislocated approach in service delivery. Successive governments have encouraged all agencies to work in partnership in order to provide more joined-up thinking in service planning and service delivery.

Devolution of some powers to the Scottish Parliament and the Welsh Assembly following the Labour victory in 1997 has permitted these regional governments to deal with issues of service delivery and deprivation at a more local level. In England the British government has continued to take the lead.

Five years ago the government introduced the concept of Local Strategic Partnerships in England, where the statutory agencies and other stakeholders would come together on a voluntary basis to plan services and share information and outcomes. In 90 areas the government made it a requirement that a

Local Strategic Partnership be formed, and in these areas announced that a grant would be given to enable the new partnerships to address the issues of deprivation in their areas. This grant, called the *Neighbourhood Renewal Fund (NRF)*, was to enable the statutory partners to change the way they carried out their mainstream services in order to improve the outcomes in the most deprived areas, and to narrow the gap between the most and least deprived areas in a region.

The government was working on the principle that the most effective way to improve the outcomes for society as a whole was to concentrate on the causes of multiple deprivation in a limited number of areas, where the improvement in outcome for these communities would translate across the whole of society.

Six theme areas were chosen: education, worklessness, housing, health, safety and liveability. Their interrelationship was already acknowledged and the government published national floor targets for each one of these themes setting a basic minimum standard of performance/outcome. The Local Strategic Partnership was then required to analyse its local data to see where the greatest gaps in outcome currently existed at a neighbourhood level, and to determine whether current services were closing the gap or whether the gap was widening.

Initiatives to address local need would be developed in partnership and the grant would be used to assist in changing service delivery. As many of the floor targets set by government were by their nature long term, e.g. health outcomes, the partnerships were required to establish short-term targets and milestones for monitoring progress.

Unlike previous initiatives, the partners were asked to share data and analysis, and to plan service changes in a broader consultative manner which engaged all stakeholders including the voluntary and community sectors. Similarly, the partnerships were expected to carry out a full evaluation of interventions as they proceeded, and again to share their conclusions both locally and nationally.

Progress to date has been mixed. Although the areas without Neighbourhood Renewal Funding are not required to have a local Strategic Partnership they are still encouraged to do so. However these voluntary partnerships tend to be much weaker, and it is questionable whether they are properly addressing the issues of multiple deprivation with their limited resources. Equally, some of the funded partnerships have not made the best use of the opportunity or the funding, and have made little use of the available data to evidence need or to measure progress.

However, many who have taken full advantage of the initiative have some interesting stories to tell. For example, a housing investment to bring properties up to the Decent Homes Standard in an area in the South West can now evidence a drop in worklessness, improvement in education outcomes for 16 year olds, improvements in health and reductions in crime. In another area in the East Midlands, a family learning centre at a primary school has helped young black minority ethnic group (BME) women to improve their basic literacy and numeracy and seek employment.

These partnerships are now developing to the next stage, through the introduction of Local Area Agreements, which are designed to move away from the centrally driven agenda and to start building in local priorities alongside those set by central government. Nevertheless, whilst partnership working by the public sector and their partners engages with the business, voluntary and community sectors, it is still led by central government and is still seen as a top-down approach by many.

Local self determination

In 1998, following the publication of the Social Exclusion Unit's report, *Bringing Britain Together*, a new programme was introduced in England by Central Government called New Deal for Communities (NDC). This programme was to concentrate on the 39 most deprived neighbourhoods in England. It would run for ten years with a total budget in excess of £1.5bn

The New Deal project was intended to introduce the concept of community-led regeneration, where local people would be in control of the change agenda. The partnerships were usually set up as companies limited by guarantee, with one of the public agencies, usually the local authority, appointed as the accountable body to ensure probity. The governance arrangements were introduced in a broadly similar way across all 39 NDCs with Boards of between 15 and 25 members. The local community representatives, who would be in the majority, were elected by their communities, while the other Board members would be nominated by the public agencies. The NDCs normally employ a small team of specialist staff often drawn from the public agencies who work with other stakeholders in the area.

The purpose of this approach was to enable people in the community to drive forward the regeneration programme in a way that fits with that community, rather than the failed attempts of the past where initiatives have been introduced from outside and not received support or ownership by people in the neighbourhood. In many ways the NDC concept is to operate in a similar way to the Local Strategic Partnership, but at a more local level, where the grant, significantly higher in the NDC area, is intended to address the same principal causes of deprivation.

One of the first tasks for any NDC was to ensure that the resident Board members were adequately skilled to take decisions using the information provided. To ensure that this was the case the NDCs undertook intensive training programmes, whilst the Board members from the public agencies generally offered support.

The NDCs were expected to be innovative and to act as test sites for initiatives which would be evaluated and, where successful, adopted more widely elsewhere. The interventions were expected to be based on need, determined by analysing data for the neighbourhood. Performance management systems were required to be in place to ensure delivery.

An important change in the last three years has been the introduction of a commissioning process, rather than seeking bids from other groups, where the NDC uses its knowledge and data to establish priorities and commission work under the six themes that are likely to directly affect the outcomes for people

Another issue yet to be resolved is the difficulty of getting some of the public agencies to take on the long-term commitment to carry on with a project once funding has ceased and the NDC is dissolved; in some cases, with the first NDCs, this will be within the next four years. Public agencies have also been reluctant to commit themselves to bending mainstream services towards these areas of multiple deprivation, possibly due to pressure from elsewhere, if other services are to be cut. Further issues have occurred where the NDC money has replaced expenditure that would have otherwise been incurred by a public agency, although the intention had always been for the NDC money to be additional.

Another form of community-led regeneration has recently been developed. Where small pockets of deprivation exist in otherwise relatively affluent areas, rather than create a statutory partnership the government two years ago established small Neighbourhood Management Pathfinders based on individual communities. These can operate like NDCs outside the Local Authorities and have a small grant allocation administered directly by the local community. Their management and governance structures are similar to those of the NDCs, but with far smaller budgets they are far more dependent on the cooperation of the public agencies. It is too early yet to see if they are making a substantial difference.

Evaluation of NDCs and some implications

Evaluation

Sheffield Hallam University was appointed by the government to carry out an annual evaluation of progress for each of the NDCs and to make this report available to the NDC Board and government. The evaluation was also intended to review the interventions and to promote best practice.

Not all NDCs have progressed equally well. In some cases the Boards started their programme by seeking bids from community groups for activities that did not always fit with the known priorities in the neighbourhood. By contrast, some Boards have also spent a significant proportion of their allocated funds on large new landmark projects, with the likelihood of only limited benefit to the wider community. Others have undertaken major housing renewal schemes, where much of the existing population has been decanted, never to return, merely transferring the deprivation elsewhere.

Evaluation, both within the NDC and by Sheffield Hallam, has looked at governance issues, sometimes problematic performance, exemplars of good practice and value for money. Comparators have been assembled, information shared and an NDC support network established. Many think that the NDC programme has been a qualified success, although others hold the view that it is too early to say.

Two substantial issues remain unresolved. The first is what happens to the initiatives and fixed assets when the NDCs disappear. The second is whether it has really made a difference.

In the first case many of the NDCs are looking at different models for their area, to ensure that what they have achieved is sustainable over the longer term. These can include community land trusts, housing associations, parish councils, not-for-profit companies and so on.

However, in the second case we need to go back to the Local Strategic Partnerships and their role in narrowing the gap between the most and least deprived areas within a region to see if the NDC programme has been successful. This Local Strategic Partnership approach concentrates on six themes: education, health, crime, liveability, housing, and worklessness. It may be recalled that the government set minimum standards, or floor targets, for each of these themes. Progress against some of these floor targets can only be evaluated after a significant period of time has elapsed. For example, it will take some time beyond the end of the NDC programme to see whether cancer death reduction targets have been met.

It would therefore seem desirable to establish some proxy targets now, with milestones towards the longer term evaluation against the floor targets, to establish whether this programme has started to make a difference, and whether locally-determined regeneration has worked better than the more directive approach employed hitherto.

Learning from and sharing experience

We have come a long way in a hundred and fifty years, from a time where, for much of the population, life represented little more than a bare existence with no say, through to local democracy and then to local self-determination.

But will the poor always be with us? There is no denying the efforts made to tackle the underlying causes of deprivation. It is noteworthy that successive British governments since the Second World War have moved progressively from a top-down approach to one that is more inclusive. It may also be observed that the Blair Government has experimented more than most and is intent on evidence-led solutions to problems. Experience to date from the limited evaluation that is available suggests that deprivation can be reduced and the gaps between the most and least deprived areas narrowed, such that poverty as a term is relative.

It is also apparent that many of the initiatives in the UK can be witnessed elsewhere in the world. This reinforces the need to be clear about what we are trying to achieve and assessing whether or not we are succeeding. There is also concern that we don't share the knowledge – either through the lack of reflective analysis or through some misplaced attitude of protectionism arising from a fear of failure.

We need to record success and failure in equal measure. Community initiatives are costly, not only in terms of money but also in terms of social capital. If the programme fails it is likely that the social capital within the community will also diminish. To minimise the risk and ensure success we need to put in place robust data analysis, plausible interventions and good evaluation; and to share and learn from the experience. Has evaluation kept pace with innovation?

Useful links

Office of the Deputy Prime Minister   www.odpm.gov.uk

Neighbourhood Renewal Unit   www.neighbourhood.gov.uk

Renewal Net   www.renewal.net

Urban Forum   www.urbanforum.org.uk

Sheffield Hallam University   http://ndcevaluation.adc.shu.ac.uk

Notes

[1] This paper is written by a former public servant with over twenty years of experience in the development and implementation of community regeneration policies and initiatives and is a personal reflection on the progress made in the UK to address multiple deprivation. Useful websites and references are included for those who wish to explore this further.

Chapter 11

Vocational education and training: implementing innovation

Paul Carter and Sue Dunn

Introduction

The complexities of the English 14–19 education and training agenda at national, regional and sub-regional levels are overwhelming. The multitude of competing organisations involved in the delivery of programmes, coupled with the convoluted arena of academic and vocational qualifications, makes the prospect of innovation in vocational education a significant challenge for schools in England. Local Authorities such as Kent are well positioned to deliver and drive the changes in the vocational education agenda. They have the capacity together with the broad prospective, depth of experience and knowledge needed to create new ways of delivering learning. Despite this Local Authorities are increasingly disempowered through recent government policies to take on this role.

This chapter explains how Kent County Council is seeking to address these significant challenges to deliver a flexible, demand-led, innovative vocational programme. It is intended that the proposed changes will contribute to the long-term transformation of vocational education and training nationally. The new vocational programme intends to provide variety in the curriculum to meet learners' needs, opportunities for different forms of learning, a range of progression pathway and new forms of achievement and qualifications.

This chapter is in three parts. The first section explores how effective collaborative partnerships can develop, the second section examines some determining factors for the successful delivery of the 14–16 programme and the third identifies the practical interventions which support innovation at national, regional and sub-regional levels.

The aim of Kent's vocational programme is to raise achievement in vocational subjects, to increase the diversity of vocational subjects on offer at 14–16 and to increase the number of learners progressing into further learning opportunities at 16, which will include the development of an in-house Kent apprenticeship scheme. To achieve this transformation it is recognised that developing capacity within organisations to facilitate collaboration is critical to the success of the programme. To provide maximum choice and diversity for learners, successful inter-organisational networks will need to be established and to function at a number of levels. The potential obstacles to progress are numerous. They present real challenges, but there is a genuine belief in Kent that a new vocational programme is needed to fulfil learner entitlement and to ensure that all schools and learners have the opportunity for success.

How are collaborative partnerships developing in Kent?

Kent Local Authority recognised three years ago that although there was outstanding good practice in secondary schools, with many learners reaching high levels of achievement, there were also too many learners failing. The curriculum was inappropriate for a significant minority of learners, good practice was not shared between schools and excellent leadership in schools remained inconsistent. To address these inequalities in provision, 23 collaborative clusters of schools with devolved resources were established and federated schools and new academies were introduced. The model of cluster working in Kent provides head teachers with the opportunity to make collective decisions to reshape how the local authority works. Head teachers are interacting with each other's schools, informing LEA policy and have the ability to determine what clusters of schools need to do locally to improve standards. This is partly achieved by sharing good practice, developing a local identity and determining how cluster resources are allocated and deployed.

The purpose of developing these collaborative arrangements between providers was based on the need to get schools and colleges to move beyond the notion of being a single institution operating within a competitive frame-work and towards a collaborative model that would bring about improvements within the whole system. Currently, collaboration between schools is evident between a range of providers and there is a perceived cultural change where mutual trust between organisations can exist. The rate of this progress is significant, given a decade-long national agenda that promoted competition, examination league tables and autonomy. The implementation of the vocational programme in Kent and the government's 14–19 Education and Skills implementation plan are predicated on the successful establishment of collaborative partnerships and inter-organisational learning at a number of levels. The establishment of robust collaborative partnerships between institutions – schools, colleges and work-based learning providers – is a central theme of the national government's agenda for the delivery of 14 new specialised diplomas. There is, however, an unresolved tension within the competitive market between schools, colleges and work-based learning providers that could easily undermine the collaborative partnerships.

Determining factors for success

What precipitates cultural shifts in developing partnerships that enable inter-organisational exchanges based on mutual trust?

Schools and colleges within the pilot phase of the vocational developments have been identifying quality ideas or solutions that will really make a difference. This has been achieved in Kent within the context of the Kent Secondary Strategy and the 14–19 Education and Skills framework. Certain conditions need to be in place between institutions for this to happen. If a school or college is confident with its own performance and progress, then it is likely that meaningful collaborative partnerships and inter-organisational learning will take place allowing interdependence based on mutual trust. Therefore, it is important that all schools succeed, so that organisations can engage in a meaningful way in partnership working. Significant resources have been identified within the local authority to provide a supportive challenge to all schools, including the development of the Secondary Trans-formation Team, a group of head teachers who have been given a specific role to capacity-build in secondary schools.

Fullan (2004) stresses the importance of schools transcending the individual institution to produce a high quality of organisations and of the system itself. He talks about public service with a moral purpose. He makes the point that school improvement has plateaued; only by collective engagement in the system will schools significantly improve. He goes on to talk about lateral capacity-building through networks. In this case lateral capacity means deliberate strategies where peers learn from one another across schools or, in essence, reflective relationships and inter-organisational learning. Building and developing 'lateral' capacity within organisations particularly at head teacher and senior manager level is an underpinning principle of the vocational changes in Kent.

The need for mutual trust between organisations is recognised for developing meaningful collaborative partnerships within Kent's vocational programme. Partners who trust each other will not need to control each other. Instead they will cooperate, be committed to the collaborative arrangements, communicate openly and accept each other's points of view. The issue for many schools is about trusting another organisation with 'their' learner. There are fundamental issues around the need for schools to have absolute security in terms of the quality of the provision in which a learner is involved. This has been highlighted within the implementation of Phase I of the vocational programme. At head teacher level there is without question a commitment to developing the collaborative partnerships, but this investment and commitment to the partnership can be easily undermined if participating schools display mistrust. This happens where the quality of provision is not maintained, or ethos and culture differ widely between participating institutions. This highlights the need for robust quality assurance methodologies, reporting mechanisms and formative evaluation frameworks between organisations. It is important within the development of new collaborative arrangements that mutual distrust is not allowed to grow up. If it does partners behave quite differently and will stifle any innovation. With mutual distrust organisations attempt to control each other's behaviour, minimise their contribution, are not committed to the partnership, communicate only at a strategic level, and are not receptive to each other's views. Such behaviours render collaborative partnership ineffective.

The vocational arena in England is complex. Institutions involved can have different mental models of what the vocational offer for 14–16 year olds should be. Effective communication and a common understanding of the language used are critical, especially between schools and colleges. Schools participating in Phase 1 of the pilot have established a range of ways of communicating and gained a common understanding of each other's organisation. Most influential in this context are not the strategic groups of head teachers and college principals but the operational groups – assistant head teachers, curriculum or vocational centre managers and college directors of studies. These groups have been established to implement common curriculum frameworks, delivery mechanisms and support structures for learners.

Examples of good practice emerging in terms of joint developments include joint school marketing materials under a partnership logo or badge, so that no one school is seen as taking the lead, for all learners across the participating institutions, co-ordinated options evenings and recruitment and allocation processes. At this point when collaborative partnership becomes operational, common understanding and use of language is critical. The most effective partnerships within the vocational programme have ensured that communications systems have enabled all institutions to be kept informed, provided accurate feedback, explained decisions and policies, been able to be honest about problems and resisted the temptation to withhold information in order to keep the 'competitive edge' over collaboration. Partner schools/colleges must work towards gaining a true perception of each other's organisation, taking account of the varying institutional pressures, needs and cultural differences.

The success of these operational groups has been determined by the following interventions, which have enabled innovative practices to develop at the operational level:

- Ensuring that all partners are involved in the identification of the most appropriate curriculum offer, rather than what is best for individual institutions. This means considering local and national trends in terms of skills shortages and developments.
- Developing ways to synchronise delivery mechanisms between partner institutions to enable learners to engage effectively in the vocational offer. (This becomes more complex the more learners are involved.)
- Establishing and implementing clear protocols between organisations which are not too bureaucratic, adding value to the process.
- Articulating clearly the progression routes post-16. This may mean destabilising the current post-16 offer. There could be fewer learners in particular institutions, particularly as apprenticeships are developed. This will have major budgetary implications for some institutions, which, if not managed in a transparent way, could destabilise the collaborative arrangements.
- Undertaking quality assurance of the programme jointly and dealing effectively with outcomes.
- Undertaking a formative evaluation at the start of the programme.

How are innovative practices identified and refined?

To bring about sustainable innovation, particularly within the complex vocational arena, the soundness of the decision-making process is important. The soundness of new ideas and the building of a body of knowledge each need intense scrutiny. There is a sense of déjà vu for some educationalists within the UK system, as they believe that the current vocational developments are no different from previous attempts. In Kent there is an absolute commitment at the highest political level to making the vocational programme different this time and offering young learners the personalised curriculum that suits their needs. Head teachers understand that the current system does not meet the needs of all learners. They now have access to a vast array of information and knowledge about their school's performance, and information and knowledge outside education, for example about the Kent economy in relation to national employment trends and skills. This information needs to be used to inform a vocational offer. Head teachers, through the collaborative partnerships between schools and other partners, can see what is going on in their schools, having engaged in reciprocal exchanges of knowledge and information, all strengthening the body of knowledge that enables them to continue innovation. Arguably the vocational programmes being developed in Kent have a much firmer platform and an informed body of knowledge. Relevant research from the UK and elsewhere should be used to continually build and refine knowledge about why some innovations succeed and others do not. The Pascal Observatory will be invaluable for accessing relevant studies and similar operational vocational programmes.

Practical interventions that support innovation

The national government aspires to having half a million 14–16 year olds (one in every three learners) involved in vocational education as part of their 14–16 learning programme by 2012. This is a significant challenge. Expanding the vocational curriculum and introducing 14 new specialised diplomas requires a paradigm shift in the way schools design and deliver the 14–16 curriculum. The expectation is that the 14 new diplomas will be developed within localities. No one single school is expected to deliver the full range of vocational qualifications.

Expanding the vocational curriculum will require 14–16 year old learners to be educated off site, away from their base school. The national framework is clear and quite prescriptive but provides a good platform for reform. At a sub-regional level there is much local discretion over delivery methods for the new curriculum. Schools and colleges will have to negotiate who provides which course, the curriculum framework and associated support systems such as transport arrangements, protocols and procedures. In this context Kent's vocational programme has established a range of innovative delivery frameworks. The capacity for local innovation across the collaborative partnerships has seen three delivery models emerging:

Distributed provision across schools
This is where groups of schools have agreed to take a lead in particular subject areas. There has been some capital investment, mainly expansion and refurbishment of existing provision as at Sittingbourne, Sittingbourne Community College, Westlands School and Fulston Manor School

Vocational centres on a school site
Two new purpose-built vocational centres, which offer up to four subjects, have been built at Whitstable Community College, Canterbury and Thamesview School, Gravesham. These centres offer the core provision of most new subjects. Partner schools in the locality supplement the vocational offer with their own specialisms. New practical workshops and facilities have been provided in these partner schools, but generally only on a single subject basis.

Free-standing vocational centres
Two large vocational centres, which are housed in light industrial units, have been developed at Tonbridge (North Farm) and Margate, Thanet. These centres offer a wide range of vocational subjects and can support a large number of schools.

To promote and raise the profile of vocational developments in Kent there has been significant capital investment including £6.5 million by Kent County Council, £2 million by the Office of the Deputy Prime Minister, £180k by Gateway Knowledge Alliance and £270k by the Learning and Skills Council, to provide new high quality facilities. This capital investment for high quality workshops is pivotal to the vocational offer being attractive to all learners.

These models differ vastly from normal curriculum delivery for 14–16 year olds; the impact will mean a re-evaluation of the entire 14–19 curriculum offer. Planning the phasing of this expansion in the vocational curriculum and undertaking formative evaluations over the next five years will be essential for the collaborative working groups. Schools have taken significant risks to get to this position over the past 12 months, not only in patterns of delivery but also in terms of curriculum content.

The development of external school networks is also critical to vocational innovation, to ensure that the curriculum is based on best practice, that it is relevant, and meets industry and employers' needs. Most Kent vocational partnerships rely on transferring good curriculum practice from post-16 courses to the 14–16 age range. The emerging pedagogy, assessment method-ologies and range of vocational qualifications will require further significant refinement. No one institution can do this independently. It is intended to establish five centres of vocational excellence across Kent to support local partnerships and sustain the progress made to date. This scale of curriculum reform requires significant professional development and the full engagement of employers and skills sector councils. The dissemination of good practice at local, national and international level is also important and will be the core function of these centres of excellence.

Vocational education in England is still seen as the poor relation to the academic route. Recent initiatives have failed to gain the confidence of employers, higher education and parents. In many advanced industrial countries including France, Holland and Australia young people pursue vocational routes from 14 onwards and employers are engaged in the vocational curriculum. Employer engagement and endorsement is a priority for Kent's initiative. The engagement of employers is needed to permeate the traditional boundaries between school and working life, and for employers to gain confidence in the vocational programme.

The next phase, and the greatest challenge, will be actively to engage employers in developing specialist facilities and real work curriculum projects. There are examples of good practice in employer engagement in the French and Australian vocational programmes. If vocational learning is to succeed it must be perceived as a high quality alternative to the academic route; the low interest of employers must be challenged. If vocational programmes at 14 are to be successful, learning needs to be practically based, providing opportunity for the application of skills and their development appropriately to industry needs. For this employer engagement is essential. Celebrating the vocational and the applied as much as the academic and theoretical must be a constant theme of vocational development.

In developing the vocational programme in Kent a number of key issues have been identified which will ultimately determine the success of the programme. These include:

- Mapping a coordinated area curriculum offer with the most appropriate provider delivering the programme.
- Developing vocational programmes in schools for 14–16 year olds, which necessitates 16+ providers reviewing the post-16 offer within the locality to ensure appropriate progression routes. The pathways into higher education, apprenticeships and employment need to be clearer, as they are in countries such as Denmark, The Netherlands, Australia and Canada.
- Developing Apprenticeship Scheme programmes.
- Employers and Skills Sector Councils being more directly involved in determining the content delivery and assessment of vocational courses.
- The retraining and professional development of teachers delivering vocational courses is critical to successful delivery of the programme. Thus in Victoria, Australia, teachers delivering a vocational programme are required to have experience working in a related industry within the last five years. This is updated through industrial placements, ensuring that teaching is embedded in commercial and industry-related practice.
- Vocational programmes should be delivered in good quality accommodation which reflects the real workplace environment.
- Work experience placements and work-related learning activities need to be more structured and vocationally relevant.
- Learners need to be fully engaged in the vocational offer and in developing future provision.

What factors support and enable innovation within vocational development? Which interventions have worked most effectively to achieve the vocational programme goals? A number of emerging interventions at rational, regional and sub-regional level have moved the programme forward. They are identified below. Although they relate specifically to the vocational programme, it is hoped that the general tenet of these themes can be transferred to other projects.

National level needs to:

- Develop a framework, which is robust but allows discretion at a regional and local level.

Regional level policy-makers need to:

- Provide political drive and commitment at the highest level
- Declare a vision, policy and overall statement of intent
- Undertake open and transparent consultation on vision, principles, strategies, aims and objectives
- Refine vision and iterative process
- Take responsibility for implementing the strategy and checking progress
- Provide physical resources
- Capacity-build in schools by providing supportive challenge
- Develop knowledge alliances which allow inter-organisational learning.

Sub-regional level schools need to:

- Develop the ability to build lateral capacity
- Engage in collaborative partnerships underpinned by mutual trust
- Accept that no single institution can deliver all the vocational programmes, that only by working together collectively will the national agenda be achieved
- Have a common vision and share a common language
- Develop sub-structures with clear reporting lines both strategic and operational, to implement the programme and develop the collaborative partnerships that enable them to make collective decisions
- Network with employers to engage them in the delivery of the programme
- Ensure that good quality assurance systems are in place.

Summary

Kent's strength in developing the programme has been its declared strategy and overall evolving policy entitled *Nurturing Autonomous and Creative Learners – The Kent Secondary Strategy*. The vision is explicit: 'in Kent's successful learning communities, achievement will exceed expectations and no child or school will fail'. This identifies the key issue for all schools. The strategy document goes on to identify the prime issues and the key players, and to explore a number of ways to improve the system. Kent County Council is actively promoting this agenda.

Head-teachers will need to develop the skills for purposeful creative exchanges with other heads and professionals. School leaders will need to think in bigger terms, not seeing themselves as leaders of separate schools but as system thinkers. The 23 Kent clusters support this principle.

The collaborative partnerships being established within the vocational programme further develop the idea of cluster working. Trust is implicit to the success of these partnerships, to enable transfer and implementation of the best ideas and practice. To maintain progress, schools must continue to evolve strategies and create new networks and partnerships. School leaders will increasingly need the capacity to build networks outside their school – lateral capacity.

As learners become increasingly autonomous in determining their own learning, schools will be challenged to establish alternative ways of learning. As young learners have greater choice of curriculum and progression routes the traditional school structures are challenged. This not only requires schools to offer jointly a rich and diverse curriculum, it also highlights the need to review the traditional school term, day and physical environment. Schools cannot continue as institutions educating young people only between nine a.m. and three p.m. (there are vocational programmes in Kent offered only between eight and five). We need continually to ask *are schools designed and managed for adults or for learners?* Schools need to accept continuous change as the norm. This is particularly important in relation to vocational developments, if the vocational curriculum is going to equip young people with the knowledge and skills they need for further learning and employment.

How young people learn in the vocational arena is constantly evolving. Do our delivery methods, pedagogies and assessment frameworks recognise this evolution; and can school leaders embrace the change? As technology is increasingly used in the classroom, teaching styles and strategies are challenged to the point where teaching and technology actually diverge. This in turn changes the role of the teacher or tutor and the way in which teacher and learner interact – an interesting dilemma for the vocational curriculum, which is biased towards the acquisition of skills.

Perhaps the way for the education system to develop new ways of learning is by developing its model of thinking further. Fullan (2004) believes that breakthrough and innovation will be achieved via the concept of *system thinkers in action*. Fullan takes Senge's (1990) system thinking a step further, developing a tri-level reform perspective: school, local authority and national level – three levels that are evident in Kent's vocational development programme. Fullan writes that system thinkers in action experience and embrace all three levels of operation for two reasons: first because they know that all three levels impact on each other; second because they are aware that in order to transform a large system, you have to engage in it.

Chapter 12

Active citizenship and the third age of learning: economic and social dimensions[1]

Brian Findsen

This chapter addresses the issue of what it means to be an active citizen in the third age (Laslett, 1989) and how learning may facilitate this process. Necessarily, the economic and social dimensions of life are considered because an individual's capacity to engage proactively in later life is strongly linked to constraints and opportunities emanating from economic, cultural or social bases. In analysing third age learning, I propose that it is important to consider not just formal learning, but also non-formal and informal learning (Jarvis, 1985), much of which occurs in social institutions, as exemplified by the private sphere of the family and the public sphere of the workplace. I argue that in the informal and non-formal learning arenas particularly, the prospects for active citizenship are strongest.

Third age learning in a lifelong framework

The third age of learning, according to Laslett, occurs once the pressures of earlier life are minimised at the curtailment of paid work. In *A Fresh Map of Life*, Laslett (1989) describes four main phases to the lifespan. The *first age* is essentially one of early socialisation in which a person is dependent on others (usually parents); the *second age* is one of adult maturity where a person typically takes on responsibilities such as established social relationships, career and financial independence and perhaps childrearing; the *third age* is that of fuller autonomy wherein an individual is freer of constraints imposed in the second age. The person has the opportunity to enhance intellectual and spiritual capacities. The *fourth age*, one of dependency and ultimately death, is usually short.

Laslett argues for conceptually aligning the considerable years ahead of most older adults after the second age with profitable activity, and especially with active learning. While his ideas are closely linked to the institutional context of learning via the University of the Third Age (U3A), they transcend this setting as an exhortation for seniors to lead a heightened quality of life. However, this depiction by Laslett is overly-romanticised as he assumes that older adults will have the necessary financial resources and social support to uphold this dream. In the neo-liberal Westernised world of the new millennium, the gaps between rich and poor have increased and there are growing numbers of marginalised older adults who are disenfranchised from much educational provision and freedom of choice in how to conduct their lives (Glendenning, 2000). Laslett's perspective is essentially middle-class and primarily male in its emphasis.

As the global economy has materialised, respective governments have tended to emphasise the need for a competitive workforce to be 'upskilled' and more knowledgeable in an international marketplace. In the UK context, according to Hodgson (2000, p. 11), at least in rhetoric, the New Labour Government has embraced lifelong learning as 'a central strategy for ensuring the future prosperity of the UK, as well as building a more just and inclusive society'. However, the lifelong learning agenda is dominated by economic and vocational concerns and is a threat, because 'it celebrates and promotes a fragmented and distributed view of learning' (Field, 2002, p. 14). In the more localised Scottish scene, policy reports such as Wendy Alexander's *A Smart, Successful Scotland* (2001) reinforce the importance of gainful employment and vocationalism in the way forward for a better Scotland. What is missing from this kind of public policy is an acknowledgement both of other forms of life's activities in which older citizens can enrich their lives contributing to communities, and that older adults need any consideration as citizens – witness their invisibility in lifelong learning reports.

To adult educators, the notion of lifelong learning has been treated as a given: adult learning/education is that endeavour occurring after an individual's compulsory education experiences – it is hardly anything new. Equality of educational opportunity, another well trumpeted myth of many governments, should mean just that – whether a person is just beginning life or nearing its end, regardless of circumstances, should not affect one's right of access to education. Hence, older adults' learning can be seen as part of the larger framework of opportunity open to individuals across the life-course.

In the area of older adults' learning there is increasing recognition that much of this is related to day-to-day life away from formal educational institutions (Jarvis, 2001). At an earlier date (1985, p. 3), Jarvis pointed to three contexts for learning:

- *informal learning* – the process whereby every person acquires knowledge, skills, attitudes and aptitude from daily living;
- *nonformal learning* – any systematic, organised, educational activity carried on outside the formal structure to provide selected types of learning to particular sub-groups of the population;
- *formal learning* – the institutionalised, chronologically graded and hierarchical educational system.

While the boundaries of each mode of learning are more porous than the definitions suggest, this typology enables adult educators to consider the relative emphases of each context for individuals and/or groups of older learners in their lives. The reality is that many seniors undertake non-formal learning through engagement with numerous social agencies and undertake informal learning incidentally in their lives. Many older people, especially those from higher socio-economic status, and from more extensive social networks and group membership, contribute significantly to their communities through volunteering (Lamdin and Fugate, 1997).

In one significant attempt to conceptualise the learning needs of older adults McClusky (1974), a pioneer in educational gerontology, categorised these as follows:

- *coping* needs: adults engaged in physical fitness, economic self-sufficiency, basic education;
- *expressive* needs: adults taking part in activities for their own sake and not necessarily to achieve a goal;
- *contributive* needs: adults deciding how to be useful contributors to society;
- *influence* needs: adult becoming agents for social change.

While I acknowledge that a needs-based approach to (older) adult education is fraught with moral and ethical difficulties (Collins, 1998), the point to be stressed from the above typology is that older people tend to function effectively to fulfil coping and expressive needs; indeed, much of what adult education providers offer this section of the population are programmes in these very arenas. Courses in preparing for retirement and enhancing leisure pursuits exemplify this approach. Contributive needs are significant when older adults seek to give something back to society by volunteering in third sector agencies and engaging in civil society via inter-generational exchanges. Such exchanges may be intra-familial (as grandparent to grandchild) or within organisations as mentors to less experienced workers. A largely missing dimension in many older adults' lives is the opportunity to be influential as part of a collective in the political and cultural configurations of societies, at least in comparison with prior historical cohorts. Exceptions include Grey Power or Grey Panthers. While there is considerable potential to effect social change as seniors (given the advance of new technologies and its greater familiarity amid young-old), this is more than counter-balanced by the ostracising of older adults from active participation as citizens and their own propensity to self-segregate, ostensibly for support. Most Western societies are oriented towards the glorification of youth where to be old is to be 'other' – a largely invisible entity (Biggs, 1993).

Much of the literature on educational gerontology has unfortunately focused on the limitations of older adulthood, emphasising physiological and cognitive decline, and locating older adults in a deficit model of dependence and decrepitude. While this view of older adulthood has limited validity, the untold story is that the vast majority of older adults live fairly autonomous lives where learning plays a key role in successful aging and contributes towards active citizenship.

The meaning of active citizenship in later life

The phrase *active citizenship* can mean different things to different groups in society. In a society in which all individuals contribute equally to its welfare and benefit commensurately, the issue of fairness in active citizenship is redundant. However, this notion of equal contribution and benefit is mythical. There are always dominant and subordinate groups in all societies (for instance, the Marxist capitalists and proletariat; men in the business world and women in the private domain of family) and power is not readily available to disenfranchised groups. And what kind of contribution are we acknowledging? Financial (as through taxes); social (as in volunteering in voluntary groups); cultural (as in helping mentor young people to assimilate a set of values of an ethnic group)?

In most nations, the term *citizen* qualifies a person to have basic rights such as freedom of expression and protection from the State, yet there is an expectation that something is given back too. In the third age, most but not all older adults have 'retired' and theoretically have a choice whether to continue (part-time) work, to volunteer in social agencies, to focus on family matters, to partake in leisure activities, perhaps previously suppressed. In this instance, an active citizen is one who positively engages with the wider social world, maintains effective networks, and continues in work, not necessarily paid – 'productive activity' in the Marxian sense. Using the framework above of needs, such a person is more readily identified as involved in contributive and influence needs-fulfilment. Citizenship implies a membership of society wherein older adults can connect meaningfully to other groups and challenge stereotypical exclusion from a youth-oriented culture.

Conventional perspectives on older adult participation and provision

A central component of the argument in this chapter is that older adults learn in a variety of contexts outside the conventional framework of formal education opportunities, allowing that these opportunities are differentially allocated. So it is first necessary to provide at least a brief commentary on what constitutes conventional participation for older adults, and who provides learning opportunities for them. This portrayal illustrates who benefits from current arrangements, and why a consideration of non-formal and informal learning is significant.

When we look at the participation patterns of older adults in formal education, these differ little from those of younger cohorts. Studies from all over the globe have demonstrated differential opportunity for groups of adults according to social-economic status, class, gender, ethnicity and geographical location. In the UK, the work of Sargant et al., as explained in *The Learning Divide* (1997), and of McGivney, particularly in terms of gender inequalities (1990, 1999, 2004), and more recently, Tuckett and McAulay (2005), all point to under-involvement of older adults in education. Overwhelmingly, prior education is identified as the primary indicator of subsequent success in formal education – the aging process for individuals, and the aging demographics for societies, make little difference to this truism. Hence, until such time as earlier cultural/educational inequalities are remedied across generations, this marginalisation of the majority of older adults in education will persist (Bourdieu, 1974).

Providers and provision

In terms of provision of educational opportunities for older adults, the range is enormous and generally mirrors the complexity found in other domains of adult education. Philosophical diversity is suggested by the framework of needs mentioned above – programmes can be concerned with individual development and coping skills; or focus on recreational and leisure pursuits; less often they relate to fostering vocational skills, though this might change with the growing need of retired adults to find further income; still less are they concerned with developing critical capacities of elders to challenge the social order.

In general, there are at least four types of adult education organisations in terms of provision for older people:

- those self-help agencies controlled by older adults to meet their own learning needs such as University of the Third Age (U3A);
- those agencies which develop programmes explicitly for older adults, such as Elderhostel and the Pre-Retirement Association;
- those mainstream providers that develop some courses which might appeal to older adults, such as retirement programmes run by centres for continuing education;
- those who ignore or neglect older adults – no provision is made for them and no facilities have been established to encourage their participation (Findsen, 2002).

The reality is that in most communities there are few educational agencies that have been established with older adults as the constructors of the knowledge, or that have this group as their primary target. This could reflect the relative powerlessness of older adults in youth-orientated cultures (Phillipson, 1998). However, there are certainly many mainstream providers who have provided a token level of support, that is, they establish a few courses which they hope will appeal primarily to older adults, such as preparing for retirement. The harsh reality is that there are still more agencies that have neglected these learning needs. There is an immediate challenge here for raising the consciousness of such providers to their responsibilities of working with traditionally marginalised groups, inclusive of older adult sub-populations.

In the provision of older adult education, the distinct tendency among agencies is to assume a paternalistic stance of – we know what's best for you. Within the (adult) education sector, the extent of control of knowledge (curriculum) by older adults themselves has varied considerably. Some older adults, attuned to professional educators arranging education for them, are content to let this continue. On the other hand, the more politicised and assertive seniors, who argue they know best what they want to learn, have set up a range of self-help organisations. In such organisations the control of curriculum, structure and processes are in the hands of older adults themselves.

The University of the Third Age (U3A) has burgeoned in several Commonwealth countries, and in North America different versions of Institutes for Learning in Retirement (ILRs) have mushroomed. In addition, Elderhostel, a travel and learn organisation, has a distinct presence in many countries, its headquarters based in Boston. In Scotland, the success of the Senior Studies Institute (SSI) at the University of Strathclyde relates to its ability to provide meaningful educational opportunities across a wide range of human endeavours. While the degree of autonomy of older adults may vary across and within these older adult education types, the essential message is that older adults, particularly those from professional and business backgrounds, want to take greater charge of their own educational affairs.

The typology above assumes that the organisation has an *educational* role. The range of educational options reflects the degree to which these agencies are overtly making provision for older adults. Aside from this categorisation of educational purpose, there are many organisations concerned about the *social* issues facing older adults such as Age Concern, City Councils, Grey Power and Help the Aged. While their principal goals and main activities may not be explicitly related to education, it is likely that education is a means by which they would want to fulfil their mission. Education is often a supportive strategy or a subsidiary goal. Whatever the case, there is also great potential on local or national scales to encourage greater collaboration amongst such agencies and to work alongside older adults to enhance the quality of living. Learning is a close partner to living; social and educational issues can become intertwined so that by addressing older adults' social issues we are often addressing their educational needs too. The initiative taken by the Blair Government in the UK, *Better Government for Older People*, is a realisation of the need for organisations to work more effectively on a co-operative basis (Carlton and Soulsby, 1999).

When the involvement of seniors in their own administration, programme planning and pedagogical practices occurs, there is a strong tendency to avoid bureaucratic mechanisms impeding collective decision-making. U3A, an exemplar of effective non-formal learning, emphasises learner-centeredness, responsiveness to membership needs and minimal cost to afford greater participation (Swindell, 1999). This is laudable. Unfortunately, from a sociologist's framework, the membership is fundamentally white and middle-class, another testimony to established social capital in operation (Field, 2003). In the Scottish context, older adults involved in the SSI's programme and those enrolled in the University of Glasgow's Department of Adult and Continuing Education (DACE) Open Programme are not likely to be from multiple derivation zones. This is not usually the result of a deliberate disen-franchisement of minorities; rather it reflects the necessity to be financially viable in an increasingly competitive environment.

There is an obvious point to make – more learning occurs outside educational institutions than inside them (Findsen, 2005). While learning may not be an explicit goal of some organisations, it occurs as a result of older people assembling for some other purpose – to provide help as a volunteer; to consider travel interests; to address health issues; to undertake leisure pursuits. The conceptualisation of learning by most people has been too rigid. In the next section I explore how revising the major contexts in which older adults learn, those of social institutions, expands our horizons towards a more holistic perspective and provides seniors with greater prospects of becoming active citizens through non-formal learning.

Non-formal learning in social institutions

Here I focus on the environments of social institutions in which seniors, arbitrarily defined as 55 years and older, do most of their learning. From a sociological framework, social institutions are those sites in people's daily lives where certain 'functions' (Blackledge and Hunt, 1985) are performed for the individual and for society. The focus is on those institutions where older adults are portrayed as active contributors to society and where learning intersects with the socialising function of the institution. To this point, few studies have examined empirically the patterns of older adults' learning and those that do tend to underestimate the importance of social institutions as sources for learning, especially in the contributive and influence needs domains (Findsen, 2002).

In these two arenas, seniors as volunteers in non-governmental organisations and as political advocates for social change can challenge the orthodox belief that older adults are recipients of welfare and consumers of the public purse. Instead, they can be perceived as active citizens. However, these opportunities for learning are not equally dispersed across the older adult population, but are differentially allocated according to factors such as social class, gender and ethnicity. One characteristic of older adults is their heterogeneity; social inequalities developed in earlier life tend to be perpetuated and accelerated in later adulthood. Retirement is experienced very differently by the middle classes and former workers, for instance; women tend to continue living under current conditions and practices, while men more frequently adopt a discontinuous retirement pattern (Arber and Ginn, 1995; Phillipson, 1998).

The family and the workplace, amid a myriad of possibilities, provide places where seniors conduct considerable informal learning – less intentional, non-hierarchical and associated with daily living – and non-formal learning – organised learning outside a hierarchical, assessment-ridden system. Social institutions provide people with opportunities to engage in social behaviours in each of the realms of education, work and leisure (Riley and Riley, 1994). They are sites of learning in which both informal and non-formal learning are ascendant. In each case, older adults have differential opportunities to learn and there are constraints associated with their relative status and access to power (Phillipson, 1998). In this conceptual framework, I examine two social institutions as triggers for older adults' learning and evaluate the quality of the learning for both individuals and society, meaning active citizenry.

Learning in the family

The family is a fundamental societal unit for the socialisation of individuals, regardless of its shape and composition. It is where we learn prevailing cultural norms, form our initial identity, and learn the rudiments of social relationships. It has a crucial role in social and cultural reproduction, transmitting values and practices from generation to generation (Jerrome, 1998). It is not normally seen as a learning system because learning, but more especially education, tends to be attributed to the more formal institutions of schools where professionals operate as educators and carers. Yet in a family, experiential learning comes to the fore, the quality of that experience (Dewey, 1938) contingent on many factors, including financial and social capital (Field, 2003).

While norms of formality may vary considerably from family to family, as, for instance, the rituals around meal times, inter-generational learning, especially in more collective cultures where several generations more commonly co-habit, provides older adults with the potentially important tasks of historian, storyteller, mentor and disseminator of culture. However, as Riley and Riley

(1994, p. 31) point out, expectations built up around these diverse roles may become void or further enhanced by reconstituted families in the sense that relationships and roles frequently become more indeterminate and diffuse. In the post-modern world, certainties are few and expectations for older people of their traditional roles in families can be nullified.

Given changes in demographic, technological, legal, ideological and economic spheres, Jerrome (1998) argues that relationships between elderly parents and their adult children are governed more by sentiment than by obligation. She argues there is usually more choice in family relationships as a result of demographic and economic changes – smaller families, later birth of children, the complexities of relationships, rising affluence. The implications for older adults are that traditional roles as grandparents may be harder to play, given the myriad of family configurations and more complex patterns of communication. As a case in point, in the (post)modern world in which young mothers often re-enter the workforce quickly after giving birth, the child-minder frequently can be a grandparent – hence, children may learn a lot directly from older family members.

One of the key 'teaching' roles of older adults is that of mentor to at least two generations. Mentoring comes in different guises such as guide, friend and counsellor (Carmin, 1988). Typically, mentoring entails a social interaction between individuals of differing levels of experience and expertise, which may be formalised, as in many work environments, or informal and private, as in families. While the more usual flow of expertise is from older to younger, this is not necessarily the case. For instance, the example of young children showing grandparents how to operate e-mail is not uncommon.

There is a serious cultural dimension to this mentoring process. In the country where I have spent most of my life, Aotearoa, New Zealand, the indigenous Maori context provides a very good example of where both formal and informal mentoring occurs. It is customary for *kaumatua* (older men) to sit alongside their *mokopuna* (grandchildren) in public settings, advising them of tribal customs and practices. Inside the *wharenui* (communal meeting houses), the carvings on the walls of ancestors provide visual literacy, re-inforcing the *whakapapa* (genealogy) of that tribe. It is common to observe kaumatua coaching mokopuna to recite their genealogy, thus enabling the child to better understand his/her place in the *iwi* (tribe). Elders are generally revered, in the rural communities especially, but the modernisation agenda under neo-liberalism has helped to erode traditional lines of respect and authority across the generations.

The workplace as a social institution for learning

As another case study, the workplace can be interpreted as a social institution which continues to exert considerable sway in the lives of older citizens. The exigencies of economic survival and the reconfiguration of the workforce have influenced patterns of paid work for seniors, not all of whom can retire on superannuation or governmental/employer benefits. Many are part of an underclass in society as a result of poor health, inferior initial education and inconsistent work opportunities in the labour market (Thomson, 1999; Walker, 1993). The distinction between worker and non-worker is no longer as explicit as in the past. Many older adults take whatever casual work they can get to supplement a family's income. Often older adults face discrimination in the workplace and are less likely than younger workers to receive further training and professional development (Bytheway, 1995). On the other hand, more liberally-minded employers capitalise on the considerable past experience of older workers, using them as mentors and coaches in the workplace.

What happens in a workplace is influenced by a number of parties: the employer; the worker (whether under contract to the employer or independent); the state, as regulator of public policy and legal aspects. Given that older adults are often seen as part of a peripheral labour source (Thomson, 1999), their power to influence decisions affecting their paid employment is usually low. Of course, the status and position prior to retirement has a significant part to play in individuals' subsequent work lives. Professional people, more often men than women, can retain useful networks for well-paid work, and they are more likely to benefit from private pensions, thus securing financially their third age for leisure and learning. While we do not know enough about differentials, in retirement, of educational opportunity, as for adult participation trends more generally the rule of thumb is that *those who already have get more* (Benseman, 1996). It is extremely unlikely that patterns of opportunity in older adulthood, particularly related to work, will differ positively at least from those established earlier in life.

So far the focus has been on paid work. Unpaid work, in the form of housework, has been undertaken predominantly by women. Research (see Bernard et al., 1995) suggests that this pattern continues into retirement. While men sometimes steer towards greater domesticity in retirement and take on greater expressive learning activities largely ignored in a busy prior work life, women are less likely to discontinue their unpaid work tasks (Biggs, 1993). In the arena of volunteering, where fresh learning opportunities abound either through active engagement in voluntary organisations or more directly through training (professional development), both genders benefit, as does society from a huge injection of life experience and accumulated wisdom. So older people themselves, the organisations for whom they work voluntarily and the community, benefit from this input from elders (Caro and Bass, 1995).

It is a mistake to romanticise the work lives of older adults. As in other human spheres, rewards are differentially allocated, according to the political economy – gender, social class, race/ethnicity and geographical location are all variables with the potential to shape possibilities and agency (Phillipson, 1998). Some people have considerable human and material resources at their disposal; others have meagre social capital trapped in poverty and a very restricted lifestyle. The state can have a profound effect on the ability of older adults to undertake paid work, according to public policy. The position of the national economy is indeed pertinent – the ebb and flow of the production relations in capitalist societies can impact upon, for instance, employers' willingness to engage older workers, even on a part-time basis, or to invest in training for them (Lamdin and Fugate, 1997).

It is useful to distinguish between the need to learn to retire and to learn in retirement. Some, especially larger employers, run learning programmes for employees to think about the implications of future retirement. Are potential retirees' resources sufficient? Will they move residence? Who will form their primary social relationships? Given increased life expectancies, what future learning needs might they have? These are typical questions to address. On occasion, where employers do not have the resources to conduct such programmes they can call upon assistance from the likes of the Association for Pre-retirement Education, a purpose-built organisation to help with such matters in the UK. Yet these formal programmes are the tip of the iceberg. The result is that many people fall into retirement – or are forcibly placed there through redundancy – with minimal ideas about what the third age might mean to them or for close relatives.

Learning in retirement may require a major re-adjustment of 'meaning perspective' (Mezirow, 1991), the way in which they understand their world. For individuals who carry on life in a familiar pattern, the disjuncture is likely to be small; for others, perhaps a professional one Friday, and a person of enforced leisure the next Monday, the impact on self-identity can be profound. Usually the 'problem of retirement' is gender specific: retirement has been stereotypically perceived as a man's problem, since often men disengage from their major source of identity and status when they finish paid work (Phillipson, 1998). However, in the post-modern world this may be archaic, since the dynamics of retirement are much more complex than in the past.

Differential opportunity in later life

There is a tendency to equate non-formal and informal learning with greater autonomy, self-directedness and learner control of knowledge construction (Jarvis, 2001). To an extent, as demonstrated in the ways in which older adults learn from social institutions, there is undoubted truth in this assertion. Yet, on the other hand, to pretend that opportunities for learning, even in the most democratic and laissez-faire modes, are equally distributed, is to be naïve. Choices in life are always subject to prevailing societal norms, social structures and bureaucratic frameworks (Collins, 1998).

As a case in point, the position of women in later adulthood is constrained by social policy, particularly historic patterns of economic provision for them. Also, ageing and gender intersect; older age is becoming increasingly feminised (Arber and Ginn, 1995). In 'retirement' there are distinctly different trajectories linked to varied prior work experiences, education and childrearing patterns. According to Bonita (1993, p. 195), older women also have differences from men in their marital status, living arrangements and care-taking responsibilities. It is more usual for them to have fewer resources, decreasing health and mobility, loss of partners and the threat of dependency – not surprisingly, given that the life expectancy of women exceeds men in most or all societies. Hence, even though women tend to outlive men, their quality of life is nearly always at issue.

Conclusion

This chapter has traced the connections between third age learning, particularly in its non-formal and informal guises, and opportunities for older adults to be fully functioning members of society as active citizens. It argues that increased recognition should be given to situational learning contexts, such as the family and the workplace, wherein opportunities emerge for fuller engagement with society as a whole.

In both the paid and unpaid arenas, in public workplaces and private spaces, older adults engage in meaningful activity, sustaining social relationships, contributing to their own and communities' economies, at times exerting influence in public affairs (Lamdin and Fugate, 1997). The potential for significant learning in these sites of social institutions is not trivial – in the areas of the family (especially through intergenerational learning) and the work place, as examples, older adults also continue to exercise their roles as lifelong learners. Their contribution to society is frequently invisible or undervalued, often carried out in less than favourable conditions but ultimately vital for a democratic, learning society.

Because older adult education is virtually insignificant in the overall scheme of adult participation (older adults do not readily undertake education provided by an agency), the attention here has swung towards considering the relevance of less formal learning for seniors. In social institutions of the family and the workplace there is considerable learning potential, especially in those spheres where self-management is apparent and related to everyday life issues.

Learning in whatever guise is always conditioned by prevailing social structural conditions, and people's choices. This is especially true for those older adults in actual poverty and dire living circumstances – their learning is constrained by the need to cope. While there are grounds to celebrate the optimism associated with the creativity and innovation of middle-class organised older adult learning activity, exemplified in the U3A movement and the Senior Studies Institute, there are also grounds for promoting better State-provided learning opportunities for the underclass of older adults in all societies. Lifelong learning will become more than rhetoric when it includes better outcomes for the least financially positioned among us, including marginalised older people. In this way, better learning opportunities for all can assist in the development of an active citizenry, inclusive of older adults.

Notes

[1] Parts of this chapter have previously been published in the *Journal of Transformative Education*, 2006, 'Social institutions as sites for learning: differential opportunities', vol. 4, no. 1, 65–81.

Chapter 13

Policy-makers and researchers working together: dilemmas in making the connection

Bruce Wilson

Introduction

A major objective for PASCAL has been developing resources and relationships which enhance the access of policy-makers to the most useful current research in areas relevant to their work and decision-making. This is timely, as there has been a growing emphasis on the importance of 'evidence-based' decision-making, both in policy development and in challenging established ways of offering public services. This is linked closely to the understanding that learning is central to generating better evidence for choosing one course of action or another and to improving responsiveness to changing circumstances.

However, the relationship between research and policy-making is far from straightforward. Sometimes, this can reflect the different perspectives and interests of the policy community and researchers; at other times it might be that the policy process requires insights which cannot be readily induced from the research literature which is available. Often, of course, the policy formation process explicitly includes a research phase, in order to ensure that policy outcomes are as well-informed as possible.

This chapter considers a range of issues which affect the contribution of research to informing policy interventions, organisational design or programme development. The analysis suggests that there are a number of aspects of the research process which do not fit easily with the requirements of the policy process, particularly in relation to social, economic and cultural policies. The different priorities of researchers and policy-makers, the complexities of epistemology and methodology, and the time required for effective intellectual results to be achieved, all contribute to the level of risk associated with connecting research and policy (see Bessant and Watts, 2005).

The chapter concludes with some observations about the circumstances under which it can be expected that the connection between knowledge generation and policy formation will be sufficiently robust to lead to policy which is well-supported by appropriate research. It begins with an exploration of the factors that shape the effectiveness of decision-making. This applies to decision-making more broadly than that related to policy; however, a reflective approach to decision-making suggests that it is useful to consider the contextual factors, beliefs and other dynamics which influence decision-making processes and distort the impact of research.

Research evidence on decision-making

Making decisions, both as individuals and as members of collective entities, is obviously a central part of the policy formation process. There are different ways of understanding this: some have explored it from the perspective of examining how good decisions get made; others have suggested that decision-making is best seen as an arena of intense political activity, concerned with power struggles and the allocation of resources. A number of theories have been developed to account for the patterns observed in decision-making behaviour in different circumstances. A quick review of some of the theory indicates that what might at first appear as a relatively straightforward topic has various layers to it.

The foundation of much of this theorising is 'Managerial Rationality', in which:

> ... the decision-makers identify the problem or issue about which a decision has to be made, collect and sort information about alternative potential solutions, compare each solution against predetermined criteria to assess degree of fit, arrange solutions in order of preference and make an optimising choice. (Miller et al. 1996, p. 294).

Perhaps not surprisingly, the assumption of rationality in decision-making is widespread. In earlier phases of the research, considerable effort was put into the development of mathematical models and computer applications designed to support rational approaches in the face of seemingly impossible complexity. Even where the value of some of these models was questioned, they were defended on the grounds that they provided managers with 'psychological insurance'; in other words, they gave the appearance that decision-making was rational even where that was not the case (see, for example, Dickson, 1983).

However, the complexity of contemporary policy issues makes it very difficult to gather and to analyse sufficient, relevant evidence, and the scope of the policy framework itself may well be quite unclear. Evidence about alternatives might be unavailable and the criteria against which policy decisions are evaluated unclear or not agreed.

As early as 1960, Simon advanced a thorough critique of 'managerial rationality', noting that while much decision-making might be 'reasoned', it is difficult to prove that it satisfies the test of rationality. He noted, however, that many decisions fit a relatively routine set of circumstances and are often made in a rather straightforward manner. When unfamiliar circumstances arise this is not possible, and less certain guidelines exist to shape the ways in which 'new' decisions might be made.

Since then, the increasing turbulence and volatility of the international political and economic environment has meant that policy decisions are increasingly susceptible to this kind of uncertainty. Ironically, the political divisions which might have given some predictability at least to how policy decisions were approached in past decades are now equally uncertain, partly because of the inability of ideologies to speak to contemporary circumstances, partly because of the implications of advances in information and com- munication technologies and partly because of increasing sensitivity to shifts in public opportunities.

Other writers have emphasised that policy-making often has less to do with rationality and more to do with the exercise of power. Many factors affect the ways in which people choose to exercise power. Perceptions of interests (including self-interest), control of resources, claims to particular expertise, gender and language proficiency have all been identified as factors which shape the struggle to assert specific viewpoints over and against those of others when differences of viewpoint occur. People exercise 'leadership' in decision-making not only on the basis of positions of formal responsibility, but also by virtue of the coherence of their logic, or of their charisma.

This is exacerbated in situations where the policy-making apparatus is structured across different governmental departments, or divisions within a department. Pfeffer and Salancik have argued that the arrangement of internal divisions of authority and of labour leads inevitably to fragmentation and a narrowing of focus. In this context, groups jockey for position with varying intensity, depending on the actual topics that are on the policy agenda at the time. Over time, internal differences amongst organisational units can consolidate so that different assumptions and views of the world influence the approaches adopted to particular topics (see Pfeffer and Salancik, 1978).

The one other dimension of this discussion to be noted is whether 'decisions' do get made. Much of the research on decision-making processes has been called into question by Mintzberg and Waters (1990) who have argued that the concept of 'decision' is no longer useful. Their view is based on the observation that actions can be taken without deliberate decisions being made. Hence, a policy strategy might emerge from a series of actions rather than being decided in advance. From this perspective, understanding policy formation depends on recognising the complex interactions and relationships which influence how certain patterns in actions unfold, leading with hindsight to an acceptance that a particular policy strategy has been adopted.

Research in policy-making processes

Policy formation involves the determination of an appropriate direction of legislative framing of how social, economic and cultural life will be approached. Sometimes this requires minor adaptation of existing arrangements. On other occasions it leads to fundamental redefinition of people's rights and of the processes through which various aspects of public life will be managed. Changes in industrial relations regulation, and of the rigid processes for assessing requests by refugees for residency status, represent two recent examples of major policy redirection in Australia.

While political ideas and values are a central part of policy formation, use of evidence is also important. Indeed, there are many areas where the development of evidence over a period of time has prompted policy initiatives that might not otherwise have occurred. Much of this is part of the normal process of public service monitoring and review of official statistics.

However, one of the significant consequences of the pressures to contain government expenditure has been to reallocate resources away from administrative and research resources within public service agencies to service delivery. Consequently, there has been a significant increase in the amount of research and advisory work that is tendered to university or consultancy researchers. This means that research briefs are framed often from the perspective of policy-makers who sometimes specify not only the kinds of insights or outcomes which they are seeking, but even the methodology which is to be used. The subsequent reports have variable impact on the policy process, with the overriding determinant of influence typically being the political context rather than the quality of the research. The research process itself is subject to the confines of formal contracts, and specifications regarding the scale, quantum and timelines of research, irrespective of the way in which the actual research agenda might unfold.

Partly because of this kind of framing, research knowledge can provide only limited assistance in policy formation. Where policy issues with considerable public significance are concerned (such as drug and alcohol, migration, income support, company regulation or education, in the Australian context), the impact of research findings will always be shaped by lobby groups or social movements, depending on the scale of the issue. Significant policy development in these areas depends on work which develops over the longer term, linking public confidence in the direction of policy formation with 'political learning' about what is possible.

In this respect, there is a parallel in policy formation with tensions that Sandberg has observed between the value of research, as a scientific methodology, and the conflicting priorities of trade union action. The more specific tensions to which Sandberg referred included differences in the objectives of trade unions and researchers:

> a short time perspective versus a long term perspective; problem solutions and clear guidelines versus a study of problems and a widening of perspective; the articulation of views and demands through the organisational hierarchy versus through the research process; locally useful knowledge versus theories and generalisations. (Sandberg, 1985, p. 88)

Clearly, there are similar tensions with policy formation. In Sandberg's view, these tensions lead one set of priorities to be subordinated to the other. The issues here are not dissimilar to the tensions around maximising the impact of research projects mentioned by Duke and Charles in the final chapter in this volume. The fundamental tension is that research is intended primarily to lead to the production of new knowledge. This is, unfortunately, a tortuous process, in which the tasks of defining research questions, gathering data and trying to make sense of it all can be very untidy. It can be a real struggle to fit into the framework necessary to meet contractual obligations.

Sandberg proposed, therefore, the adoption of an approach to union-oriented research that seems to be relevant also to policy formation. He referred to this approach as 'praxis' research: 'an activity that contains a dialogue, and has an action part subordinated to an action practice and a conceptual or reflective part subordinate to a scientific practice' (Sandberg, 1985, p. 89; see also Sandberg et al., 1992). The interplay between the two is essential, but it should be understood more as an exchange rather than a combination or an integration of the two types of activities.

> Knowledge is <u>used</u> in the dialogue/action and knowledge is <u>produced</u> there, and in the subsequent analysis and conceptualisation. Praxis research is thus characterised by a conscious and <u>planned</u> interplay between an action and dialogue phase in research and a phase characterised by distanced conceptualisation and reflection... The two parts of praxis research must be carefully <u>developed</u> to make possible this interplay. (Sandberg, 1985, p. 89)

The concept of praxis research provides a framework for addressing the twin priorities of producing effective policy formation *and* of ensuring the intellectual rigour that can make the outcomes of local activities more generally useful in informing theories about change and in developing social and political theory. It points to a framework that leads away from the empiricist character of narrowly-construed policy-oriented research towards the development of more general theoretical insights, which not only have more general application, but genuinely deepen our understanding of social, political and economic life.

The central part of Sandberg's concept of praxis research, in this regard, is his emphasis on an *intellectual* dialogue, in which the priorities of the policy formation process can be seen apart from, yet engaged in, intellectual exchange with the key relevant theoretical knowledge. This dialogue contributes not only to better policy advice, but also to enhanced theoretical formulation. The evidence on which policy recommendations are based depends on the resources that the policy-makers are prepared to fund, and can be positioned as being apart from, yet interpreted within, a wider theoretical context. The one is not reduced to the other, but is seen in relation to it, through a frame of dialogue.

Ironically, given the more rigorous emphasis on dialogue, one other significant tension arises from the use of language itself. It is not uncommon for the language of research to be at odds with the language of policy and politics. Even the notion of 'research' can be understood as the use of secondary sources, rather than engaging with the very generation of knowledge itself. When researchers and policy-makers are working together, the clarification of key concepts and meanings can be very important. This issue arises also in Duke and Charles' chapter, where they refer to the researcher's challenge of finding appropriate language to describe the insights which they have generated and the use of metaphors to share those insights with others.

Action/praxis research

Given these concerns, it is useful to consider the value of participatory action research (PAR) as a methodology for undertaking policy-oriented research, in contrast to more formal methodologies. Action research is common in settings that are oriented towards change, because of the way in which 'groups of people can organise the conditions under which they can learn from their own experience, and make this experience accessible to others' (Kemmis and McTaggart, 1988, pp. 8–9). Participatory action research, often inspired by the STSD approach, has been used in a variety of other circumstances. Whyte and Lazes have demonstrated the particular benefits for unions and management in the introduction of the Quality of Working Life (QWL) initiative in Xerox during the 1980s, while Greenwood and others have applied the strategy to understand the issues of apathy and alienation in quite another context, the Fagor Cooperatives Group in Mondragon, Spain (Whyte et al., 1991). In their report, Greenwood et al. commented on the advantages of participatory action research. It:

> ... subjects normal research approaches to a special kind of test. The results must be convincing and informative to members of the organisation under study. Results must also point in the direction of intelligible actions to correct important problems. While this is, in a certain sense, restrictive, it also serves to reduce complex social theories to essential and important propositions and subjects local views and analyses to group

> review. In this way PAR pools the power, knowledge, and energy of many minds, all engaged in a process of reflection, discussion and action. (Greenwood et al., 1992, pp. 9–10)

While pointing to certain strengths of this approach for policy formation processes, it also implies its constraints. Policy formation is not necessarily about achieving a consensual or logical outcome. There will be many other influences, other than the 'power, knowledge, and energy of many minds' that will shape policy outcomes. Nevertheless, in those circumstances in which policy is intended inevitably to lead to new arrangements, Sandberg's concept of praxis research can be particularly useful. It provides not only a framework for generating valuable new knowledge, but of mobilising public support for a policy initiative. This applies especially where the action research is linked with key organisations and representative institutions (such as local government) rather than individuals. In these settings, action researchers have used typical research methods, such as surveys, interviews, participant observation and historical studies; however, the dialogue and common action which have occurred as part of the action research process have been extremely useful also in obtaining certain types of data, and in exploring understandings about the processes of change.

Case studies: research for policy formation in action

There are a variety of ways in which research is included as part of the policy formation process. Perhaps the most formal example is the Commission of Inquiry, with formal terms of reference and commissioned research. With such inquiries, a substantial body of independent research is commissioned, and there is an expectation that the Commissioner(s) will provide formal recommendations for governments to implement.

Many countries also have formal schemes for allocating funding for research. Typically, most of this funding is won by universities and formal research institutes. Increasingly, an important criterion for selecting projects for funding is the potential that they have either to benefit industry, or to contribute evidence in support of public policy ('national priorities'). At the other end of the scale, policy officers themselves draw on secondary sources from departmental libraries, or draw on official statistics. Generally, specific policy-related research initiatives are let by tender, with the scale of the project depending on the resources available.

In Australia, at least, there is relatively little experience in the use of action research specifically to support policy formation. It is much more likely to be used in the context of community or organisational change, or in the implementation of policy. However, there are a number of examples where a form of *praxis* research can be observed, especially where policy initiatives are a response to pressure from non-government stakeholders for government action. One recent example in Victoria has been in response to growing concerns about violence against women.

In 2002, the Victorian Government released its Women's Safety Strategy and established three State-wide Steering Committees, including one to Reduce Violence Against Women in the Workplace. The aim of the latter was to improve the prevention of, and responses to, violence against women occurring in a workplace setting, including workplace violence, bullying and sexual harassment (OWP, 2005).

The membership of the Committee included representatives from the following agencies: Victorian Trades Hall Council, WorkSafe Victoria, Equal Opportunity Commission, Women Against Sexual Harassment (WASH), Centres Against Sexual Assault (CASA) Forum, Victorian Employers' and Chamber of Commerce and Industry (VECCI), Working Women's Health, Victorian Aboriginal Legal Service, the Union Research Centre on Organisation and Technology (URCOT), Job Watch, Community and Public Sector Union (CPSU), Victoria Police, Women's Health Victoria, and the Office of Women's Policy (OWP).

Some of the activities undertaken by the Committee have included:
- the establishment of a centralised research and data base to pool resources and knowledge into an accessible and structured base;
- forming a Research Sub-Committee to categorise research and conduct a preliminary gap analysis of the material;
- a series of information sessions by URCOT, Jobwatch, Equal Opportunity Commission, WorkSafe, and Victorian Trades Hall Council to inform Committee members of the roles and responsibilities of the range of agencies addressing violence against women in the workplace; and
- identifying the limitations and strengths of current practice and systems to respond to violence in the workplace (URCOT, 2005).

Based on its 'gap analysis', the Research Sub-Committee proposed a major research project on a range of questions about the character and scale of workplace violence against women in Victoria. An applied research organisation with experience in this type of research, the Union Research Centre on Organisation and Technology, URCOT, was contracted to undertake the research, with support from Working Women's Health (in Victoria). After the contract was let, there continued to be ongoing communication between the researchers and the State-wide Committee.

The research itself was framed by an appreciation of the methodological challenges posed by this type of research and by the particular need for a gendered analysis and a process that respected the traumatic implications of workplace violence for many women. Specific data-gathering resources were developed, including a large-scale telephone survey, focus groups with specific categories of women workers and case studies of firms in particular industries. Reports to the State-wide Committee were presented iteratively, by method and by theme.

The distinctive feature of this project, then, was that it was governed not only by the policy agency itself, but by a group that was constituted formally, with representation from a range of government agencies, from non-government advocacy groups, and others with specific expertise (see OWP, 2005). This group was responsible for:

- overseeing a review of the available research literature, and for identifying gaps both in the research in general and in Victoria in particular;
- refining specific research questions to be addressed through a research project which was subsequently tendered;
- reviewing progress reports on the research;
- engaging politicians, including the Minister, in discussion about the issues emerging; and
- engaging in debate of the research findings, and in formulating policy recommendations to be put to the Office of Women's Policy.

In this sense, the process of policy development was more inclusive not only of key policy officers, but of key stakeholders involved in public debate, service delivery and the political process. The two women who were accountable formally for delivering on the research contract, the Directors of URCOT and of the Working Women's Health, were members of the State-wide Committee because of their organisation's expertise, and therefore were involved actively in all aspects of the process, including the debate about policy options. Alongside the more formal work of the Committee, there was an ongoing process of networking and advocacy, with various organisations pursuing their own particular interests and campaigns, partly at least with the intention of influencing Government to adopt the policy recommendations.

The case study illustrates the way in which an active involvement of stake-holders and policy officers can facilitate the development of a more comprehensive understanding of both issues and of research findings, leading to policy recommendations that have broad, consensual support. The process adopted reflected Sandberg's notion of dialogue, and allowed for the relative rigour that can come from sustaining an iterative process of dialogue amongst those responsible for policy formation, those involved in action (both advocacy and service delivery of one kind or another) and the researchers. The formal processes of bringing together current knowledge and then undertaking research to generate new knowledge are separated from the debates about policy outcomes, values and interests; the latter were positioned largely in the domain of the Steering Committee, yet were held in dialogue with the Research Sub-Committee.

Conclusion

These case studies demonstrate that notwithstanding the best of intentions, policy-makers face a fundamental problem in both commissioning and taking advantage of research. As was foreshadowed earlier, part of this problem is framed by the complexities and uncertainties of the research process itself. Part of it results from the variable priorities of policy-makers and part from the difficulties of creating the climate in which policy initiatives can be implemented.

Ultimately, the political context of most policy formation remains a critical determinant of the extent to which research evidence can contribute to policy formation. To assume that knowledge or technique alone can resolve policy difference is to assume that conflicts in interests and values can be reduced to technocratic solutions. For better or worse, this is not the case. However, the example above does demonstrate that there are models for making these issues transparent, and for facilitating processes for ensuring that appropriate research knowledge can inform policy formation. Policy debates which are driven by values should at least be better informed than has often been the case.

Praxis research attempts, at least, to create an intellectual environment in which the distance between policy-making and generating knowledge is not collapsed, but framed in a way which facilitates understanding, builds congruence and builds clarity in communication. How widely can this approach be adopted? It does involve a substantial investment of time and of other resources. However, there is no reason on major issues at least, why such an approach cannot be adopted. Given the issues in linking policy and research, perhaps the more important question is whether we can afford not to pursue these kinds of approaches.

Chapter 14

Old wheels and new: cyclical progress in the use of language, metaphors, networks and projects to enhance learning and city governance

David Charles and Chris Duke

Introduction

This concluding chapter steps outside the immediate operating framework of the Pascal International Observatory. It reflects on the learning processes and outcomes – the deliverables, in the language of the European Commission (EC) – of an EC research project involving four European cities and universities together with an ancillary Australian partner. This coincided with the first years of the life of the Observatory, concluding in the first quarter of 2006. In reflecting on the process and progress of this CRITICAL (hereafter referred to for convenience in small case as Critical) project – *City Regions as Intelligent Territories: Inclusion, Competitiveness and Learning* – the chapter also invites consideration of the way that the Pascal virtual community and expanding network can support productive partnership between regional policy-makers, social planners and scholars. How do we go about the business of 'making knowledge work', the theme title of the Pascal Stirling Conference in October 2005? More broadly, it invites readers to examine the fast-changing creation, use and often disposal of language; the tensions inherent in working across theory and practice, social and economic, short and long term, products and processes; and to be aware of the cyclical and erratic character of understanding and acting in this complicated arena.

It is not often that project managers write a reflective account of such a project: it can be difficult to be objective and dispassionate about a process in the final days of a project and the writing of final reports. All too often at this point the emphasis is on presenting a positive spin and satisfying the sponsor. On this occasion the authors of this chapter bring together the two roles of project manager (Charles) and that of a participant observer (Duke). The chapter therefore largely presents the more objective view of a participant unencumbered by the responsibilities of advocacy, but with the reflections and inputs of the project manager. In places, to clarify these two positions the reflections of Charles are inserted as direct quotations in italics where a personal view is necessary.

The Critical project

The Critical project was one of a number of socio-economic research projects funded by the European Commission within its Fifth Framework Programme. It was a response to a general call for proposals against a broad set of funding priorities. One of the last round of projects under the programme, it was of a different character than what was to follow. In its Sixth Framework Programme the Commisison was more prescriptive in setting themes and allocated a substantial proportion of its budget to much larger five-year projects and networks.

In this particular circumstance it was possible for a small group, Professors David Charles, Klaus Kunzmann, James Wickham and Markku Sotarauta, to submit a bid for a three-year project. Three of the partners had collaborated previously on an EU project on universities and regional development (Charles, 2001), whilst the fourth, Sotarauta, was known to Charles through other means, including a period as a visiting researcher from Tampere to Newcastle.

The notion of the project emerged from a project in the UK on the challenges facing provincial city-regions (Charles et al., 1999) and a desire to extend this to an international scale. At the same time previous work on the regional role of universities had stimulated an interest in processes of learning and engagement. The proposal sought to bring together these strands of work and examine learning processes in city-regions across a group of European cities. The selection of the cities was shaped therefore by the personal connections between the team members and the desire to focus on city-regions outside of the world cities such as London, Paris and Berlin.

Main intentions, processes and intended outcomes

The formal aim of the project was 'to test the concept of a knowledge, or learning society within the context of city regions, in order to assess how knowledge and learning can be utilised by cities within integrated strategies for their future development'. Five more detailed objectives sought: (a) empirically to investigate forms of knowledge and learning within the four selected and represented cities, Newcastle in England, Dortmund in Germany, Dublin in Ireland, and Tampere in Finland; (b) to identify key roles of cities in wider economies and the types of knowledge resources used by different city-region networks; (c) to examine how tertiary education institutions and other forms of educational provider contribute to collective learning processes and community learning and development; (d) to assess the success of existing strategies, identifying good practice and lessons susceptible to wider dissemination; and (e) to develop indicators that would help local and regional authorities in developing appropriate intervention strategies.

The project also built upon the notion of city-regions having to address five main 'elements or challenges'. These helped frame the project and the methodology for empirical research and analysis. They were: knowledge and economic competitiveness; image and cosmopolitanism; social cohesion; sustainability; and governance. The rationale connected the purposes and expected outcomes to European Union policies and emphasised dissemination within the 'urban policy community'. The scientific description reflected policy-makers' over-optimism for policy innovation in learning, and 'a desire to find a solution that is generalisable and can be rolled out nationally or even internationally'.

Research methodology

The selection of medium-sized, what were termed ordinary rather than globally significant, cities noted that these account for a high proportion of Europe's urban populations and problems. The core of the project was to be case studies of (initially seven but subsequently eight) networks, or what came to be called arenas, in each of the four city regions. Alongside and informing these case studies were to be an attempt to identify and map different forms of knowledge centres; to develop approaches to investigating community learning processes; to develop tools or indicators of tertiary education sector outreach learning activities; and to take forward work on local authorities' strategy development. Apart from a final synthesis report after three years, the last project deliverable was to be a set of indicators of learning that city authorities could use to assess their own performance as learning cities, by means of a 'learning city toolkit'.

The project commenced formally in February 2003, with a final report to the Commission due before Easter 2006. Most of the attention in the last of the series of intensive working sessions that punctuated and connected the work in the linked cities and partnering academic groups, held in Barcelona in January 2006, focused on the so-called toolkit and on a fully refereed co-authored book. The latter was to be produced from, but outside the terms and time period of, the work for the EC contract that was about to conclude.

The more informal story of knowledge-making within the framework

As the project acquired a life and energy of its own, through the shared website, the succession of usually two-day meetings and by means of regular email and occasional telephone conversation, it was enriched and varied as opportunities and insights arose, and as conceptual and empirical data posed new problems and suggested new possibilities. Looking back to the detailed text of the proposal over three years later, one is struck both by the accuracy with which a path of inquiry was charted, and by the extent of acceptable and sensible deviation and accretion along the way:

> *There is always a tension between sticking with a pre-designed research programme and responding to opportunity. The EC tends to expect an adherence to planned 'workpackages' and 'deliverables' and also expects projects to feed into practice during the process as well as after. In the case of CRITICAL we had to balance the need to satisfy the Commission that we were doing what we promised, with a shift to a more reflective and uncertain stance as the research unfolded and methodologies evolved.*

The first periodic progress report to the Commission after six months explained how building out a wider research and policy network had come to include a fifth city and university partner, RMIT University and Melbourne in Australia, where a parallel, associated and complementary, self-financed study was being developed, tracking and where possible integrating with the main EC-funded work. It was this extension that created an informal and initially essential personal link between Critical and the Pascal Observatory. RMIT was a foundation member and one of the two key 'nodes' for the Observatory, and several, ultimately all, of the senior members of the four original Critical city teams came to make substantial intellectual contributions to the Observatory, in turn using it as one unanticipated means of dis-seminating the work of the Critical project.

Trust emerged during the project, not for the first time, as an important element in building partnership between different community and governmental partners as a prerequisite for confident learning and development. An unspoken understanding in framing the EC bid, and in winning the confidence and contract of the EC, was that the research partners shared mutual confidence and trust – that they were already in effect a team, and a 'community of practice', to use an expression that become pivotal as the work proceeded. The inclusion of a fifth, unknown and untested, team from distant Australia was an exercise in trust and confidence on the part of the contracting parties. It also symbolised, and could serve as something of a metaphor for, much that the project addressed at the formal, substantive level.

> *Trust is particularly important in such collaborative projects. I was keen to keep the project to a modest scale and only include partners I could trust to deliver interesting insights and stick to the workplan. The need for interdisciplinarity also reinforces the need for trust – funding is dependent on demonstrating different disciplinary inputs in the team, but this leads to the absence of a common shared intellectual foundation and hence a need to rely more on each other's conceptual inputs and insights.*

Other changes were less obvious, growing up mainly through the empirical studies as these went ahead, some smoothly, some with great difficulty and what might be called running repairs. The initial design referred to seven networks per city. These became eight arenas – learning in informal clusters, cultural learning, community-based learning, learning sustainability, learning in urban regeneration, access to learning for the disadvantaged, facilitated learning among SMEs and policy learning. When it came to drawing the results together and interrogating the case study findings within the commissioned framework, these eight arenas had to be located back within the higher level five key elements. In most instances a case study was relevant to more than one of these five thematic elements. The purposeful emphasis on *learning* – echoing through the arenas listed above – was a preoccupying theme of the later of the combined team meetings. Ultimately it led to a sixth core element being drafted into the outline of the book proposed to come later: learning to learn.

With these variations, however, the sustained structure and focus is more remarkable than the diversion from or embellishment of the central themes. There were other alterations. In particular a 'month 33 deliverable milestone' for a conference for city administrations and academics was broken out into no less than six separate conferences at this penultimate phase: a 'roadshow' for each of what were then the five participating cities, using a common disseminate-and-discuss template, with local variations; and a wider one-day academic conference in Berlin. We return below to the question of dissemination and impact.

The Barcelona discourse – an empirical snapshot

The meeting over two days in January 2006 was the culmination of a singularly collegial and convivial three-year project involving four central teams (known as Team Tampere, Team Dublin etc.) together with the fifth, more part-time and ancillary, Team Melbourne. The special central interest of all involved, irrespective of their diverse academic disciplines of origin, was in learning. This interest encompassed ideas about reflexivity, the processes of learning how to learn organisationally, applications of learning and the relevance of social context. It called for repeated vigilance however, as the project drew to a close, to sustain this concentration and not be tempted away into studies of, in particular, administration and policy-making. One dialectic played out throughout these discussions was between learning and governance: was the project essentially about governance itself, or about governance as learning? Given the position of governance as the fifth, logically culminating, of the five key elements in the research design, and the intention to contribute to more capable governance through more capable learning, this threat of displacement was endemic.

> *At early stages in the project, team meetings usually commenced with a ritual discussion and questioning of the aims of the project, the meanings of terms and a renewal of consensus building. Whilst sometimes frustrating to members new to this kind of collaboration, these discussions are essential to the orientation and synchronisation of teams that meet only occasionally. We can see some of the work of building communities of practice which we mention below in this kind of behaviour.*

Ten commandments or eight?
The penultimate project meeting had sought to re-centre the work firmly on learning. A brainstorming session threw up two dozen essential features for a learning city-region which were reanalysed, redefined and pulled together

by local work and correspondence between full meetings into ten key characteristics or aspects of learning. This number was agreed to balance self-denial of complexity and sub-division with something short and clear enough to connect with the more busy and less reflective world of practice: both for communication and for using as the skeleton of the intended toolkit. The ten starting propositions (*Intelligent cities should*), included for example *have an ability to value and build up an inheritance of knowledge culture and institutions without being trapped in the past*; and *respond effectively to crisis and with an ability to generate a sense of urgency and avoid complacency.*

These ten propositions were reconsidered at the Barcelona meeting, in the context of shaping the toolkit for the use of cities in appraising their capacity as learning cities. This built on trialling of the application by team members before the meeting. The idea was to develop perhaps eight measures or indicators that could be used by all cities in all network settings or arenas. This would leave room for one or two further measures particular to that arena. Using all of these, workshop groups in the different areas could examine and assess together their performance, and consider ways of doing better.

A highly energised, sustained, creative and ultimately gruelling discussion followed, in which the checklist of ten was made, remade and made again. Each iteration led to questions about the scope and meaning of the reshaped item, sometimes about the scope, meaning and assumptions of familiar words; and to the recognition that in solving some problems of redundancy, duplication or omission, the revised checklist had in the process left out other important elements that has been included previously.

All this triumphantly illustrated the interconnectedness of each and all of the elements of learning, including conditions, processes, contexts and style characteristics. It displayed the infinite possible formulations of lower and higher order elements into different combinations, and the deep ambiguities of language and underlying assumption that many familiar terms contain. The long working session triumphed thus, illuminating again the limitations of simple terms and phrases in capturing complexity. As a quest for the best or one right answer it proved frustratingly, perhaps inevitably, elusive. In the end the ten starting propositions came out as *local knowledge, external knowledge, experiments/risk, involvement (inclusiveness), vision, foresight, neutral places of dissent and discussion – agora/debate,* and *valuing individuals.*

Distinctive mission, existential doubt

Perhaps the task, though innately difficult, would have been easier and solvable had it not been for the location of this work within a Mode Two rather than a Mode One approach (Gibbons et al., 1994). We were forever looking over our shoulders at what 'those who do' would make of the outcome, at how it could be used to examine and improve practice. We acknowledged the reality of short attention span. This limited the number of items that could be included, and the length of scale that might reasonably be used to distinguish between very good and very poor performance. And yet, even without the ambiguities of language, the task of capturing the complexity of community and organisational learning in a few checklist items is daunting. The reaction of even a sophisticated reader, looking at the outcome without having shared the blood and tears of its making, is 'so what? – all these terms have been spoken, written and regrouped a hundred times before'! Uninhibited by such utilitarian considerations, it would have been so much easier to refine and elaborate the concepts, using the abstractions and special argot with which academics address themselves through their myriad of specialised journals.

It is not surprising that here, as throughout the life of the project, there was recourse to metaphors. Nor is it to be wondered at that a frisson of existential doubt was acknowledged during these concluding sessions, despite three years of productive and often exhilarating collaboration: what if anything have we actually learned and are able to say after three years' hard labour? A different but almost simultaneous manifestation of this was the temporary refuge taken in this session in the known and published world of others. How do we locate and relate all that we have done in published, and thereby legitimated, and thereby safer, academic structures of saying and knowing? It required the sharp reminder that our primary reference for what we had to offer others – both scholars and practitioners – was what we had discovered empirically. The relevant secondary consideration was how to connect this with and locate it in 'the literature'; but not just make our finding and experience fit into that which was already legitimated. If so experienced and well-functioning a team can be tempted thus, spare a thought for the lonely novitiate doctoral student who tries to play safe by taking refuge in a standard 'textbook' thesis structure.

Iterative progress

This chapter makes no attempt to summarise or discuss the findings of the

Critical research project as such. Readers interested to pursue the substance of that work can visit the website, the reports and, in due course, the book, which will be prepared later this year. The focus here is on the deliberations and learning processes involved in the project itself. Can implications for knowledge making and knowledge using of this kind be generalised to other applied and developmental social science research that sets out to influence practice?

Metaphors and language

The Critical Team engaged periodically in a quest for metaphors that would encapsulate and bring to life essential understandings about human behaviours that sustain, or conversely negate, the possibility of 'intelligent territories'. Even here there lurk booby traps. Familiar, taken-for-granted terms of scholarship have different connotations in daily public language. The benefits of familiarity can make for other kinds of miscommunication. Such terms in this instance include *clusters* and *networks*. More politically fraught are the different uses of other familiar terms as *consultation, participation,* and *empowerment.*

One expression on which much of the formative and empirical midlife work of the project turned was *communities of practice.* Treated for brevity as *CoPs*, this term and concept, derived from the work of Wenger (2001), was a frequent touchstone and a reference point for interpreting field findings. Which of these cases have the characteristics of CoPs, and are therefore in some sense better – more grounded and integrated, more likely to produce results and sustain themselves over time? Later on, limitations were found in the explanatory power of this work and metaphor.

Two specific difficulties can be mentioned. The notion of the community of practice rooted in the workplace proved difficult to apply to some of the more nebulous and evolving, multi-layered associations investigated in the project, especially when contrasted with more structured formal groupings often within the same case studies. In addition the use of the word *communities* – another deceptively familiar term – created confusion given the proliferation of different communities and senses of that term experienced within the work of the project.

The team instead searched for another metaphor for a community and adopted, from the behaviour of dolphins, the term *pod*. A pod is a collective noun for dolphins, but more than that refers to a family community, which incorporates other individual animals at times, exhibits learned behaviour including language, and is re-scaleable as pods combine together into bigger units from time to time. The behaviour of dolphins seemed to manifest many of the essential features that explain the capacity to learn, to collaborate and so to work together well. Curiously, this apparently ideal metaphor drifted out of use for a while.

> *There is a degree of self-consciousness about the use of a metaphor such as the pod, and sometimes difficulty in communicating meaning to audiences not used to it. There is a tendency in presentations to introduce such terms in a light-hearted way, when what is often needed is a detailed account of the need for such a metaphor and the meanings incorporated into it. In the roadshow events we should perhaps have been much more emphatic about the use of the pod concept.*

In the end, in Barcelona the team had to remind itself of the pod. Possibly doubt was sown by a roadshow question as to the meaning of the word, the term being unfamiliar to some non-English speakers, suggesting that unfamiliarity undermined precisely its intended utility for transferring familiar understanding from one setting to another. The conversation at Barcelona took a brief excursion into other organised life forms, from bee swarms to ant colonies and beyond. By the end of the main project both CoPs and pods had survived, along with more familiar terms inhabiting the shared space between popular and specialised language, One term that got adopted in preference to *forum* was the Greek term *agora*, to connote a place, and indeed a culture, where open public discourse can take place. Whether this, like the pod, can catch on and serve us well remains to be seen.

Beyond the temptations and the risks of using metaphors to capture and breathe life into complex ideas and meanings, we ran into the corruption of language, which is a common feature of modern discourse, both public and scholarly as well. This takes more or less benign and malignant forms. It includes the almost purposeful and destructive wastefulness that accompanies the invention of new terms and meanings. Waste creates redundancy, draining good words of their meaning. It may also cost us our memory, much in the way that frequently changing bases for the collection of statistical data make sustained time series analysis impossible, obscuring changes in public policy behaviour and its outcomes.

Creating and recognising the spontaneous generation of new words and terms is part of living language, culture and scholarship – witness the recently celebrated expansion of the English language to exceed a million words. Less laudable is the sometimes innocent and well-intentioned colonisation of terms that then become unusable in their earlier sense. More reprehensible, and commoner still, are the uses of fashion to command support or curry favour, which in politics sits with sound bites rather than sustained argument.

Absolutely central to the Critical project is the (expanded later twentieth-century) notion of learning as social, contextual, grounded in experience and exercised by systems at levels above the individual learner: organisations and communities, cities, regions or territories. Around it floats the rich but nebulous concept of lifelong learning, the subject of serious if spasmodic intellectual and public policy analysis since the late 1960s. Both are undermined by the casual use of learning as a synonym for education or even training and the double reduction of lifelong learning to mean, also, no more than this. It is as politically *de rigeur* to speak of lifelong learning as it is to talk of 'going forward (into the future)', as also to speak in fashionably folksy estuarine. We need to be clear what essential terms mean and to use them consistently enough to create rather than to bury meaning.

A similarly unhelpful academic contribution to this trend is fuelled by a different quest for success: finding a new metaphor, a choice phrase or a crisp management tool can earn citations and recognition in the global seminar room, enhancing success. Snappy metaphorical titles and new terms can greatly assist – the empty raincoat, the creative classes, Mode Two knowledge production, bowling alone, even social capital and risk society. But as the Critical team found yet again, they can help understanding but may also obstruct inquiry.

The hard and the soft

We have called this section *iterative progress* , acknowledging many seemingly chronic and timeless tensions that presented themselves during the work of Project Critical. Several may be seen as repeating manifestations of essentially the same tension. They can be expressed as different paired terms, depending on the direction of approach. They feel uncomfortably familiar from projects in other times and places; for example:
- Quantity and quality;
- Product and process;
- Long-term and short-term;
- Economic and social.

At the most simple level these tensions can be summarised, and they are parodied as hard and soft. The dichotomy of philosophy, values and even style applies not only to academic orientation or scholarly preference, but equally to the making, implementing and evaluation of policy. The quest for accountability, value for money, and return on public no less than private investment demands exact measures of cost and benefit. Quantitative measurement cannot simply substitute for qualitative judgement. This desire for certainty tends to marginalise social changes and gains, unless they can be quantified. Thus the capacity to quantify social changes has become imperative. Some social indicators may be proving sensible and robust, but often we risk reducing subtle and complex social factors to those elements that can be lifted out and measured. The tendency of politics and the media to require immediate demonstrable gains, if not indeed the instant gratification thought to be necessary for popular support, adds to the difficulty. Wanting quick results further exacerbates a tendency to measure, only in economic terms, demonstrably direct products on a short timescale. Thus, too, products which are tangible and can be seen and weighed or measured are naturally favoured over process changes which are by contrast soft, intangible and, realistically speaking, often not honestly and fully measurable.

Managing the buried agenda
The Critical project, with sustainability as one core theme, confronted this as a recurrent dilemma at the heart of policy making. The team was concerned with how to recommend good practice in a world that leans to product rather than process, unintentionally lowering the value of learning – as process – that sat at the heart of this study. What this meant in practice was a kind of verbal horse-trading as the toolkit was deliberated: if there were not a suite of familiar (quantitative, economic-oriented, product-focused) indicators to command attention and respect, would the more important, deeper, longer-term changes in the capacity to learn, collaborate, evaluate and change, ever command serious attention from the administrations to whom the work was to be addressed?

Unless these timeless dilemmas can be resolved, they suggest that progress in understanding how policy can be made better and implemented more effectively will be at the best iterative, looping around the same predetermined circuit for the same reasons of orientation and style. If the behaviour patterns are essentially repetitious and 'programmed', progress and productivity may depend more on good or bad fortune to do with changing factors in the wider environment than on any learned capacity for improvement.

Part of the work of Critical had to do with getting a handle on these somewhat intangible factors, asking what kinds of 'toolkit' might allow administrators to move into a more reflective, confident, less instinctually self-protective, 'learning space'. Not only that, but how in reality would different places take it up and use it effectively? Other benchmarking and indicator devices have been produced, only to sit it out on the bench awaiting a call while the game moves on. Benchmarks are essentially comparative in a world that has been made essentially competitive. Can ways be devised for using a toolkit that sidesteps defensiveness and invidious public comparison, when reputation and publicly perceived performance rate so high? Is a toolkit of any practical use without an external facilitator? The same kinds of question confront the Pascal Observatory if it is to be a medium for enhancing learning and policy-in-action, rather than just for its scholarly discourse.

Making change happen – dilemmas of dissemination and diffusion

Practical difficulties
Among the more tangible factors thrown up by the Critical project, we may briefly add to those already mentioned above, technical problems involved in achieving comparability across cities, even within Europe. Not only is each context and story unique in important ways (historically, culturally, economically, geographically, politically), but the 'basic facts' within which comparison might take place are inaccessible, flawed or simply non-existent, despite the large volume of cross-European data collection throughout the EU era.

The principle of taking learning to practitioners also proves elusive. Some are too busy, indifferent or even complacent. For those 'owning' the learning, there are tensions between transparency on the one hand and efficacy on the other. There are very practical considerations about who to 'target' when and how: which leadership, which key players, at what opportune moment? In terms of benchmarks, indicators and other tools, what works for whom? In principle the wide and open sharing of everything with all stakeholders seems attractive. This would however be naïve. It would deny realities about the exercise of power and the limits of participation that the Critical research exposed.

Indeed, questions of politics, power and governance represented another, largely unsurfaced, 'existential crisis' for the project team. The focus on governance rather than politics, even the creative and consensual, intelligently egalitarian, management and life of the project itself, may have tended to avert attention from the implications of deep inequalities uncovered in some of the case studies. Community and network participation in shared public learning is often, maybe brutally, limited by what those in power will tolerate.

Commissioning and disseminating agencies and approaches

The purpose of the Pascal International Observatory is to enable better movement and use of knowledge about place management, social capital, and learning city-regions and communities in the context of a new global knowledge economy, lifelong learning and the need for sustainability. The objectives of Critical as set out at the beginning of this chapter are close and relevant. Its primary purpose was the creation of new knowledge about the learning and governance of intelligent (or learning) city-regions, with a view to generating and disseminating understanding useful for better practice. Pascal is centred on an intention to locate the agenda with policy-makers and practitioners and to explore ways whereby scholars and their universities as knowledge-makers can create more productive and more mutual partnership with those who are mainly knowledge-users.

Pascal employs what might be termed passive means with active intent, based on a website that carries news and Hot Topics, together with other relevant information and data linkages, while encouraging discussion of issues raised especially by Hot Topics through this medium. It also conducts living conversations and more active learning through conferences, seminars, site visits and by means of different forms of mutual learning exchange and consultancy. It is considering more extended brokerage services and the evaluation, dissemination and perhaps more active promotion of indicators and toolkits, as its experience of and ideas about the dissemination and use of innovation mature.

The European Commission, the body that commissioned the Critical research project, also takes a keen interest in the dissemination of its work. One needs to ask however how far this intention is and can be translated into purposeful and active, rather than essential passive, dissemination. The EC works within political constraints. It must judge how far it can risk provoking the protective principle of subsidiarity and jealousy about local autonomy without provoking hostility. It would be fair to say that while dissemination is written into the contest for its research grants, this takes a fairly passive form: website and published materials, occasional conferences and seminars, rather than a highly strategic or targeted, active approach.

The same is true for the English Higher Education Funding Council (HEFCE), working between the latent jealousies of the central government Department for Education and Skills (DfES) and a universities clientele jealous of institutional autonomy, irritable about interference and even light-of-touch steering. The Research Councils, notably in this case and for the UK the Economic and Social Research Council (ESRC), have become increasingly clear, strategic and assertive in seeking the application and active use, not merely the passive and more leisurely journal and monograph-based scholarly dissemination, of the research that they cause to be produced. End-users feature in bids. Dissemination is seen in progressive and formative terms, along with evaluation, as the project proceeds. Some groundwork is now funded to prepare the way (for example create the networks) for more programmatic research initiatives to gain purchase and have impact.

These demands for active application of knowledge within research projects again often confuse product and process. In my experience the project is likely to be just one element in a broader portfolio of work that evolves over time, and the transfer of knowledge into practice may take place across this wider process and not just within the scope of an individual project. Research Councils betray their own insecurity and limited experience of knowledge application by expecting such outcomes within the timescale of projects that are simultaneously expected to yield academic outputs. In reality application is more likely to take place in the consultancy study that follows on from the research project or through the flows of staff and students in the longer term.

Making knowledge work

Without question the world has turned, compared with the heyday of traditional exclusively academic research. The mourners grow fewer with the passing years. Co-production, the shared utilisation and exploitation of knowledge, is increasingly normal and often big core business for more universities and some parts of some private and public sector corporations. And yet, reflecting back on the discussion of the Critical project, the quest for effective dissemination is not all over; we have some way to go before we really know how to 'make knowledge work'. The worlds of academic scholars and 'those who do' are still often poles apart; mutual stereotyping has not ended. The realities of different roles and reward systems persist. Division is not assisted by repeated failure to take 'joined-up government' beyond rhetoric into instinctual good practice. It is exacerbated by tightly sectoral audit and accountability requirements on both sides. The cultural pulls of different values, traditions, *mores* and tribal elders remain. Looked at thus, one might well ask whether Mode 2 knowledge production really is attainable, other than in small corners and for short periods of time.

Towards the end of the Barcelona meeting a session dedicated to dissemination was brief and uncontroversial, attending mainly to which outlets were most fitting for which parts of what had been or was being written. In fact the main discussion about dissemination had already occurred much earlier, under cover of the creation and use of a toolkit. The reality was acknowledged that Critical was a temporary organisation without the resources (however wistful the desire) to continue working together. A self-financing summer school was all that could be considered beyond the period of life-according-to-EU-funds: not so much sustainability as a temporary EU fillip for one part of a loose and larger scholarly network. If the ideas were to be carried further into action, other probably local means are required; or purposeful, preferably inbuilt, partnership with ongoing institutions like Pascal, which have the capacity to sustain learning-in-action across the thinking-and-doing divide.

This consideration uncovered one further relevant consideration – the important and honourable role of *opportunism* in permitting innovation and sustaining development. It was a barely acknowledged disappointment about the modestly attended but vigorously engaged Critical roadshows that policy-makers and administrators were less prevalent than those who were themselves engaged academy-based scholars, with a sprinkling of others of similar persuasion working with regional and local authorities or in relevant consultancy companies. It would be fanciful to consider the roadshows as powerful direct dissemination events from research into its application.

On the other hand, the participation of one or two key players strategically located in a key regional or local body is enough to give leverage, and for the constituent teams of Project Critical, back in their home bases, to carry the process forward into city-region learning and perhaps changed behaviour. Where the soil is 'opportunistically fertile', the past and future of the informal 'Pascal college' may provide authority, expertise, and robust stimulation to carry on. As was suggested above, such inter-city and inter-regional comparison is only possible where there is enough trust and self-confidence to share and compare. Then a benevolent spiral of learning and enhanced governance may be possible, and knowledge may indeed be made to work.

Notes

[1] Handy, 1994; Florida, 2002; Gibbons et al., 1994; Putnam, 2001; and Beck, 1992.

References

Accent (2006). *Service Priority, Accessibility and Quality in Rural Scotland.* Edinburgh: Scottish Executive (in press).

Alexander, W. (2001). *A Smart, Successful Scotland: Ambitions for the Enterprise Networks.* Edinburgh: Scottish Executive.

Alford, J. and O'Niell, D. (eds) (1994). *The Contract State: Public Management and the Kennett Government.* Geelong: Deakin University.

Alheit P. and Dausien B. (2002). 'The "double face" of lifelong learning: two analytical perspectives on a "silent revolution"', *Studies in the Education of Adults,* 34(1): 3–22.

American Studies (2002). *Social Movements and Culture.* Pullman WA: Washington State University.

Anastacio, J., Gidley, B., Hart, L., Keith, M., Mayo, M. (2000). *Reflecting Realities: Participants' Perspectives on Integrated Communities and Sustainable Development.* Bristol: Policy Press:

Arber, S. and Ginn, J. (eds) (1995). *Connecting Gender and Ageing: A Sociological Approach.* Buckingham: Open University Press.

Aucoin, P. (1990). 'Administrative reform in public management: Paradigms, principles, paradoxes, pendulums', *Governance,* 3(2): 115–37.

Australian Learning Communities Network (2002). *A Lifetime of Discovery .* 2002 Australian Learning Communities Conference.

Australian National Training Authority (2004). *National Industry Skills Report.* Sydney: ANTA.

Bailey N., Flint, J. Goodlad, R., Shucksmith, M., Fitzpatrick, S., and Pryce,

G. (2003). *Measuring Deprivation in Scotland*. Edinburgh: Scottish Executive Central Statistics Unit.

Ball, C. and Stewart, D. (1995). *An Action Agenda for Lifelong Learning for the 21st Century*, Report from the First Global Conference on Lifelong Learning (ed N Longworth), European Lifelong Learning Initiative, Brussels.

Bauman, Z. (2000). *Liquid Modernity*. Cambridge: Polity Press.

Beck, U. (1992). *Risk Society: Towards a New Modernity*, Cambridge: Polity Press.

Bélanger, A. and Côté, J.F. (eds) (2005). 'Le spectacle des villes' *Sociologie et Sociétés*, XXVII: 5–13.

Belanger, P. and Federighi, P. (2000). *Unlocking Peoples' Creative Forces. A Transnational Analysis of Adult Learning Policies*, Hamburg: UNESCO Institute for Education.

Bélanger, P. and Tuijnman, A. (ed.) (1997). *Shifting Patterns in Adult Education Participation*. London: Pergamon Press.

Bélanger, P. and Valdivielso, S. (ed.) (1997). *The Emergence of Learning Societies. Who Participates in Adult Education?* London: Pergamon Press.

Bélanger, P. (1994). 'Lifelong Learning: The Dialectics of 'Lifelong Education', *International Review of Education,* 40(3–5): 353–381.

Bélanger, P. (2003). 'Learning environment and environmental adult education', in Clover, D. 2003, (coll.) *Environmental Adult Learning*. San Francisco: Jossey-Bass.

Bélanger, P. and Paetsch, B. (2004). *Montréal, Ville Apprenante*. Montréal: UQAM/CIRDEP.

Benfield, J., Terris, N, and Vorsanger, N. (2001) *Solving Sprawl: Models of Smart Growth in Communities across America*, FK – Islandpress.org.

Benseman, J. (1996). 'Participation in the fourth sector', in Benseman, J., Findsen, B. and Scott, M. (eds). *The Fourth Sector: Adult and Community Education in Aotearoa/New Zealand* pp. 274–284. Palmerston North: The Dunmore Press.

Berkman, L.F. and Glass, T. (2000). 'Social integration, social networks, social support, and health', in Berkman L.F. and Kawachi I. (eds) *Social Epidemiology.* Oxford: Oxford University Press.

Bernard, M., Itzin, C., Phillipson, C. and Skucha, J. (1995). 'Gendered work, gendered retirement', in Arber, S. and Ginn, J. (eds). *Connecting Gender and Ageing: A Sociological Approach.* (pp. 56–68). Buckingham: Open University Press.

Bessant, J. and Watts, R. (2005). *Talking Policy.* Melbourne: Longmans.

Biggs, S. (1993). *Understanding Ageing: Images, Attitudes and Professional Practice.* Buckingham: Open University Press.

Blackledge, D. and Hunt, D. (1985). *Sociological Interpretations of Education.* London: Croom Helm.

Blackmore, J. (2002). *Learning Networks as New Educational Spaces and Strategies of Educational Reform in Response to Risk and Interdependence.* Lisbon: Deakin University.

Bonita, R. (1993). 'Older Women: A Growing Force', in Koopman-Boyden, P.G. (ed). *New Zealand's Ageing Society: The Implications.* (pp. 189–212). Wellington: Daphne Brasell Associates Press.

Botkin, J. (2002) *Towards a Wisdom Society* [online] http://www.swaraj.org/shikshantar/ls2_botkin.pdf

Bourdieu, P. (1980) 'Le capital social: notes provisoires', *Actes de la Récherche en Sciences Sociales,* 2–3

Bourdieu, P. (1986). 'The forms of capital', in Richardson, J., *Handbook of Theory and Research for the Sociology of Education*, pp. 241–258, Westport, CT: Greenwood.

Brown, P. and Lauder, H. (2001). *Capitalism and Social Progress. The Future of Society in a Global Economy*, New York: Palgrave.

Burns, D. and Taylor, M. (2000). *Auditing Community Participation*, York: Joseph Rowntree Foundation:

Bytheway, B. (1995). *Ageism.* Buckingham: Open University Press.

Campaign for Learning (1998–2006). *Why Learn?*

Campbell, C., Wood, R. and Kelly, M. (1999). *Social Capital and Health.* London: Health Education Authority.

Candy, J. (2003). *Planning Learning Cities. Addressing Globalisation Locally.* http://www.kas.de/upload/dokumente/megacities/LearningCities.

Capello, R. (2002). 'Knowledge, innovation and economic growth. The theory and practice of learning regions', in Book Reviews. *Papers in Regional Science*, 81: 131–137.

Cara S., and Ranson S. (1998). *Learning Towns and Cities – "The Toolkit" – Practice, Progress and Value – Learning Communities: Assessing the Value They Add*. Birmingham: DfEE.

Cara, S. (1993). *Learning Towns and City* (conference report), Leicester: NIACE.

Cara, S. (2003). *The Learning Community: Background and Models*. e-mail communication.

Carlton, S. and Soulsby, J. (1999). *Learning to Grow Older and Bolder: A policy discussion paper on learning in later life*. Leicester: NIACE.

Carmin, C. (1988). 'Issues on research on mentoring: definitional and methodological', *International Journal of Mentoring*, 2(2):9–13.

Caro, F.G. and Bass, S.A. (1995). 'Increasing volunteering among older people', in Caro, F.G. and Bass, S.A. (eds). *Older and Active: How Americans over 55 are Contributing to Society*. (pp. 71–96). New Haven, Connecticut: Yale University Press.

Castells, M. (2003). 'The new historical relationship between space and society', in Cuthbert, Alexander R. (ed.) *Designing Cities: Critical Readings in Urban Design*, pp. 59–68. Oxford: Blackwell.

Castels, M. (2000). *The Rise of Network Societies*. Oxford: Blackwell.

Cavaye, J. (2002). *Learning Town Evaluation Framework*. Melbourne: Victorian Learning Communities Network.

Cavaye, J. (2005). 'Social capital: a commentary on issues, understanding and measurement' in Duke, C., Osborne, M., Wilson, B. (eds.) (2005) *Rebalancing the Social and Economic: Learning, Partnership and Place*. Leicester: NIACE.

Chanan, G., Gilchrist, A., and West, A. (1999). *SRB6: Involving the Community*. London: Community Development Foundation Publications.

Charles D.R. et al. (1999). *The Core Cities: Key Centres for Regeneration*, Report to the Core Cities Group (representing the cities of Birmingham, Bristol, Leeds, Liverpool, Manchester, Sheffield and Newcastle).

Charles, D.R. (2001). *Universities in Regional Development (UNIREG) TSER project final report*, CURDS, Newcastle.

Chavagneux, C. (1997). *Les Institutions Internationales et la Gouvernance de L'Economie Mondial*. Paris: La Découverte. coll. Repères

Christoforou, A. (2004). 'On the determinants of Social Capital in Countries of the European Union', *ESPAnet Conference*, Oxford.

Clark, J. (2001). *Glasgow the Learning City: Lifelong Learning and Regeneration*. Glasgow: Scottish Enterprise.

Colebatch, T. (2004). 'Unemployment rate drops', *The Age*. Melbourne, 9 April.

Coleman, J.S. (1988). 'Social capital in the creation of human capital', *American Journal of Sociology*, 94: S95–S121.

Coleman, S. and Gotze, J. (2001). *'Bowling Together: online public engagement in policy deliberation'*, Hansard Society, London. www.handardsociety.org.uk accessed September 2004.

Collins, D. (2005). 'Are we breaking down the Silos?' in Pascal, *Making Knowledge Work, Conference Proceeding*, Stirling, p. 53–60.

Collins, M. (1998). *Critical Crosscurrents in Education*. Malabar, Florida: Krieger Publishing.

Commission of the European Union (2001). *'Memorandum on Lifelong Learning for Active Citizenship in a Europe of Knowledge'*, DG Education and Culture, Brussels.

Commission of the European Union (2001). 'The local and Regional Dimension of Lifelong Learning: creating learning cities, towns and regions', A European Policy Paper from the TELS project (ed Longworth, N.), DG Education and Culture, Brussels.

Communities Scotland (2005a). *National Standards for Community Engagement*, Edinburgh: Communities Scotland http://www.communitiesscotland.gov.uk/stellent/groups/public/documents/w ebpages/lccs_008411.pdf (accessed 18/03/06).

Communities Scotland (2005b). *National Standards for Community Engagement Guidance,* Edinburgh: Communities Scotland http://www.communitiesscotland.gov.uk/stellent/groups/public/documents/ webpages/cs_006607.hcsp (accessed 18/03/06).

Considine M.P. (2004). *Community Strengthening and the Role of Local Government*. Melbourne: Local Government Victoria.

Considine, M. (2003). 'Networks and inter-activity: making sense of front-line governance in the United Kingdom, the Netherlands and Australia', *Journal of European Public Policy'* 10(1): 46–58.

Considine, M. (2004). '*Building Connections: community strengthening and local Government in Victoria*'. Melbourne: Department for Victorian Communities.

Cooke, P. and Morgan, K. (1998). *The Associational Economy: Firms, Regions and Innovation*. Oxford: Oxford University Press.

Cooke, P. (1999). *Social capital in the learning region*. <http://www.ebms.it/SS/documents/cooke_1999_social%20capital%20in%20the%20learning%20region.pdf.>.

Dasgupta, P. (2000). 'Economic progress and the idea of social capital', pp. 325–424 in P. Dasgupta and I. Serageldin (eds), *Social Capital: A Multifaceted Perspective*. Washington DC: World Bank.

DCITA (2005). *The Role of ICT in Building Communities and Social Capital*. Canberra: Australian Government, Department of Communications, Information Technology and the Arts.

Dempster, T.L. (2001). Proposal to establish Stirling Business Panel. Scottish Enterprise Internal Document, March.

Department for Victorian Communities (2002a). *Community Capacity Building*. Melbourne: Victorian Government.

Department for Victorian Communities (2002b). *Overview, Department for Victorian Communities*. Melbourne: Victorian Government.

Department for Victorian Communities (2004). *Department for Victorian Communities*. Melbourne: Victorian Government.

Dewey, J. (1938). *Experience and Education*. New York: Collier Books.

DfES (2005). *14–19 Education and Skills Implementation Plan*. London: HMSO.

DfES (2005). *14–19 Education and Skills, White Paper*. London: HMSO.

Dika, S. L. and Singh, K. (2002). Applications of social capital in educational literature: a critical synthesis, *Review of Educational Research*, 72(1): 31–60.

DPC (2001). *Growing Victoria Together*. Melbourne: Department of Premier and Cabinet, State.

Duke, C., Osborne, M., Wilson, B. (2005) 'Beyond the economic: finding balanced development in a global environment' in Duke, C., Osborne, M., Wilson, B. (2005) (eds) *Rebalancing the Social and Economic. Learning Partnership and Place*. Leicester: NIACE.

Dunn, S. (2005). *A Study of Leadership Styles that Encourage Self-Scrutiny in Schools*. Unpublished MSc Dissertation Salford University

DVC (Department for Victorian Communities) (2004). *Indicators of Community Strength in Victoria*. Melbourne: Department for Victorian Communities. www.dvc.vic.gov.au/spar.htm accessed November 2004.

Ebers, M. (2002). *The Formation of Inter-Organisational Networks*. Oxford: Oxford University Press.

Edinburgh City Council (2005). 'City in business for a successful Edinburgh'. News release, May 4. Retrieved 10 March 2006 from http://edinburghguide.com/edgforum/viewtopic.php?p=2947&sid=3a9d78dc f5cd5282cb1e3d0af91b96b1.

Eger, J.M. (1996). 'Building Smart Communities: a new framework for an American information initiative', address to the *International Telecommunication Union*, Rio de Janeiro, June 1996 [online] http://www.smartcommunities.org/library_newframe.htm

Euridyce (2002). *Citizenship education at school in Europe*. Brussels: European Unit.

European Commission (2005). *The Luxembourg Declaration*. Online at http://www.eu2005.lu/en/actualites/documents_travail/2005/04/26declalux/y outhforum.pdf

European Foundation for Management Development (2005). *Globally responsible leadership – a call for engagement*. Brussels: EFMD.

Faris, R. and Peterson, W. (2000). *Learning-Based Community Development: Lessons Learned for British Columbia*. Ministry of Community Development, Cooperatives and Volunteers.

Faris, R. (2001). *The Way Forward: Building a Learning Nation Community by Community*, draft for Walter & Duncan Gordon Foundation.

Faris, R. (2002). *A Model for Developing Learning Communities*. Annual Meeting, Albury Wodonga. Australian Learning Communities Network.

Farmer, J., Hinds, K., Richards, H. and Godden, D. (2004). *Access, Satisfaction and Expectations: A Comparison of Attitudes to Health Care in Rural and Urban Scotland*. Edinburgh: Scottish Centre for Social Research.

Faure, E., Herrera, F., Kaddowa, A., Lopes, H., Petrovsky, A., Rahnema, M. and Ward, F. (1972). *Learning to Be: The World of Education Today and Tomorrow*. Paris: UNESCO.

Field, J. (2001). Lifelong Education, *International Journal of Lifelong Education*. 20(1–2): 3–15.

Field, J. (2002). *Lifelong Learning and the New Educational Order*. Stoke on Trent: Trentham Books.

Field, J. (2003). *Social Capital*. London: Routledge.

Field, J. (2005). *Social Capital and Lifelong Learning*. Bristol: Policy Press.

Field, J. (2005). 'Social networks, innovations and learning: can policies for social capital promote both dynamism and justice', in Duke, C., Osborne, M., Wilson, B. (eds.) 2005, *Rebalancing the Social and Economic. Learning Partnership and Place*. Leicester: NIACE.

Fife Economic Forum (2006). Business Partnership Initiative Progress Report. Fife Economic Forum Meeting Agenda Item No. 6. Scottish Enterprise Internal Document, February 26.

Findsen, B. (2002). 'Developing a conceptual framework for understanding older adults and learning', *The New Zealand Journal of Adult Learning*, 30(2): 34–52.

Findsen, B. (2005). *Learning Later*. Malabar: Krieger Publishing Co.

Florida, R. (1995). 'Toward the Learning Region', *Futures*, 27(5): 527–536.

Florida, R. (2002) *The Rise of the Creative Class and how it's Transforming Work, Leisure, Community and Every Day Life*. New York: Perseus Books group.

Fullan, M. (2004). *System Thinkers in Action; Moving Beyond the Standards Plateaux,* Department for Education and Skills. London: HMSO.

Gibbons, M., Limoges, C., Nowotny, H., Schwatzman, S., Scott, P. and Trow, M. (1994). *The New Production of Knowledge*. London: Sage.

Gibson, T.A. (2005). 'La ville et le spectacle: commentaires sur l'utilisation du spectacle dans la sociologie urbaine contemporaine', *Sociologie et Sociétés*, XXVII: 171–196.

Giddens, A. (1994). 'Risk, trust, reflexivity', in U. Beck, A. Giddens and S. Lash, *Reflexive Modernization. Politics, Tradition and Aesthetics in the Modern Social Order*. Stanford: California.

Glaeser, E.L., Laibson, D. and Sacerdote, B. (2002). 'An economic approach to social capital', *The Economic Journal*, 112: 437–58

Glaser, H. (1991). 'Mythos und Realität der Stadt' [Myth and Reality of the City], in: *Deutsches Institut für Urbanistik* (ed.), Berlin: Kohlhammer, pp. 11–29.

Glendenning, F. (ed.) (2000). *Teaching and Learning in Later Life: Theoretical Implications.* Aldershot: Ashgate.

Goldsworthy, J. (2001). *Resurrecting a Model of Integrating Individual Work with Community Development and Social Action.* International Community Development Conference.

Granovetter, M. (1974). *Getting a Job.* Cambridge MA: Harvard Uni Press.

Greenwood, D., Gonsalez Santos, J. L., et al. (1992). *Industrial Democracy as Process: Participatory Action Research in the Fagor Cooperative Group of Mondragon,* Social Science for Social Action: towards organisational renewal, Vol. 2. Stockholm: Arbetslivscentrum/van Gorcum, Assen.

Grossman, G.M. and Helpman, E. (1992). *Protection for Sale.* N.J.: Princeton.

Hall, P. (2000). Creative Cities and Economic Development, *Urban Studies,* 37(4): 639–649.

Halpern, D. (2001). 'Moral values, social trust and inequality: can values explain crime?', *British Journal of Criminology,* 41(2): 236–251.

Handy, C. (1994). *The Empty Raincoat: Making Sense of the Future.* Hutchinson.

Hannigan, J. (2003). 'Symposium on branding, the entertainment economy, and urban place building: Introduction', *International Journal of Urban and Regional Research, 27*: 352–360.

Harvey, D (1989). *The Urban Experience.* Baltimore, MD: Johns Hopkins University Press.

Harvey, D. (1990). *The Conditions of Post-modernity.* Oxford: Blackwell.

Healy, T. and Côté, S. (2001) *The Well-Being of Nations: The Role of Human and Social Capital.* Paris: OECD.

Henderson L, Castles, R., McGrath, M., and Brown, T. (2000). *Learning Around Town: Learning Communities in Australia.* Canberra; Adult Learning Australia (ALA).

Hess, M. and Adams D. (2001). 'Community in public policy: fad or foundation?', *Australian Journal of Public Administration,* 60(2): 13–24.

Hess, M., and Adams, D. (2002). 'Knowing and skilling in contemporary public administration', *Australian Journal of Public Administration*, 61(4): 68–79.

HGLV (2004). *Learning Together – An Introduction to the Hume Global Learning Village and our Strategy – 2004–2008*. Hume City: Hume City Council.

Hodgson, A. (ed.) (2001). *Policies, Politics and the Future of Lifelong Learning*. London: Kogan Page.

Howard, J. (1998). 'Speech to the World Economic Forum Dinner', Melbourne, 16 March 1998.

Howard, J. (1999). 'Building a Stronger and Fairer Australia: Liberalism in Economic Policy and Modern Conservatism in Social Policy', speech to the Australia Unlimited Roundtable, 4 April, 1999.

http://www.demos.co.uk/catalogue/networks/ Accessed February 2005.

http://www.dfes.gov.uk/publications/14-19educationandskillsria.shtml/ reference1268-2005DCL-en(accessed 1/02/06)

http://www.dfes.gov.uk/publications/14-19implementationplan(accessed 6/03/06)

http://www.jrf.org.uk/knowledge/findings/foundations/169.asp) (accessed 14/03/06).

http://www.standards.dfes.gov.uk/innovation-unit/pdf/SystemThinkersin Action.pdf?version=1(accessed 1/08/05)

Hyppä, M. and Mäki, J. (2001). 'Why do Swedish-speaking Finns have a longer active life? An area for social capital research', *Health Promotion International*, 16(1): 55–64

iEARN International Education and Resource Network (2005). http://www.iearn.org/projects/index.html

Ife, J. (2002). *Community Development*. Frenchs Forest: Pearson Education Australia.

Inglehart, R. (1977). *The Silent Revolution: Changing Values and Political Styles among Western Publics*. Princeton: Princeton University Press.

Jarvis, P. (1985). *Sociological Perspectives on Lifelong Education and Lifelong Learning*. Athens, Georgia: Department of Adult Education, University of Georgia.

Jarvis, P. (2001). *Learning in Later Life: An Introduction for Educators and Carers*. London: Kogan Page.

Jerrome, D. (1998). (2nd ed) 'Intimate relationships', in Bond, J., Coleman, P. and Peace, S. (eds) *Ageing in Society: An Introduction to Social Gerontology* (pp. 226–254). London: Sage Publications.

Jessop, B. (2004). Critical semiotic analysis and cultural political economy, *Critical Discourse Studies*, 1(2): 159–174.

Joseph Rowntree Foundation (1999). *Developing Effective Community Involvement Strategies – Guidance for Single Regeneration Budget Bids,* York: Joseph Rowntree Foundation.

Judd, D. and Swansttrom, T. (1994) *City Politics: Private Power and Public Policy*. New York: Harper Collins.

Kearns, P. (ed.) (2001). *Australian National Training Authority Learning Communities National Project 2001 – Briefing Notes for Communities.* Canberra: Global Learning Services.

Kearns, P. (2004). *Journey Down a Shifting Path – Learning Communities in Practice*, Be Shaken – Learning for Change, The 3rd Australian Learning Communities Conference, Newcastle.

Kearns, P., McDonald, R., Candy, P., Knights, S. and Papadopoulos, G. (1999). *VET in the Learning Age: The Challenge of Lifelong Learning for All.* NCVER 2.

Kemmis, S. and McTaggart, R. (1988). *The Action Research Planner*, 3rd ed., Deakin University.

Kenny, S. (1994). *Developing Communities for the Future: Community Development in Australia*. Australia: Thomas Nelson.

Kenny, S. (1999). *Developing Communities for the Future: Community Development in Australia*. Australia: Thomas Nelson.

Kent County Council (2005). *Nurturing Autonomous and Creative Learners Secondary Strategy Phase 2*. Maidstone: Kent County Council

Kent County Council (2005a). *The Kent Virginia Project*, Summary available from Principal Regeneration & Projects Officer, Strategic Planning, Kent County Council

Kent County Council (2005b). *KCC European Strategy summary*, available from Principal Regeneration & Projects Officer, Strategic Planning, Kent County Council

Kenyon, P. (2006). *Behaviours and actions that develop community health, resilence and sustainability – some useful checklists*. Bank of Ideas.

Konvitz, J. (2006). *Cities: Challenges for Growth and Governance* (Pascal Hot Topic). Melbourne: Pascal.

Korpi, T. (2001). 'Good friends in bad times? Social networks and job search among the unemployed in Sweden', *Acta Sociologica*, 33(2): 157–70.

Kosky, L. (2002). Knowledge and Skills for the Innovation Economy – A statement by The Hon. Lynne Kosky, MP, Minister for Education and Training on the future directions for the Victorian education and training system. Melbourne: Department of Education and Training.

Kosky, L. (Minister for Education) (2003). *Blueprint for Government Schools*. Melbourne: Department of Education and Training.

Kumlin, S. and Rothstein, B. (2005). 'Making and breaking social capital: The impact of welfare-state institutions', *Comparative Political Studies*, 38(4): 339–365.

Lahrèche-Révil, A. (2002). *Intégration Internationale et Interdépendances Mondiales*. Paris: La Découverte. coll. Repères.

Lamdin, L. and Fugate, M. (1997). *Elderlearning: New Frontier in an Aging Society*. American Council on Education: Oryx Press.

Landry, C. (2000). *The Creative City*. London: Earthscan Publications.

Landry, C. and Matarasso, F. (1998). *The Learning-City Region: Approaching Problems of the Concept, its Measurement and Evaluation – A Discussion Document*, Gloucester: Comedia.
http://www.ala.asn.au/conf/2003/melville.pdf

Lash, S. and Urry, J. (1994). *Economics of Signs and Space*. London: Sage.

Laslett, P. (1989). *A Fresh Map of Life: The Emergence of the Third Age*. London: Weidenfeld and Nicholson.

Le Bas, C., Picard, F., and Suchecki, B. (1998). 'Innovation technologique, comportement de reseaux et performances: une analyse sur données individuelles', *Revue d'Économie Politique*, 108(5): 625–44.

Léveque, M. and White, D. (2001). 'Capital social, capital humain et sortie de l'aide sociale pour des prestataires de longue durée', *Canadian Journal of Sociology*, 26(2): 167–192.

LILARA project (2006). Details from University of Stirling Centre for

Research into Lifelong Learning, Airthrey Castle, Stirling

Lin, N. (2001). *Social Capital: A Theory of Social Structure and Action*. Cambridge: Cambridge University Press.

Livingstone, D. (2001). *Mapping the Iceberg. The Research Network for New Approaches to Lifelong Learning*. http://www.oise.utoronto.ca/depts/sese/csew/nall/res/54DavidLivingstone.pdf.

Loch Lomond and the Trossachs National Park Authority (2005). *National Park Plan 2005 Consultative Draft*. Balloch: LLTNPA.

Longworth, N. (1999). *Making Lifelong Learning Work: Learning Cities for a Learning Century*. London: Kogan Page Limited.

Longworth, N. (2001). *Towards a European Learning Society (TELS)*, Project Report presented to the European Commission Nov 2000, also available on www.tels.euproject.org

Longworth, N. (1999). *Lifelong Learning at Work – Learning Cities for Learning Century*. London: Kogan Page.

Longworth, N. (2003). *Lifelong Learning in Action: Transforming 21st Century Education*. London: Kogan Page.

Longworth, N. (2006). *Learning Cities, Learning Regions, Learning Communities: Lifelong Learning and Local Government*. London: Taylor and Francis.

Longworth, N. and Allwinkle, S. (2005). '*The PALLACE project: linking learning cities and regions in Europe, North America, Australasia and China*'. Final Report to the European Commission, Napier University, Edinburgh, [online] www.pallace.net

Longworth, N. and Davies, W. K. (1996). *Lifelong Learning: New Visions, New Implications, New Roles for Industry, Government, Education and the Community for the 21st Century*. London: Kogan Page.

Martin, J. and Faris, R. (2005). *Learning Communities and Regions in British Columbia, Canada and Victoria*, draft paper.

Maskell, P., Eskelinen, H., Hannibalsson, I., Malmberg, A. and Vatne, E. (1998). *Competitiveness, Localised Learning and Regional Development: Specialisation and Prosperity in Small Open Economies*. London: Routledge.

Massiah, G. (2003). *Dans le Chaos de L'Après-Guerre. Le G8, Un Club de Riches Très Contesté.* www.monde-diplomatique.fr

McClusky, H.Y. (1974). 'Education for aging: The scope of the field and perspectives for the future', in Grabowski, S. and Mason, W.D. (eds). *Learning for Aging.* Washington, D.C.: Adult Education Association of the USA.

McGivney, V. (1990). *Education's for other People: Access to Education for Non-Participant Adults.* Leicester: NIACE.

McGivney, V. (1999). *Excluded Men: Men who are Missing from Education and Training.* Leicester: NIACE.

McGivney, V. (2004). *Men Earn, Women Learn: Bridging the Gender Gap Divide in Education and Training.* Leicester: NIACE.

McNulty (2004). Keynote Presentation: *Overview of 2003 Australian Tour and where are we heading: What are some of the pitfalls and signposts? Reflections from abroad: What's happening with UK Learning Communities?*, Be Shaken – Learning for Change, The 3rd Australian Learning Communities Conference, Newcastle.

Medel-Añonuevo, C., Ohsako, T., Mauch, W. (2001). *Revisiting Lifelong Learning for the 21st Century.* Hamburg: UNESCO Institute for Education.

Mezirow, J. (1991). *Transformative Dimensions of Adult Learning.* San Francisco: Jossey-Bass.

Miller, S., Hickson, D. and Wilson, D. (1996). 'Decision-making in organizations' in S. Clegg, C. Hardy and W. Nord, *Handbook of Organization Studies.* London: Sage.

Mintzberg, H. and Waters, J. (1990). 'Studying deciding: an exchange of views between Mintzberg and Waters, Pettigrew, and Butler', *Organization Studies* 11(1): 2–16.

Moen, P., Dempster-McClain, D. and Erickson, M.A. (1992). 'Successful aging: a life-course perspective on women's multiple roles and health', *American Journal of Sociology.* 97(6): 1612–38.

Morgensen, U.K, Lenain, P. and Royuela-Mora, V. (2004). *The Lisbon Strategy at Midterm – Expectations and Reality.* Warsaw: Centre for Social and Economic Research.

Morrissey, M. and McGinn, P. (2001). *Evaluating Community Based and Voluntary Activity in Northern Ireland: Interim Report.* Belfast: Community Evaluation Northern Ireland.

Mott, G. (2004). *14–19 Education and Training: New Patterns of Provision*. Strood: EMIE at NFER

Mowbray, M. (2005). 'Community, the state and social capital impact statement', in Duke, C., Osborne, M., Wilson, B. *Rebalancing the Social and Economic: Learning Partnership and Place*. Leicester: NIACE.

Nash, V. (2004). 'Public policy and social networks: just how "socially aware" is the policy-making process?' in C. Phillipson, G. Allan and D. Morgan (eds), *Social Networks and Social Exclusion: Sociological and policy perspectives*, pp. 219–35. Aldershot: Ashgate.

National Economic and Social Forum (2003). *The Policy Implications of Social Capital*. National Economic and Social Forum Report 28, Dublin: NESF.

Newton, K. and Kaase, M. (1995). *Beliefs in Government*. Oxford: Oxford University Press.

Neyer, F. J. (1995). 'Junge Erwachsene und ihre familiaren Netzwerke', *Zeitschrift für Sozialisationsforschung und Erziehungssoziologie*, 15(3): 232–48.

Nicholls, R.G., Stevens, L.A., Bartolome, F. and Argyris, C. (1999). *Effective Communication*. Boston: Harvard Business School Press.

Noah, H.J. and Eckstein, M.A. (1969). *Towards a Science of Comparative Education*. London: Macmillan.

OECD (1996). *Lifelong Learning for All*. Paris: OECD.

OECD (2001a). *Cities and Regions in the New Learning Economies*. Paris: OECD.

OECD (2001b). *The Well-being of Nations: The Role of Human and Social Capital*. Paris: OECD.

OECD (2003). *The Sources of Economic Growth in OECD Countries*. Paris: OECD.

Office for Youth (2002). *Respect: The Government's Vision for Young People*. Melbourne: Department of Education and Training.

OWP (Office of Women's Policy) (2005). *Safe at Work? Women's Experience of Violence in the Workplace*. Summary of Research Report, Melbourne: Department for Victorian Communities, September.

Pedler, M., Burgoyne, J. and Boydell, T. (1991, 1996). *The Learning*

Company. A Strategy for Sustainable Development. London: McGraw-Hill.

Perkins, D.D., Brown, B.B. and and Taylor, R.B. (1996). 'The ecology of empowerment', *Journal of Social Issues*, 52(1): 85–110.

Pfeffer, J. and Salancik, G. (1978). *The External Control of Organizations: A Resource Dependence Perspective*. London: Harper and Row.

Phillipson, C., Allan, G. and Morgan, D. (eds) (2003). *Social Networks and Social Exclusion: Sociological and Policy Issues*. Basingstoke: Ashgate.

Phillipson, C. (1998). *Reconstructing Old Age: New Agendas in Social Theory and Practice*. London: Sage Publications Inc.

Piore, M.J. and Sabel, C.F. (1984). *The Second industrial Divide: Possibilities for Posterity*. New York: Basic Books.

Pollard, R. and Bradley, M. (2004). 'Poor urban design weighs heavily on health', *Sydney Morning Herald,* 20 August 2004.

Porter, M. (2000). 'Location, competition and economic development: local clusters in a global economy', *Economic Development Quarterly*, 14(1): 15–34.

Porter, M.E. (1998). 'Clusters and the new economics of competition'. *Harvard Business Review*. 76 (6): 77–90.

Putnam, R. (1993). *Making Democracy Work: Civic Traditions in Modern Italy*. Princeton: Princeton University Press.

Putnam, R. (2000). 'Bowling alone: America's declining social capital', in *Journal of Democracy*, 6(1): 65–78.

Putnam, R. (2000). *Bowling Alone: The Collapse and Revival of American Community*. New York: Simon and Shuster.

Raffo, C. and Reeves, M. (2000). 'Youth transitions and social exclusion: developments in social capital theory', *Journal of Youth Studies*, 3(2): 147–66.

Reich, R.B. (1991). *The Work of Nations. Preparing Ourselves for 21st Century Capitalism*. New York: Knopf.

Rhodes, R. (1997). *Understanding Governance: Policy Networks, Governance, Reflexivity and Accountability*. Buckingham: Open University Press.

Riley, M. and Riley, M. (1994). 'Structural lag: past and future', in Riley, M.W., Kahn, R.L. and Foner, A. (eds). *Age and Structural Lag*. New York: John Wiley & Sons Ltd.

Robins, K. (1997). What in the world is going on? in P. Du Gay (ed.) *Production of Culture/Cultures of Production*. London: Sage.

Roxburgh, C. and Tuffs, A. (in press) *Community Futures: Community Engagement in Scotland's first National Park* . Balloch: LLTNPA

Rubenson, K. (2003). Adult Education and Cohesion, *Lifelong Learning in Europe*, 8(1).

S&RD (1999). Ministerial Statement on Connecting Victoria – The Victorian Government's Strategy for Information and Communications Technologies. Melbourne: Department of State and Regional Development, Victorian State Government.

Salagaras, S. (2004). 'The South Australia PALLACE Report on Schools and Learning Communities', in *PALLACE Report to the European Commission* (Longworth and Allwinkle eds), Napier University, Edinburgh

Sandberg, A. (1985). 'Socio-technical design, trade union strategies and action research', in E. Mumford, R. Hirscheim, G. Fitzgerald and T. Wood-Harper (eds), *Research Methods in Information Systems*. Amsterdam: North Holland.

Sandberg, A., Broms, G., Grip, A., Sundstrom, L., Steen, J. and Ullmark, P. (1992). *Technological Change and Co-Determination in Sweden*. Philadelphia: Temple University Press.

Sargant, N., Field, J., Schuller, T. and Tuckett, A. (1997). *The Learning Divide*. Leicester: NIACE.

Sassen, S. (1991). *The Global City*. Princeton, NJ: Princeton University Press.

Sassen, S. (2000). *Cities in a World Economy,* Thousand Oaks: Pine Forge Press.

Scottish Enterprise (2002a). *Issues for Consideration by the Business Assembly*. Scottish Enterprise Internal Document.

Scottish Enterprise (2002b). *Community Planning and Local Economic Forums*. Network Executive paper (for discussion). Scottish Enterprise Internal Document, May.

Scottish Enterprise (2005). *Issues for Consideration by the Business Assembly*. Scottish Enterprise Internal Document.

Scottish Executive (2000). *Civic Participation, a Policy Unit project*, Edinburgh: Scottish Executive http://www.scotland.gov.uk/library3/government/civicp.pdf   (accessed 14/03/06).

Scottish Executive (2000a). *Rural Scotland: A New Approach.* Edinburgh: Scottish Executive.

Scottish Executive (2000b). *The Quality of Rural Services in Scotland.* Edinburgh: Scottish Executive.

Scottish Executive (2002). *Availability of Services in Rural Scotland.* Edinburgh: Scottish Executive.

Scottish Executive (2002). *Community Planning, Making it Work for Scotland.* Guidance to the Local Government in Scotland Act 2003. Scottish Executive (Work Draft Paper), October 28.

Scottish Executive (2003). *The Local Government in Scotland Act: Community Planning/Statutory Guidance,* Edinburgh: Scottish Executive http://www.scotland.gov.uk/library5/localgov/cpsg-00.asp   (accessed 18/03/06).

Scottish Executive (2004). *Scottish Executive Urban Rural Classification.* Edinburgh: Scottish Executive.

Scottish Executive (2004). *Consultation Good Practice Guidance,* Edinburgh: Scottish Executive http://www.scotland.gov.uk/Resource/Doc/1066/0006061.pdf   (accessed 18/03/06).

Scottish Executive (2006) *Rural Development Programme for Scotland 2007–2013 – The Strategic Plan.* Edinburgh: Scottish Executive.

Scottish Executive Enterprise and Lifelong Learning Department. (2001). *Local Economic Forums National Guidelines.* Scottish Enterprise Internal Document, March.

Scottish Parliament (2001). asp 10 Housing (Scotland) Act http://www.opsi.gov.uk/legislation/scotland/acts2001/20010010.htm (accessed 20/03/06).

Scottish Parliament (2005). Planning (Scotland) Bill, Edinburgh: Scottish Executive http://www.scottish.parliament.uk/business/bills/51–planning/b51s2-introd.pdf (accessed 18/03/06).

Scottish Parliament Committee (2000). Enterprise Committee unveils radical proposals for Economic Development services. News release, May 10 2000.

Retrieved 10 March 2006 from
http://www.scottish.parliament.uk/nmCentre/news/news-comm-00/cent00-015.htm.

Senge, P. (1990). *The Fifth Discipline: the Art and Practice of the Learning Organization.* New York: Doubleday.

Sheed, J., and Bottrell, C. (2001). *Learning Towns Network Program Evaluation.* Melbourne: ACFE.

Shi Long (2004). *Beijing Learning City,* address to PALLACE Canadian conference, Edmonton 2004, in *PALLACE Report to the European Commission* (Longworth and Allwinkle eds), Napier University, Edinburgh

Shire of Melton (2005). *Shire of Melton Community Learning Plan 2005–2007.*

Simon, H. (1960). *The New Science of Management Decision.* New York: Harper and Row.

Simons, J. (2005). 'Mount Evelynn – a learning town in action', in Pascal (2005) *Making Knowledge Work,* Conference Proceeding, Stirling, pp. 375–382.

Skinner, S. (1997). *Building Community Strengths.* London: Community Development Foundation Publications.

Skinner, S. and Wilson, M. (2002). *Assessing Community Strengths.* London: Community Development Foundation Publications:

Smyth, P., Reddel, T., and Jones, A. (eds) (2005). *Community and Local Governance in Australia.* Sydney: UNSW Press.

Sodoti, E. (2003). *National Policy Commitment.* Dusseldorp Skills Forum.

Sotarauta, M. (2005) 'Tales of resilience from two Finnish cities: self-renewal capacity at the heart of strategic adaptation', in Duke, C., Osborne, M., Wilson, B. *Rebalancing the Social and Economic. Learning Partnership and Place.* Leicester: NIACE.

Steiner, M. (2002). *Learning city Vienna,*
<http://www.equi.at/pdf/swsartikel.pdf>.

Stirling Council (2000). Community Planning Overview at November 2000. Presentation. Scottish Enterprise Internal Document.

Swindell, R. (1999). 'New directions, opportunities and challenges for New Zealand U3As', *New Zealand Journal of Adult Learning,* 27(1): 41–57.

Szreter, S. and Woolcock, M. (2004). 'Health by association? Social capital, social theory, and the political economy of public health', *International Journal of Epidemiology*, 33: 1–18.

Sztompka, P. (1999). *Trust: A Sociological Theory*. Cambridge: Cambridge University Press.

Taylor, P. (2001). *Involving Communities – Handbook of Policy and Practice*. Glasgow: Scottish Community Development Centre.

Taylor, C. (1994). *Multiculturalism: Examining the Politics of Recognition*. Princeton: Princeton University Press.

TELS (2003). *Towards a European Learning Society. Learning initiative*. <http://tels.euproject.org/index.cfm>.

Thomson, D. (1999). *The Ageing Workforce in the New Millenium: Benefit or Burden?* Public lecture delivered at Maidment Theatre, the University of Auckland, 27 July.

Tomison, A.M. (1996). *Child Maltreatment and Substance Abuse*, National Child Protection Clearing House Discussion Paper No 2, Australian Institute of Family Studies: Melbourne.

Touraine, A. (1988). *Return of the Actor: Social Theory in post-industrial Society*. Minneapolis/Minn: University of Minn. Press.

Tuckett, A. and McAuley, A. (2005). *Demography and Older Learners: Approaches to a New Policy Challenge*. Leicester: NIACE.

Tuijnman , A. and Bostrom, A. (2002). 'Changing Notions of Lifelong Education and Lifelong Learning', in *International Review of Education*, 48(1–2): 93–112.

Tuijnman, A. and Boudard, E. (2001). *International Adult Literacy Survey: Adult Education Participation in North America – International Perspectives*. Ottawa: Statistics Canada.

UNESCO (1997). *The Hamburg Declaration on Adult Learning: Adult Education and Development*. Paris:Unesco.

URCOT et al. (2005). *Analysis of Workplace Violence Research Frameworks* For the Statewide Committee to Reduce Violence Against Women in the Workplace, Melbourne: Office of Women's Policy, Department for Victorian Communities.

Victoria, (2001). *Growing Victoria Together. Innovative State. Caring Communities*. Melbourne: Department of Premier and Cabinet.

Vinson, T. (2004). *Community Adversity and Resilience: The distribution of social disadvantage in Victoria and New South Wales and the mediating role of social cohesion.* Melbourne: Jesuit Social Services.

Vinson, T., Baldry, E. and Hargreaves, J. (1996). 'Neighbourhoods, networks and child abuse', *British Journal of Social Work.* 26(4): 523–43.

Viscarnt, J. J. (1998). 'EU Programmes: a 'bridge' between education and employment', in A. Walther and B. Stauber (eds), *Lifelong Learning in Europe: options for the integration of living, learning and working*, pp. 242–47. Tübingen: Neuling Verlag.

Walker, A. (1993). 'Poverty and inequality in old age', in Bond, J., Coleman, P. and Peace, S. (eds). *Ageing in Society: An Introduction to Social Gerontology.* (2nd ed.) (pp. 280–303). London: Sage Publications.

Walsh, P. (2001). 'Improving Governments' Response to Local Communities – is Place Management an Answer? – group of 2', *Australian Journal of Public Administration*, 60(2): 3–12.

Wellman, B., Haase, A.Q., Witte, J., and Hampton, K. (2001). 'Does the internet increase, decrease or supplement social capital? social networks, participation and community commitment', *American Behavioural Scientist*, 45(3): 436–55.

Whiteley, P.F. (2000). 'Economic growth and social capital', *Political Studies*, 48(3): 443–66.

Wollebaek, D. and Selle, P. (2002). 'Does participation in voluntary associations contribute to social capital? The impact of intensity, scope and type', *Nonprofit and Voluntary Sector Quarterly*, 31(1): 32–61.

Yarnit, M. (2000). *Towns, Cities and Regions in the Learning Age – A Survey of Learning Communities.* London: LGA Publications, DfEE, LCN, pp. 92.

Yarnit, M. (2000). *A Survey of Learning Communities,* http://www.ala.asn.au/learningcities/LGALearningCover.pdf.

Yarnit, M. (2006). *Building Local Initiatives for Learning, Skills and Employment: Testbed Learning Communities Reviewed.* Leicester: NIACE.

Yarra Ranges (2003). *Yarra Ranges Learning: a Learning Communities Strategy.* Shire of Yarra Ranges.

Young, F. and Glasgow, N. (1998). 'Voluntary social participation and health', *Research on Aging,* 20(3): 339–362.

Youth Affairs Council of Victoria (2003). *Taking Young People Seriously.* Melbourne: Youth Affairs Council of Melbourne.

Index